THE WOLF MAN'S BURDEN

THE
WOLF MAN'S
BURDEN

Lawrence Johnson

CORNELL UNIVERSITY PRESS

ITHACA AND LONDON

First published 2001 by Cornell University Press.

Printed in the United States of America.

Library of Congress Cataloging-in-Publication Data

Johnson, Lawrence, b. 1967
    The Wolf Man's burden / Lawrence Johnson.
    p. cm.
    Includes bibliographical references and index.
    ISBN 0-8014-3875-6
    1. Psychoanalysis 2. Freud, Sigmund, 1856–1939. 3. Pankejeff, Sergius,
1887–1979. I. Title.

BF173 .J55 2001
150.19'52—dc21
                                                                                2001028902

Cornell University Press strives to utilize environmentally responsible suppliers and materials to the fullest extent possible in the publishing of its books. Such materials include vegetable-based, low-VOC inks and acid-free papers that are also either recycled, totally chlorine-free, or partly composed of nonwood fibers. Books that bear the logo of the FSC (Forest Stewardship Council) use paper taken from forests that have been inspected and certified as meeting the highest standards for environmental and social responsibility. For further information, visit our website at www.cornellpress.cornell.edu

Cloth printing   10 9 8 7 6 5 4 3 2 1

This book is dedicated to the memory of those who have been lost, and will continue to be lost, as an index of the fragile mortality of those of us yet surviving.

(Without which life, and writing, would be senseless.)

CONTENTS

ACKNOWLEDGMENTS

Immediate acknowledgment and my deepest gratitude go to Tony Thwaites, who supervised my doctoral project in the English Department at The University of Queensland from 1995 to 1999. I want to thank Jo-Anne Johnson, for having endured more and longer diversions on Freud's rivals, family, dogs, and other trivial things than any human being should ever be required to sit through. I would also like to acknowledge the balanced involvement of John Frow, whose door was always open, and who freely provided advice and feedback at crucial stages of this project. In a similar vein, I want to take this opportunity to recognize the staff and postgraduates of the English Department of the University of Queensland, for listening to seminar papers in which I tested the ground for some of the material included herein, and in some cases for giving me valuable extra clues and conclusions. It is in this respect that I wish to acknowledge Catherine Howell, who seemed throughout this project to understand what I was doing and who told me as much constantly.

I also extend particularly special thanks (in order of appearance) to Christine Watson, Jo Robertson, John Gunders, and Helen Tiffin, for giving me the notion that I should complete this analysis of Freud and his cohorts—an analysis which threatened at times to become interminable. In addition, there are of course so many other people, friends and family, past and present, to whom I wish to express my gratitude and my love, that I cannot list them all here. Instead, I simply hope that you all know who you are, and accept that this text (which writes "me") has been written "to, for, with, and/or against" you all.

L. J.

THE WOLF MAN'S BURDEN

INTRODUCTION

Getting Reacquainted: The Wolf Man, Sergei Pankeiev, and Sigmund Freud

This book is about Sigmund Freud and psychoanalysis. It describes how Freud's textual presentations of himself and others give to the institution of psychoanalysis its principal concepts, structures, and processes. The compass of such a task is of course ambitious, from exploring the deep individual psychic histories expressed in textual presentations to mapping the vast networks of an institution that has become one of the defining intellectual and cultural movements of the last century. Given the dimensions of the task, I have opted for depth rather than breadth. My methodology, as spelled out in greater detail in the latter half of this introduction, is geared toward being thorough with respect to the relations between individual, textual, and institutional structures and processes, rather than in the range of events, individuals, and texts to be covered.

The title of this book will already have suggested to the reader that the particular relations on which I intend to focus are those surrounding the Wolf Man, a patient who both fascinated and vexed Freud. Despite the master analyst's special attention—or perhaps, as we shall see, just because of it—Sergei Pankeiev (a.k.a. the Wolf Man) remained in analysis, sporadically, throughout his adult life (he died 7 May 1979). Pankeiev's first analaysis lasted from 1910 to 1914, and he returned to Freud for a second analysis in 1919, after which he was passed from Freud to Ruth Mack Brunswick, with whom he was in-

1

termittently in analysis from 1926 to 1938. Later, he received treatment from a number of analysts including Kurt Eissler and Wilhelm Solms (president of the Vienna Psychoanalytic Society). His treatment was the primary source for several major essays on method, including "From the History of an Infantile Neurosis" (1918), the long case history written by Freud after the end of the first treatment in 1914 but not published until four years later.

It may seem difficult to reconcile these two aspects of Pankeiev's analytic situation: on one hand, his continued reliance on treatment suggests that he was never "cured" satisfactorily; on the other hand, references to him in essays written *in defense* of psychoanalysis and its principal tenets suggest that his case is indeed an exemplary one. Rather than attempt to resolve this conundrum, I will explore the conditions that enable the Wolf Man to be situated in relation to psychoanalysis in such a way as to be at once Freud's (and therefore, by inheritance, also his disciples') greatest prize *and* his archnemesis. If Pankeiev made a gift of himself to psychoanalysis under the guise of the "Wolf Man," then it was not unconditional, and neither were the gifts that Freud and other analysts gave in return. What I am calling the Wolf Man's "burden" is this conditional status attached to self-representation, or the giving over of oneself to the other, in psychoanalysis. The burden is that which self-representation leaves behind— its remainder. Yet it is not tangible, in the sense that a gift or even a representation has its object. The burden is an effect of loss, if you will, which might best be described as a promise (or an obligation) of the return. I recognize that in attempting to *describe* the Wolf Man's burden it becomes necessary to speak in riddles. This may be because the burden is a concept that has only emerged out of an attempt to describe something—the relationship between Freud and the Wolf Man, or a particular analytic mode of representation for which this relationship served as prototype—which is itself already "riddled."

In order to explain what I mean by this, it will be necessary initially to lay some groundwork. In January 1910, Pankeiev was referred by Leonid Drosnes to Freud. The twenty-three-year-old Russian began treatment in February of that year for phobias occasioned by a strong castration complex and a severe depression, manifestations of which included intestinal problems and the need for enemas. Four years later, apparently under the impression that the patient was cured of the condition with which he had entered into his analysis, Freud arbitrarily terminated the treatment. He claimed that Pankeiev's adult condition had been brought about as the result of an obsessional neurosis which had "come to an end spontaneously" but which "left a defect behind it after recovery" during the patient's childhood (Freud 1918, 8).

We know of Freud's reckoning in this matter because he tells us explicitly in the case history. In effect, he discusses the patient's adult condition only in so many words as it takes to justify *not* discussing the condition at all, since he is concerned primarily with the patient's childhood neurosis. In the first footnote to the case history, Freud explains that the content has been reprinted as it was "written down shortly after the termination of the treatment," while Freud himself supposedly remained "freshly under the impression of the twisted reinterpretations which C. G. Jung and Alfred Adler were endeavouring to give to the findings of psycho-analysis" (1918, 1n1). Thus, the justification of his subject matter several pages later is already cast in a polemical light: if he is mainly concerned with the patient's childhood neurosis, it is not because *this* patient's adult condition was determined by the circumstances of his childhood; rather, it is because this patient's childhood circumstances support Freud's *general* hypothesis of infantile sexuality, against the detractions of Jung and Adler.

While I discuss Freud's troubled relationships with these two men later, I should question whether the Wolf Man's case history is *primarily* a polemic against Jung and Adler, as Freud tells us in this footnote that was added four years after the case history had been written down. One rule that practitioners of textual criticism have learned from Freud is that representations of any kind invariably manifest themselves under conditions beyond the control of their makers (and that these makers are just as often blind to their own lack of control, convinced instead as they are of their own agency). Thus, I think we need to remain cautious of presuming that the polemical aspect of "From the History of an Infantile Neurosis" is its principal feature. Having stated this much, I also want to foreshadow what may well be one of the more important claims this book makes. *From a psychoanalytic perspective*, we must consider that it was Freud, after all, who gave us this particular insight about our own blindness to the conditionality of representation. In other words, it would be unwise to presume that anything we find by applying psychoanalytic tools to

Freud's own writing was not already revealed to the man whose self-analysis gave rise to these very tools.

Instead, I offer a reading in which psychoanalytic writing is cast in the mode of what Stephen Greenblatt, in *Renaissance Self-Fashioning: From More to Shakespeare*, calls "*improvisation*, by which I mean the ability both to capitalize on the unforeseen and to transform given materials into one's own scenario" (Greenblatt 1980, 227). Improvisers are those rare individuals who are able to recognize the conditions for representation, who accept that these conditions are beyond their control, yet who are sufficiently gifted in the use of various modes of representation—or in inventing modes of representation—to take advantage of the fact that others remain blinded by a belief in their own agency. Of course, not all improvisations are successful, and the best improvisations depend as much on the odd stroke of good fortune—whereupon all the conditions come together in just the right combination—as they do on the genius of the improviser. My reading of "From the History of an Infantile Neurosis" demonstrates that this case history, in particular, is a highly successful improvisation in view of the extraordinary range of materials that it calls into play, at a time when Freud seems to have felt himself to be besieged from numerous quarters, and the way that it transforms these materials into concepts and structures of writing that are still influential today.

Of course, even as we attempt to restore to Freud some semblance of the genius that several waves of "Freud bashing" have caused many to dismiss, we should not lose sight of the fact that the picture of Freud as an improviser may not be that unwelcomed by some camps in which the validity of his work is always being questioned. After all, the improviser's *modus operandi*, as it were, is a deceit. For many, the slightest hint of any impropriety is enough to discredit psychoanalysis, so claims of this nature will be grist for the mill. Yet my own hope is that more even-minded readers will recognize in the present exercise an intent neither to discredit nor to laud Freud. Where there are clear signs of impropriety in Freud's work, as is the case with his account of the Wolf Man, I am less concerned with either taking Freud to task or playing the apologist than I am with exploring the very condition of propriety, or of property, that manifests itself in our responses to Freud.

In a recent review of *Der Fall Freud: Die Geburt der Psychoanalyse aus der Lüge* by Hans Israëls, Mikkel Borch-Jacobsen argues that it is insufficient to simply expose a fabrication and call it a lie in order to undo psychoanalysis (Borch-Jacobsen 2000). It is one thing to say that Freud falsified his clinical material, but it is a much bigger task altogether to explain the intense investment that so many analysts and analysands have made, and continue to make, in the practices Freud elaborated with the support of this material:

> Psychoanalysis was, from the very beginning, a purely speculative (a purely "metapsychological") enterprise in which facts and evidence played, at best, a role of marginal importance. In that respect, to establish that Freud lied about clinical matters is not enough to account for that "longest error," psychoanalysis. . . . Indeed, we all but forget that Freud's patients and colleagues swallowed his lies, including the biggest and (to us) the most blatant. Now this is precisely what must be explained if we want to account for the extraordinary cultural success of psychoanalysis: how come the fib fared so well? (Borch-Jacobsen 2000, 7)

By characterizing Freud's writing as improvisation, I suggest that we can begin to get at the heart of the matter. As Borch-Jacobsen explains the situation here, the falsification of clinical material is less likely to seem improper when clinical material is considered to be of only marginal importance. What is "proper" to psychoanalysis, instead, is the mode of speculation framing the metapsychological enterprise.

As the proponent of a "meta-" psychology, Freud knew that he had to speak in a language that was at once "proper" to psychological inquiry—hence the use of clinical material seemingly as a matter of convention at times—*and* completely unbound by the rules of this same discourse. In other words, psychoanalytic writing could appear to be proper, yet it would not be "property" in the sense that psychological discourse (or any other discourse for that matter) could contain its speculations. Freud had invented a mode of speculation in which nothing, including psychoanalysis itself, remained within traditional discursive boundaries. As we shall see, this situation presented a problem for Freud when it became apparent that he himself would be unable to contain "his" metapsychology—"his" by virtue of the degree to which he had invested his own self-representation in the contours of its theoretical speculations.

"From the History of an Infantile Neurosis" bears testimony to Freud's powers of improvisation in that it transforms a situation in which all seems to have been gambled and lost into a vehicle for securing Freud's personal legacy and the perpetuation of his metapsychology into the future. The key to this transformation is the representation of the analysand in the case history, which is ostensibly a record of the interpretation of a dream that Pankeiev recalled in analysis. He claimed that in the dream he had been gazed upon by a number of wolves from a tree outside his bedroom window. Freud's interpretation of the dream involves the reconstruction of a "primal scene" involving the infant Sergei's being witness to repeated acts of coitus *a tergo* by his parents. This scene returns several years later in a distorted form (the dream) in keeping with the principle that Freud called *"Nachträglichkeit"* (deferred effect).

As this dream and the patient's drawing of it were central to the interpretation—and therefore, we might guess, central to the treatment of the adult condition to which the infantile neurosis gave rise—Freud labeled his patient the "Wolf Man" in letters and elsewhere, and Pankeiev himself adopted the lupine pseudonym in his own writing. Yet the fact that Pankeiev is not named *in the case history* must strike us as significant, given Freud's predilection for using invented names in referring to other patients (for example, Anna O., Cacilie, Dora, Elizabeth von R., Emmy von N., Katharina, Little Hans, Lucy R., and Rosalia H.) It may seem doubly significant when we consider that Freud had demonstrated particular interest in this patient, taking up collections after Pankeiev was bankrupted, allowing him free sessions, and giving up other patients so as to make time available for him when he returned for help. Of course, the Wolf Man was not the first subject of a major case history to be given no name; prior to the start of Pankeiev's treatment, Freud published "Notes upon a Case of Obsessional Neurosis" (1909), in which the celebrated "Rat Man" is only ever referred to as the "patient."[1] What sets the Wolf Man apart from the Rat Man, and indeed from Freud's other cases (with the possible exception of Anna O.), is the degree to which this case is generally

[1] I would like to point out that some of the associations that I will be foregrounding in the Wolf Man case history were already present in the Rat Man case history, although I have elected not to deal with this case in detail in the interests of concision. Given that many associations are absent from the earlier study, there may be scope for yet another investigation into the possibility that the Rat Man case represents a failed prototype for the synthesis which, as I argue here, Freud accomplishes in the Wolf Man case history.

thought to have subsequently contributed to the development of the central concepts and practices of psychoanalysis.

It may indeed be impossible to overstate the importance of this single case to the institution of psychoanalysis. At the very least, we might agree with James Strachey's estimation of "From the History of an Infantile Neurosis": The editor of *The Standard Edition of the Complete Psychological Works of Sigmund Freud* begins his editorial note to the text by stating that this document "is the most elaborate and no doubt the most important of all Freud's case histories" (Freud 1918, 3). He justifies this assessment by listing a number of later psychoanalytic concepts that were foreshadowed in the case history: the relation of "primal scenes" to "primal phantasy" leads to the "obscure problem of the possibility that mental content of primal phantasies could be inherited" (5); the suggestion of cannibalism in early oral-libidinal formations paves the way for Freud's later theorization of "interconnections between incorporation, identification, the formation of an ego-ideal, the sense of guilt and pathological states" (6); and the role of the primary feminine impulses in the patient's infantile neurosis confirms Freud's existing views on bisexuality and gives rise to the emphasis he would later place on "the fact of the universal occurrence of bisexuality and on the existence of an 'inverted' or 'negative' Oedipus complex" (6).

In addition to the influence that the concepts developed in the Wolf Man case history were to have on Freud's own thought, we find the case continuing to play a major role in the development of psychoanalytic theories throughout the twentieth century. Examples of this are many, although I shall limit myself to listing but two of what may be the most significant examples in terms of the establishment of schools of thought within psychoanalysis: the Kleinian and Lacanian schools. In 1932, Melanie Klein published her early major work *The Psychoanalysis of Children*, paving the way for generations of disciples in the field of child psychotherapy. Klein uses the Wolf Man to illustrate the concept of "primary anxiety," stating that the fear of being eaten by wolves is not simply a "substitute by distortion for the idea of being castrated by his father," since this idea itself is a "relic" of some anxiety which has persisted in an unchanged form from the very earliest stages of psychical development (Klein [1932] 1975, 223). This distinction between the content of an idea and the anxiety that is attached to it enables Klein and her followers to develop the concept of "projective identification," which characterizes Kleinian analysis.

Projective identification involves splitting off a hostile object from within oneself and projecting it (together with the destructive impulses attached to it, directed toward the self) into another object. As Ricardo E. Bernardi suggests, the concept of primitive anxieties enabled Klein to emphasize the immediacy of repetitions in the present, rather than the embeddedness of repeated content in a deferred past event (Bernardi 1989, 346). Had Klein revisited her rereading of the Wolf Man case after the later development of the concept of projective identification, according to Bernardi, she would have "directed her attention to those other wolves whose wombs are open in order to take out the devoured objects, and also to hiding in the clock-case in the transference situation. Transference and countertransference, not history, would have been the chosen field of observation" (346). Bernardi's supposition is a pertinent one, since the example of the Wolf Man enabled Klein to initially articulate her point of departure from the master's teachings. Implicit in the development of the concept of projective identification along the lines of this departure is the assumption that all analyses (beginning with those by the master himself) are situations in which primitive anxieties are likely to surface in a patient.

It was against such departures that Jacques Lacan responded with his so-called "return to Freud" in France in the 1950s and 1960s. While the Wolf Man was not a pivotal component of this "return," Lacan did cite the case on several occasions and was not backward in his assessment of its importance: "one of Freud's great psycho-analytical cases, the greatest of all, the most sensational" ([1973] 1994, 251). These words of praise were expressed during Lacan's seminar at the École Normale Supérieure in Paris in 1964, in a series of lectures that would later be published as *The Four Fundamental Concepts of Psycho-Analysis* ([1973] 1994). Earlier, in 1953, when Lacan first addressed the newly formed Société Française de Psychanalyse—at which time he also first used the expression "return to Freud"—the case of the Wolf Man was among the five famous cases (together with Dora, Little Hans, the Rat Man, and Schreber) that Lacan used to support his elaboration of the concepts of the Symbolic, Imaginary, and Real registers (Marini 1992, 153).

Lacan's next address was delivered at the 1953 Rome Congress and his report is generally regarded as a major contribution to French psychoanalytic thought. Indeed, "Function and Field of Speech and Language in Psychoanalysis" (1955) was greeted at the time as the "S. F. P.

manifesto," an articulation of the terms of the return to Freud around which the split within the French psychoanalytic community was organized (Marini 1992, 152–54). In this "manifesto," Lacan cites the Wolf Man case first of all to ground psychoanalytic methods in the assumption of a history by the analytic subject, "in so far as it is constituted by the speech addressed to the other" (Lacan 1955, 48). Psychoanalysis relies on the field of speech, in the domain of concrete discourse, in order to highlight the discontinuity introduced into language by the unconscious.

Fifty pages later, the Wolf Man's case is cited for the same reason: to highlight the role of the analyst as the addressee toward whom the analysand directs the speech in which subjectivity is constituted: "we re-establish in the subject his original mirage in so far as he places his truth in us" (96). Yet Lacan argues that in the case of the Wolf Man, the termination of the analysis imposed a "moment of concluding" that was out of time with the patient's own "time of understanding" (48, 96). From the perspective of the patient's scientific value as a case for study, the termination provided a valuable lesson to which Freud would return in later essays on method. Yet from the perspective of the transference, the termination revealed an "unresolved subjectification" reversing the effects of the gifts of money, that is, the intervention of reality in the analysis (96–97).

It may be no surprise, then, that when Lacan returns to the Wolf Man in his 1964 seminars, his concern is with the repetition of content inasmuch as these repetitions of the event constitute different moments in the restructuring of the subject, and this only inasmuch as they are revealed in the transference. The "thread" that leads Lacan to reintroduce the Wolf Man as the greatest and most sensational of Freud's cases takes him from a discussion of analytic interpretation (what interpretation reveals about the ordering of the subject) to the structure of analysis, according to which the analyst is always implicated in the transference as "the subject who is supposed to know" (1994, 251–53). The case of the Wolf Man illustrates more clearly than any other the degree to which fantasy and reality converge in what Lacan calls "non-sense," or "an originally repressed signifier," as representative of the loss of the subject (251). The transference posits this "subject who is supposed to know" as given component of each analytic relation. Yet *this* subject must be understood as a function of the analytic relation, not as the person of the analyst. The analysand's identification of the analyst with the knowing subject in each analysis directs the analysand's individual non-sense toward a given point, enabling this non-sense to be treated representatively within analysis.

Lacan's language may of course be difficult for the uninitiated to master. This is because he is less concerned than Freud had been with trying to speak the language of the psychological sciences. Lacan's discursive antecedents are linguists, philosophers, and sociologists. Nevertheless, his message with respect to psychoanalytic practice is clear: the case of the Wolf Man, the most exemplary of all cases, suggests to us that in the field of psychoanalytic interpretation nothing proceeds without the transference. Not even Freud, who we are told is legitimately the one who did know and who "gave us this knowledge in terms that may be said to be indestructible," could force analysis to proceed without the establishment of a transference relation in each individual case (1994, 232–33).

While Klein and Lacan may differ in their rereading of the Wolf Man, they agree in the extent to which they hinge the elaboration of their positions, vis-à-vis the master, on this particular case history. Bernardi makes the point that the difference between a Kleinian and a Lacanian perspective is paradigmatic: they represent different ways of listening to the same material, and so they naturally find different things to say about this material, as if it were a different object altogether (1989, 347). We might add to this the recognition that what ties the two perspectives together, in spite of their paradigmatic divergence, is the link to the master expressed through the object of the Wolf Man. For both Klein and Lacan, the exemplary status of this case is unquestioned.

We should note that it is not the proliferation of what we may call Freud's "later" concepts, as identified by Strachey, that makes this case exemplary. For both Klein and Lacan, the case provides a stable point of reference through which these concepts can be interrogated. The source of this stability, I suggest, is to be found in the representation of the Wolf Man, which I have already indicated to be the key to Freud's improvisation. We have observed that Freud does not give a name to the patient in the case history. Yet we have also seen that, in effect, "the patient" is absent from the case history inasmuch as Pankeiev, the adult who had prostrated himself on Freud's couch, is *not* the subject of Freud's interpretation. The term "the patient" functions in the case history primarily as a designator for the origin of the stories that are the true subjects of Freud's interpretation. Any name, true or false, would transform this function from being the designation of an origin into the nomination of a persona in the here and now of the time of writing.

The distinction is an important one, more so perhaps for "From the History of an Infantile Neurosis" than for any of Freud's previous case histories, because the issue at stake in this case history is not the success or failure of the treatment of this individual but the elaboration of the theoretical principle of deferred effect. Several commentators have observed that in elaborating this principle, Freud incorporates deferred effect into his mode of writing.[2] This is to say that in presenting his material, Freud presents the standpoint of the interpreting subject (himself), within the time of writing, here and now, as being characterized by certainty. From the outset, the basis for this certainty is given as Freud's "conviction" that the causes of the patient's infantile neurosis were "concealed behind" the dream of the wolves (1918, 33). At the core of this conviction, both the principle of infantile sexuality and the neurotic pathology are assumed. What remains is for the interpreter to find them "behind" (*hinten*) the dream, toward the back of its latent content.

This is dream interpretation *à la The Interpretation of Dreams* (1900), except that the day residues are assumed to have been acted upon by much more distant material in the patient's deep past. In the case history, "the patient" designates this deep past as an origin inasmuch as we may normally presume that the term nominates a subject in the present moment. This is to say that "the patient" is what enables Freud to tie together *as a history* the jumble of stories told to us in the case history. The principle of deferred effect will only hold true if the deeply past cause and the deferred present effect can be linked together by the presumption of a single subject. Yet Freud only refers the effect to a deep past because of his "conviction" that this is the appropriate course of inquiry. This conviction is grounded in Freud's own experience, his methodological certainty, but also in his self-analysis and in his belief in the general applicability of the concepts and practices that emerged through the development of his metapsychology. Like a kind of psychoanalytic commonplace, "the patient" must therefore be sufficiently capable of containing Freud's assumptions of the general applicability of the principle of deferred effect, in addition to directing us to presume an historicized subject.

[2] For example, see the readings of the case history by Peter Brooks (1979), Whitney Davis (1995), Stanley Fish (1987), and Rainer Nägele (1987).

When Klein, Lacan, and others later refer to the Wolf Man as an exemplary case, their own convictions rely on Freud's initial approach to the material presented in the case history. By unpacking the use of the term "patient" in the case history, we see that it is indeed Freud's conviction that lends to the case its exemplary status. The more the term "patient" merges with Freud's conviction, the farther it seems that the case history gets from the analytic situation itself, and the greater the distance seems between "the patient" and the figure who bore the name Sergei Pankeiev. References to the subject of the case history using the name "Wolf Man" merely elide this distance.

For the purposes of the present exercise, I want to emphasize that I will be using the "Wolf Man" as the name *for this distance*. That is to say that the name "Wolf Man" refers to a complex figuration which emerges in Freud's analysis of Pankeiev yet which is not isomorphous with the Russian who sat on Freud's couch. The Wolf Man can be used to name the engagement of analyst with analysand. I use the name "Pankeiev" to refer ostensibly to that personage whose "life" can be said to correspond with certain biographical and historical facts. I would ideally use the term "Wolf Man" for all other purposes, to refer to that site of engagement in which the crucial rivalry between Freud and his patient was played out. It will of course become apparent that such a distinction is impracticable, since the line of demarcation between the one and the other remains highly unstable (indeed, untenable), if it is left floating here as a general principle and not submitted to specific methodological rationale.

To develop such rationale here, I shall refer to the revisionary psychoanalysis of Nicolas Abraham and Maria Torok, whose work can be viewed as a marginal response to the orthodoxies constructed around the Kleinian and Lacanian approaches to Freud. Both Hungarian Jewish origins, Abraham and Torok had immigrated to France on either side of the Second World War, and both lost their family to the genocide. They met in 1950 and soon became companions. Abraham had long been interested in Husserlian phenomenology and the psychoanalytic writings of both Freud and Sándor Ferenczi, and he attempted to elaborate a phenomenological psychology in seminars organized during his training as an analyst in the 1950s. Torok had studied psychology and was already working with maladjusted children for Family and Children's Service agencies in Paris before she also underwent analytic training. They gained membership in the Société Psychanalytique de Paris and began clinical practice as psychoanalysts in 1956. After Abraham's death in 1975, Torok undertook editorship of their writings and has been collaborating with Nicholas Rand on this and other projects for the past twenty years.

Elisabeth Roudinesco notes that Abraham "cultivated an ignorance of Lacan's work," rejecting on theoretical grounds the structuralism of the new master's written work, and being repelled by the "effects of fascination linked to an individual" in his relationship with his students (Roudinesco 1990, 598). Reconciled to adopting a marginal position in relation to the philosophical discourse of their time, Abraham and Torok committed themselves to interrogating the theories that had been handed down to them in the light of their immediate analytic situations. As Rand notes in his introduction to their first volume of collected writings, Abraham and Torok were guided by the philosophy that received theories needed to be "abandoned or revamped if inconsistent with the actual life experience of patients or the facts of a text" (Rand 1994, 1).

In 1959, Abraham met Jacques Derrida at a colloquium at Cerisy. The pair had a mutual interest in Edmund Husserl's work and similar apprehensions about the value of organized structuralist activity. Yet, as Roudinesco observes, it was Derrida who "confronted that structuralist renewal and Lacan's work," while Abraham elaborated his own "idiosyncratic reading of Freud's discovery" in collaboration with Torok (Roudinesco 1990, 599). Because they are committed to expressing their theoretical insights in terms of the lives of patients or the manifest content of written texts, as Rand observes, "Abraham and Torok expend little rhetorical energy in promoting the novelty of an idea or explaining how an approach departs from standard modes of thinking" (Rand 1994, 7). Thus, we rarely find in their writing any explicit statement of their opposition to any competing school of thought. Occasionally, on a matter of the definition of a psychoanalytic term, they voice their disagreement with another scholar. A cursory glance over the essays in *The Shell and the Kernel*, the first volume of their collected writings, makes it immediately apparent that Klein is Abraham and Torok's favorite target for this purpose (Abraham and Torok, [1987] 1994).

While they recognize that Kleinian theory represents a "rigorous, generous, and in some respects even grandiose theory," Abraham and Torok oppose the substitution of a theoretical system, particularly in the mode of descriptive structuralism, for close observation and analysis of that which is specific and contingent upon the individual whose symptom remains the first point of reference for any metapsy-chology ([1987] 1994, 135). Inasmuch as they frequently refer to the Kleinian paradigm in order to justify consideration of the original writings of Freud and his contemporaries, Abraham and Torok's "re-newal of psychoanalysis," as Rand calls it, might clearly be seen as a direct parallel to Lacan's return to Freud. Furthermore, their refusal to refer to Lacan mirrors Lacan's own initial refusal to recognise Klein's contribution.[3]

It was within this climate that Abraham and Torok undertook the most sustained application of their revisionary psychoanalysis. In 1971, Muriel Gardiner had released the Wolf Man's memoirs, which revealed aspects of Pankeiev's childhood that Freud had not dis-cussed in the case history. In particular, they revealed that in addition to the Russian Pankeiev had spoken as a first language and the Ger-man he used in therapy, a third language, English, had been at work in a rudimentary form in the child's earliest linguistic experiences, be-cause the child's governess had been bilingual, with English as a first language. Taking this polyglotism into account, Abraham and Torok traced the path of concealment not only in the dream of the wolves and other memories recalled in analysis but also in the speech act of recollecting material in analysis. They contend that when Pankeiev spoke in German, he was already also speaking English or Russian, or, more precisely, he spoke words compiled from a secret *Verbier*, a lexicon consisting of words from all three languages and behind which were concealed (by any number of modes of encryption) the unspeakable phrase which refers to a primal scene of seduction in-volving his sister Anna.

The "talking cure" was thus stymied by the capacity of the patient to find ways to say nothing. In the five years that Abraham and Torok spent studying this *Verbier*, they not only uncovered this secret world concealed behind the words that Pankeiev said to Freud on the ana-lytic couch. True to their basic desire to ground theory in individual contexts, Abraham and Torok also developed an explanation of the mechanisms that produced the Wolf Man's secret world and its pre-

[3] From Lacan's earliest public presentations in 1938, there were objections from his colleagues that he was renaming classical Freudian stages without recognizing recent Kleinian contributions. Worse still was the clear suspicion that his "mirror stage" was recasting Klein's "maternal image" and "primary fantasy" without credit. Indeed, not until the 1953 split does Lacan begin to refer to Klein's work, but then it is usually in order to articulate his contentions.

dominant modes of concealment. In doing so, they give a name to this thing by which the talking cure seemed to be short-circuited: they call it the Wolf Man's crypt. They explain that the splitting of the ego, a process normally associated with libidinal development in the Freudian model, may be undermined by a defense mechanism not recognized by Freud. If the subject loses an object which is indispensable in the early organization of the psyche, or if the idealized relationship with this object is threatened, the object may be "incorporated" into the ego, meaning that the subject presumes the object itself, rather than the words that represent the object, to have been completely internalized.[4]

The crypt is this monument of a lost object preserved intact within the split ego, although the ego continues to function as though it were intact. The subject cannot be allowed to expose to his or her self that the reality of the object is in fact a fantasy, so all representations of the object are censored. The crypt is not unconscious although it must function as though it is, filtering all material bubbling up from this nether realm before any of it may pass onto the normal secondary processes. When a cryptophoric subject speaks, then, it is only ever on behalf of the incorporated object. In place of words, a cryptophoric subject speaks in cryptonyms or word-things whose relation to each other is determined less by laws of syntax or lexis than by their relation to the object itself.

When I described the relationship between Freud and Pankeiev as "riddled," it was in reference to this cryptonymic *Verbier* through which the patient, on one side of the analysis, speaks in order to say nothing. Indeed, Abraham and Torok suggest that analysis itself provided the patient with another way to say nothing: the figure of the Wolf Man. This figure was the result of the crypt's capacity to transform the moment into the same old story, by which I mean that the people and events encountered by the cryptophoric subject are transformed into supporting evidence for the continued reality of the incorporated object in its pristine state. The crypt in this sense is the inverse of improvisation, which is a process of transforming received

[4] The theory of incorporation as a consequence of failed mourning is elaborated in two essays in *The Shell and the Kernel* (Abraham and Torok [1987] 1994): "The Illness of Mourning and the Fantasy of the Exquisite Corpse" (107–24) and "Mourning or Melancholia: Introjection versus Incorporation" (125–38). Another essay, "The Lost Object—Me: Notes on Endocryptic Identification" (139–56), elaborates the theory of the crypt in further detail.

material to suit the moment. When the crypt encountered Freud, it transformed him into what Abraham and Torok call the figure of the "Father Professor," an updated version of the father who demands that young Sergei bear witness to the scene of seduction. Pankeiev himself was never present in this encounter except inasmuch as as he re-presented the figures of "little Stanko" and "sister-Tierka," flirting with the Father Professor through the games they play in the analysis. The wolf dream was one such game through which the scene of seduction was re-presented in the analysis, and it entitled the presenter to be enshrined among Freud's most important cases.

The Wolf Man can be said to have been that figure, a composite of the many figures and cryptonyms generated by the crypt, to which Freud addressed himself. In this sense, the Wolf Man is the projection onto Pankeiev of Freud's own refusal to look beyond the figures and cryptonyms to see the thing itself. As Gilles Deleuze and Félix Guattari have observed in relation to the Wolf Man case, the Freudian ear listened for free associations "at the level of the representation of things," rather than at the level of things themselves (Deleuze and Guattari 1977, 138). In the cryptic economy of Pankeiev's self-presentation in analysis, the Freudian ear thus provided the basis for an ideal exchange. The Wolf Man could give to Freud—then to Brunswick, then to Gardiner, then to Eissler and to others—time and again, what analysis needed in order to perpetuate itself: something hidden, something left to analyze. In return, analysis enabled the crypt to continue to fashion its enigmatic façade, deferring the cure to some unspecified future time.

The product of Abraham and Torok's investigations was *The Wolf Man's Magic Word*, originally published as *Cryptonymie: Le Verbier de l'Homme aux Loups* in 1976 (after Abraham's death) with a foreword by Jacques Derrida. Not surprisingly, the text caused something of a sensation in the French psychoanalytic community, with Lacan being among the loudest detractors, although Roudinesco recalls in *Jacques Lacan & Co.* that certain Lacanians were clearly "fascinated by this baroque crypt so near and so removed from their own daily lexicon" (1990, 600). There can be no doubt that Lacan's own response was motivated at least in part by the personal affront of not having been recognized by the authors as the one "who put matters on this track" (quoted in Roudinesco 1990, 600). Yet what may have seemed even more threatening is that *The Wolf Man's Magic Word* implicitly raises serious doubts about the general validity of Freud's belief in the case history.

Abraham and Torok do not deny the importance of the Wolf Man case history in the Freudian *oeuvre*. Indeed, their whole enterprise is grounded in claims that the case history represents the momentous "break" between the "first or second topography—the early or later Freud" ([1976] 1986, 2). It was the analysis of the Wolf Man that sowed "the seeds of doubt in Freud's first views" (2). Yet they recognize that there is an apparent contradiction between Freud's explicit polemical purpose and this doubt which must have been the catalyst for the development of the second topography. Abraham and Torok therefore state their objective: "We shall attempt to link the theories, the two eras. . . . We are confident that from this imaginary voyage we will bring back a more unified view of psychoanalysis" (2). Their goal was thus to "cure" psychoanalysis of the contradictions underlining the "break" and undermining Freud's conviction. To do this, as they had done before, they listened to the patient. It is my contention, and my starting point for the present exercise, that Abraham and Torok listen so carefully to Freud's patient that they turn a deaf ear to what the Wolf Man's cryptic words could have signified, beyond the crypt, for Freud.

Foreshadowing the "False" Crypt

Over the course of five years, Abraham and Torok mapped out the Wolf Man's *Verbier*, leading them to ultimately propose the existence of a crypt in the ego as the source. The *Verbier* revealed itself only by virtue of the gaps that it left behind in the Wolf Man's words. We might be prompted by their discovery to ask the most obvious question: if Abraham and Torok were able to recognize this crypt and its *Verbier* by reading Freud's writing in the case history, why did the creator of psychoanalysis not recognize it when he himself wrote these words? It is clearly not enough to say that Freud simply missed the crypt altogether, since the crypt is patently *there*, in his own words. If Freud had missed the crypt altogether, if it had not worked upon him in the analysis, then there would have been no gaps for Abraham and Torok to find.

My argument here will be that the crypt is everywhere in Freud's words because it is precisely the crypt and its *Verbier* that form the basic materials from which Freud fashions his improvisations in "From the History of an Infantile Neurosis." In order to make this argument it will be necessary to explore some reasons why Freud took such particular interest in this patient. I will aim to show that when Freud met Pankeiev the institution of psychoanalysis had reached an impasse as a result of Freud's attempts to work through particular repressed material of his own. Thus, a "break" of sorts was inevitable at this point. It will be my contention that this repressed material found its reflection (its mirror image and its exact opposite) in the Wolf Man's crypt, leading Freud to posit the Wolf Man within his own internal drama as a rival for the control of psychoanalysis, and to take the assumed fact of this rivalry as a pathway around the impasse in psychoanalysis by using it as the basis for his legacy.

Yet it will also be necessary to solve another puzzle along the way. If Freud's improvisation does all that I claim, why would he not publish it when he had initially completed writing it in 1914? I suggest that the explanation given by Freud in the first footnote to the case history— that the 1914 war prevented publication of any material—seems to be nothing more than posturing, given that some twenty or more other essays appeared during the four years from the time Freud completed the case history to the time it was released for publication. Instead, we need to consider what is at stake for Freud in the case history, even as he makes this coy explanation for its delayed release. We may draw closer to understanding what is at stake here if we recall that improvisation, in Greenblatt's use of the term, is a mode of self-fashioning.

I have framed the first chapter of this book with a question that sets out the terms by which we might begin to map the relation between individual self-fashioning and broad institutional processes. The question is raised by Derrida in *The Post Card: From Socrates to Freud and Beyond*: "how can an autobiographical writing, in the abyss of an unterminated self-analysis, give to a worldwide institution *its* birth?" ([1980] 1987, 305). Let us unpack this question. First, we must conceive of psychoanalytic writing as having an "autobiographical" dimension. In the first and second sections of the first chapter, I outline the lineaments of a methodology that can be used to consider psychoanalytic writing as a performance of the self by the analyst through the medium of the analytic situation. This methodology begins by reiterating what Derrida has already said on the matter of casting autobiography in psychoanalysis as *heterothanatography*, that is, the construction of an autonomous selfhood upon the edifice of the dead other (a deferral of the dead self). I then delve into Freud's own explicit dislike for biography, yet this is measured against the role that biographical writing has traditionally played as a genre employed by those who wish to represent Freud and as a method by which his disciples have worked through their transference onto the master.

To retain something of this relation of biographical writing to Freud's legacy, I suggest that the particular mode of representation with which Freud improvises is the autobiographical dimension of his own metapsychological method. To develop this idea, I propose a method of reading based on a modification of the concept of "life-writing" developed by William Beatty Warner (1986). Even without modification, this approach provides a useful model for reading any written text as a contribution to an ongoing process of self-definition:

> Life and thought interpenetrate each other to become a "life-writing," or "bio-graphy" composed of letters, journals, published works and those acts which have left some written trace. Not an after-the-fact-reconstruction by a historically removed commentator, this original "bio-graphy" composes (and decomposes) the biographical subject. (1986, 30)

Warner suggests that we read all sorts of writing as an extension of oneself (one's self), a theoretical position which might seem to fit very easily alongside a psychoanalytic perspective on language use. Yet I note that Warner's use of the term "trace" here is incompatible with Derrida's understanding of trace as deferral and erasure. I suggest, however, that a modification of Warner's overall method restores to psychoanalytic writing its heterothanatographical dimension. I achieve just such a modification by taking each of the texts that I discuss to be contributions toward what Derrida calls "the abyss of an unterminated self-analysis" ([1980] 1987, 305).

This modified form of reading life-writing is thus concerned not with what each piece of writing can tell us about Freud within itself (the great hope of biography) or in relation with other pieces of writing (Warner's approach). It is concerned instead with the degree to which the texts in question combine in a mode of working-through that is ongoing and interminable. By looking at the ways in which the texts exhibit processes that psychoanalysis also describes, I focus upon the Derridean "abyss" as a constitutive function of the depth of texts and the textuality of selves conceived psychoanalytically. "From the History of an Infantile Neurosis" is thus lifted from the limited confines of the polemic against Alfred Adler and Carl Jung, and Freud's polemical statement of intent is read as symptomatic of the condition of rivalry that pervades Freud's writing. Self-analysis is read, therefore, as self-fashioning, on the principle of the deferral (and the promise) of death.

The relevance of the third part of Derrida's question—of how this writing can "give to a worldwide institution *its* birth"—should thus be apparent. The institution of psychoanalysis is perpetuated (that is, born and reborn) through the condition of rivalry identified by François Roustang in *Dire Mastery: Discipleship from Freud to Lacan* ([1976] 1982). In Roustang's account of psychoanalytic discipleship, the institution survives through the endurance of precisely that counterproductive relation which individual analyses must be required to overcome: the transference. Every disciple's transference onto Freud is predicated on usurping the master, hence the "dire mastery" to which Roustang refers in the title. The institution of psychoanalysis only survives if it is riven by the sort of internal conflict that is generally associated with institutions in decline. My reading of Freud's life-writing investigates the origins of this dire mastery and the condition of psychoanalytic rivalry in the associations and symbolism that Freud developed (perhaps unwittingly) as he lived out his ongoing self-analysis through his writings and practice.

I investigate the development of this condition of rivalry by reading Freud's life-writing according to one of Warner's strictures: life-writing often seems to have been written "to, for, with, and/or against another person" (1986, 29). The irony of this mode of reading becomes clear in the second chapter. By looking at the ways in which Freud's texts are written to, for, with, and/or against others, we find the register of his writing is almost without exception cast in the form of *nonrespondence*. Rivalry emerges inevitably in this writing only because the "correspondence" with another is predicated upon the death of the other, and is thus expressed in a refusal to write in a way that responds to the writing of another. The second chapter of this book details the development of this inability to respond in Freud's relations with Eduard Silberstein, Wilhelm Fliess, Josef Breuer, and others, and in his published writings, leading to the "break" and the rivalries with Adler and Jung (which intensified around 1910). In each case, we find that the inability to respond to another may be explained in terms of the death of the other, which has in turn been precipitated by a particular death which Freud had internalized during his own childhood: the death of his younger brother Julius, while Freud was himself not yet three years old.

In the third section of the first chapter, I discuss the psychic mechanisms that might have led Freud to declare his guilt over his brother's death in a letter to Fliess, and yet never mention the name Julius in connection with his brother in any written text that has survived the purge by which Freud had attempted to foil his biographers. I maintain that Julius's death does *not* constitute an object of incorporation in the same way that little Stanko's guilty secrets constitute the object of incorporation in advance of the Wolf Man's crypt. Indeed, I suggest that Freud's improvisation provides the very blind spot behind which the crypt may be concealed. This is to say that Freud's writing uses a language that is entirely compatible with the Wolf Man's crypt at least insofar as it is this crypt's exact opposite and complement. Whereas the crypt keeps the objects from the childhood scene of witnessing *alive* within its monumental structure, Freud internalizes the *death* of the object in what can only be described as a *false* crypt. The fantasy of incorporation manifests itself for Freud as the reality of a loss, yet this loss would not in itself be sufficient to represent the blind spot that I have just mentioned. In order for Freud's improvisation to conceal *this* very crypt, the terms behind which his own encrypted material was hiding must have been near enough to identical to those behind which the Wolf Man had hidden the "primal" scene of witnessing: the wolves or *"goulfik"* (fly) that exposed the penis, and the number six (*shiestorka*) behind which the sister-Tierka (Anna) was concealed.

I suggest, then, that it is in his troubled relations with his sister Anna that Freud's later rivalries and, in particular, his failure to come to terms with the Wolf Man's crypt had their potential origins. This situation could have emerged out of Freud's difficulty in coming to terms initially with the similarities in the words for his beloved nanny Theresa Wittek (his Amme or Nanya), his mother Amalie, and the second sibling Anna, during the oral-libidinal phase in which enduring object-relations and attachments are formed. Freud's evil wishes against his sister may have coincided with the dismissal of the nanny from the Freud household, producing a guilt reaction without a stable object. With the death of his brother made known to Freud through family remembrances, he will have displaced his evil wishes and guilt reaction onto the story of Julius, producing a false crypt or screen with which to make sense of his own ambivalence in subsequent object-relations. Thus, Julius's revenants emerge repeatedly in Freud's relationships, in the form of negations which function like secrets stored within a crypt so as to draw attention to themselves *as secrets*. This material conceals itself only so that it may be discovered, in order to divert attention from the later scene of guilt derived from the complex sister-nanny-mother object-relation (which I refer to with the reversible term, "Anna-Amme"). Thus, Freud's false crypt consists of both the crypt screen *and* the material that it screens (without which the screen and the loss that it edifies hold no significance).

In every instance of rivalry or ambivalence within Freud's writing that I discuss in the second chapter, the Julius revenant emerges as the most "visible" of the absences in the text. Yet the Anna-Amme material is often lingering in the background, either by a form of displacement or by association, and by the time of the split with Josef Breuer and the birth of Sigmund and Martha's sixth child this Anna-Amme material is frequently given more exposure. It seems that Freud's self-analysis brought to light the material that had remained buried through the formation of the false crypt and the use of a pseudo-cryptic vocabulary in his earlier writings and correspondence. The difficulty emerged when the process of working through one layer of repressed material merely laid bare the deeper strata of material that had been successfully screened for so long. Thus, the early years of psychoanalysis—in which the blueprints for institutionality were mapped out initially in Vienna and then in Switzerland and elsewhere—were characterized at the core by the master's troubled relations with material representing his own past.

By 1910 these troubled relations had reached a crisis point, one effect of which was to stifle the institution of psychoanalysis just as it promised to gain worldwide recognition (which would, of course, mark its *birth* as a worldwide institution). Freud's propensity for rivalry had begun to express itself on a broader scale, which alienated the Viennese psychoanalytic community that he had built up around him. The crisis point arrived in Freud's symbolic internal drama because in the years from 1907 to 1910 he endured a succession of "critical periods," a term that he carried over from his failed friendship with Wilhelm Fliess. In 1910, for example, he arrived at the fifty-second anniversary of the death of Julius, a number that was significant not only as a supposedly terminal age for Freud but also because it was, as I will show, directly linked to the symbolism used in the development of the Julius screen in the false crypt. The number returned to the fore at a time when this crypt was placed under great pressure by virtue of its role in Freud's rivalries in psychoanalysis.

It is at this point that Pankeiev arrives on the scene, with a personal history whose terms seem to have echoed Freud's own internal drama. The analysis of the Wolf Man thus emerged as a vehicle for Freud's own repentance, a process that would have only been completed by the synthesis of the Julius screen with the Anna-Amme material, filtered through a detailed account of someone other than himself. Yet this safeguard of concealing his own working-through behind an account of the analysis of someone else also presents Freud with the impossible situation of what I am calling the Wolf Man's *burden*: if Freud wanted to *institute* this synthetic union of displaced material, as a way of negotiating safe passage around the condition of rivalry that his own life-writing had introduced into psychoanalysis, he would have handed the text of this synthesis over to the Wolf Man. As much as the synthetic text itself, then, a significant component of Freud's improvisation was the decision to withhold the text from publication until the timing was also right. I suggest that the crucial determinant was the announcement by the sixth child Anna that she wished to enter into a training analysis of sorts. I argue in the third chapter that Anna Freud had already played a crucial early role for her father in the synthesis of the Julius material with its point of reference in the Anna-Amme complex. The daughter's entry into psychoanalysis provided the case history which completed this synthesis with its ideal audience.

By withholding the case history from the individual who would seem to represent its proper subject, Freud turned the condition of rivalry into the important precondition from which his legacy could be actualized. Before 1918, as Ned Lukacher suggests in *Primal Scenes: Literature, Philosophy, Psychoanalysis*, Freud's fear for the credulity of his arguments in the Wolf Man case history seems to have been for fear of ridicule from the patient rather than from the broader scientific or psychoanalytic community (1986, 146–48). A little later in the same section of *Primal Scenes*, describing the Wolf Man's analysis with

Brunswick, Lukacher balances the second analyst's interpretation of the patient's "debt" to Freud (and his hopes of inheritance) alongside Abraham and Torok's description of the Wolf Man's conviction of his own guilt as a key factor in his relations with the Father Professor (the substitute for the original father-accuser) (162–64). In Lukacher's hands, these contrasting approaches to the Wolf Man's relationship with Freud combine to form a delicate interplay of debt and guilt, actualized between the analyst and analysand in the exchange of gifts and the withholding of information. I am reminded here of Samuel Weber's reading of Nietzsche's discussion of *"Schuld"* as meaning both "debt" and "guilt," in his response to Derrida's "Speculer—sur 'Freud' " (1984, 47–63). Responding to Derrida's discussion of Freud's own undeclared debt to Nietzsche, Weber notes that the philosophy of *Schuld* as a dual term in translation does not remove this term—or these terms: debt and guilt—from general usage; rather, it merely testifies to the necessary relation to an other who can bear witness that *Schuld* calls upon in every instance.

I mention Weber's argument because the term *Schuld* will be a key to my picture of the development of the false crypt, given that Freud connects the term to the number "six" in a thinly veiled autobiographical reference in *The Psychopathology of Everyday Life* (1901). In the constantly shifting frames of reference for the false crypt, this is one case in which *Schuld* is made to mean something other than "debt" and "guilt" in the necessary relation to an other that Weber describes. As I suggest in the second and third chapters, this *Schuld* is given by Freud as the title of a play by Adolf Müllner so that it stands for a constellation of associations that are not meanings of *Schuld* in a strictly semantic sense: there is the number six as I mentioned, Freud's "guilt" at having failed to achieve what he might have done, the anniversary or "guilt" reactions that form the basis for the plot of Müllner's play, and these are reflected in anniversary reactions to the death of Freud's brother.

When discussing the Wolf Man's debt and guilt in his relationship with Freud, then, we might consider that these expressions of debt (*Schuld*) and guilt (*Schuld*) may have been figured in some way according to the role of *Schuld* in the development of the false crypt. This figuration seems even more important when we remember that a key term in the Wolf Man's crypt is *"shiestorka"* or "six," the very number that Freud had designated as the number of *Schuld*. As he discusses the Wolf Man's role in this relation, Lukacher hints at this twisted configuration:

> In their Nietzschean game of debt and guilt (*Schulden*), Freud and his patient may have each played out the terms of their respective primal scenes, and in each case the son would have written the terms of his own legacy; in other words, the son who pays off his debt to the father could also be the father who places his son in his debt. Whatever the underlying reasons for Freud's extraordinary interest in the Wolf-Man, they led him to the very limits of his experience as an analyst and a theorist. (1986, 166–67)

Freud's initial reluctance to publish the case history can be explained in these terms—as a refusal to let the regression of debt and guilt end with the acceptance of the legacy on the other side of analysis, fixing the analyst permanently in the role of the father's son. "Whatever the underlying reasons"—Lukacher's gesture marks the point at which I begin my investigations. Once these reasons are spelled out, it will become apparent that Freud's refusal to be fixed in the role of the father's son is in keeping with his attempt (in "From the History of an Infantile Neurosis") to fix the Wolf Man in this role, as a device for casting this crucial text within the ongoing process of his own life-writing in the improvised guise of an account of the life of someone other. The Wolf Man will thus have been Freud's perfect foil, in the sense that this composite figure enabled the Father Professor to be himself (so to speak) without giving the game (his false crypt) away.

By reading the case history as life-writing, I am able to show that the dismissal of the seduction by the sister as a primal factor in the patient's obsessional neurosis is one of the ways in which Freud writes himself through the account of the Wolf Man. With this reading, I demonstrate some of the ways in which "From the History of an Infantile Neurosis" *represents* the false crypt: Anna is named but pushed to one side, in order to assert the priority of the father, and there is no room for the brother except in the form of cryptic asides about dogs, the Julian calendar, and other things. Yet this is the very reason that the case history—this synthesis of the components of the false crypt— had to be withheld from the Wolf Man while the game of debt and guilt was still current: at no point could Freud afford to give the false crypt completely over to the Wolf Man or allow his own life-writing to become "my story" for this patient whose analysis he had only recently terminated.

It is also for this very reason that the term *Schuld*—at least in translation as *either* debt or guilt—is insufficient for our purposes here. What is needed is the term which in English may hint at the degree to which the fact of debt or guilt is always a function of the intersubjective relation, at least in the sense that particular debts or feelings of guilt (*Schuldgefühlen*) are only ever *assumed* by an individual in relation to others. The verb "to assume" (*annehmen*) is important here: as Weber reminds us—while disciplining Derrida for reading Freud's "speculative assumption" in *Beyond the Pleasure Principle* as "speculative hypothesis"—the sort of speculation through which Freud gambles with writing himself installs the activity of *taking on* (*nehmen*) assumptions, rather than the setting up (*Setzung*) of a thesis, "at the very core of psychoanalytical thinking" (Weber 1984, 57). In addition to this, I argue in the third chapter that this term *annehmen* is itself a term Freud *assumes*, insofar as it belongs to the false crypt as one of the word-things in the Anna-Amme chain. By describing the assumption of assumption, as it were, at the core of psychoanalysis, we touch upon the way in which the false crypt (the simulation of an incorporation, a taking-inside) is insinuated as a blueprint for *process* rather than for *structure* in psychoanalysis. By this I mean that the false crypt seems to offer a way into extending psychoanalysis *institutionally*, against the monumental inertia that this same false crypt seems to have introduced as Freud's primary mode of engagement with the world.

The term I have chosen to describe the way in which the false crypt is insinuated as the means for pushing psychoanalysis forward, against the same barriers to progress that the false crypt had instituted, is of course *burden*. While the translation of *Schuld* into English as either "debt" or "guilt" is incapable of retaining the oscillation between these two terms, there is in German the almost redundant term *Schuldlast*—redundant, that is, given Nietzsche's observations— which is rendered in English as "the burden of guilt." The Wolf Man's burden is the condition of assuming both debt and guilt in the intersubjective relation. Yet it is also the blueprint for inheritance or legacy, since the condition of rivalry in which the Wolf Man's burden inheres dictates that the activity of assuming debt and guilt is also the withholding of debt and guilt from another, which in turn will become the necessary rationale upon which psychoanalysis can be conceived as legacy. In English, "burden" provides a further resonance that is not at first apparent in German and it is one which enables us to imagine more easily this relation between a "concept" of legacy and legacy as "conception": I refer to the fact that, in English, "burden" belongs to the same set of words which refer to the bearing of children, that is, to the *birth* toward which Derrida's key problematic will have directed us here. What follows is grounded quite heavily at times in what may seem to be a typical psychobiographical treatment of Freud's relations with his "rivals" in psychoanalysis, yet I hope to have made it clear here that a reading of the false crypt and the burden of psychoanalysis takes as its starting point the very contradictions with which the notion of a psychobiographical subject of analysis or of writing is unhinged. While I employ psychoanalytical concepts, my intention is not to psychoanalyze psychoanalysis, in the sense that I do not purport to offer psychoanalysis a "cure" for what ails it. What I hope to demonstrate, instead, is that psychoanalysis itself proceeds from a self-analysis that contributes to a mode of self-fashioning (in which the constituted self is framed as the psychobiographical subject). In this sense, the institution of psychoanalysis may be understood as a sort of defense mechanism for preserving selves constituted in and through psychoanalysis. A reading of the Wolf Man's burden in Freud's life-writing enables us to foreground this cryptic topography of the institution of psychoanalysis, although, as with any mode of reading, the burden of proof now resides with us.

CHAPTER ONE

Bearing a "False" Crypt

If one wished to simplify the question, it could become, for example: how can an autobiographical writing, in the abyss of an unterminated self-analysis, give to a worldwide institution *its* birth?

(Derrida [1980] 1987, 305)

Instituting Rivalry—Heterothanatography

"From the History of an Infantile Neurosis," which details Freud's interpretation of the dream of the wolves recalled in analysis by Sergei
Pankeiev in 1910, was written late in 1914 but not published until
1918, when Freud included it along with numerous other essays in the
fourth volume of his *Sammlung kleiner Schriften* (1918). Reading this
text, whose argument hinges on the concept of *Nachträglichkeit* (deferred effect), the delays which delayed its availability must give us
pause.[1] Freud claims in this text that he uses his interpretation of the
patient's wolf dream—the reconstruction of the so-called "primal
scene" (*Urszene*), in which the infant Pankeiev witnessed his parents
repeatedly having sexual intercourse *a tergo*—to refute claims made
by Alfred Adler and Carl Jung that infantile sexuality is not the key to
the etiology of neuroses that he thought it to be (1918). Yet in "On the
History of the Psycho-Analytic Movement," which he actually did
publish in 1914, Freud constructs the more general argument against
claims that the approaches of Adler or Jung might be called psychoanalytic. In his reading of this latter text, Samuel Weber has shown

---

[1] In *Seductive Mirage: An Exploration of the Works of Sigmund Freud*, Allen Esterson
states that these delays were "due to the onset of the 1914–18 war" (1993, 71). Though
the dates match, Esterson is merely echoing Freud's own claims in the first footnote to
the case history, and neither explains why Freud would defer publication of what he
claims to be important evidence against Adler and Jung. Indeed, more than twenty
other essays were released during this interval, including some—such as "Mourning
and Melancholia" (1917)—which refer to the Wolf Man's case.

how the polemic into which Freud is drawn, apparently against his wishes, provides the founder of psychoanalysis with the chance to affirm his own status within the institution of psychoanalysis, as an example of superordination, and to state what psychoanalysis *is* by comparing it to what it is *not*, as an example of demarcation (1982). Opposition arises out of *and* enables the institutionalization of psychoanalysis. Indirectly, Weber thus confirms François Roustang's observation that the necessary condition of psychoanalytic discipleship, perpetuating the institution of psychoanalysis, is rivalry (Roustang 1982).

Why then, in 1914, when Freud has everything to gain by exploiting rivalries with Adler and Jung, does he withhold from publication the one text that directly affirms the principle of infantile sexuality? To answer this question, we must first interrogate the assumption—which, as we shall see, underlines almost every reading of the Wolf Man case history—that the uses Freud makes of the Wolf Man's case in "From the History of an Infantile Neurosis" are the same as the reasons for the interest that he showed in his patient from the beginning of the analysis. In other words, we must ask if Freud was at first interested in the young Russian *because* the case offered him the proof of infantile sexuality that he needed against Adler and Jung. In their respective accounts of it, both Freud and Pankeiev agree that the wolf dream was recounted very early in the analysis. William Offenkrantz and Arnold Tobin have taken this to mean that Freud's interest in the Wolf Man's story "as a case demonstration of the validity of infantile sexuality was established early in the treatment" (1973, 76). Yet Freud notes that while the dream had been recalled quite frequently during the analysis, "it was only during the last months of the analysis that it became possible to understand it completely" (1918, 33). If we take this to mean that Freud did not arrive at his final interpretation of the dream until near the end of the analysis, in 1914, we must wonder how keenly he had been pursuing the line of reasoning that later brought him to his conclusions. Specifically, we may question whether the rivalries with Adler and Jung were foremost among Freud's reasons for taking a special interest in the Wolf Man *in 1910*.

Freud mentions something about his reaction to the dream and, specifically, to the drawing provided by Pankeiev. As early as 1913, in "The Occurrence in Dreams of Material from Fairy Tales," Freud noted that when his patient had recounted the dream in analysis, he had "added a drawing of the tree with the wolves, which confirmed his description" (1918, 29). After he reprinted this essay in the case history, Freud added that "at a very early stage of the analysis," the patient "came to share my conviction that the causes of his infantile neurosis lay concealed behind [the dream]" (33). As Whitney Davis has argued, and as I have been attempting to establish here, "from the vantage point of that day in early spring of 1910 when the dream was first reported and Freud's 'conviction' was initially formed," the detail of his interpretation—which merely "confirmed" his suspicions about the infantile neurosis—remained a distant prospect: "Whence, then, Freud's 'conviction'?" (1995, 45).

In his response, Davis makes two compelling claims. He argues that along with the verbal account, the accompanying drawing became a "subjective object" for Freud, onto which a number of associations or recollections were attached (46). These associations are, for Davis, primarily visual—pictures from childhood picturebooks, portraits and family trees, scientific schema or diagrams, and other images—leading Freud to project in graphic form, onto the drawing of the dream, theories of phylogeny, infantile sexuality, and primary homosexuality that he had already been developing or had seen elsewhere. Davis claims that the chronology of Freud's "conviction" and the contradictions in the case history draw readings of the text into the general structure of *Nachträglichkeit* which informs it (46–50). The reader must share Freud's conviction because the delay between the initial formation of this conviction and the time that it is confirmed is elided in the text, such that we read Freud's early conviction only insofar as it has been already confirmed. From within the "*Nachträglichkeit* of writing," then, contradiction marks itself as the sign of certainty, not as doubt: "the extremely precise management of a local contradiction is surely a sign that the writer is hardly in doubt at all" (48).

Davis's claims are, as I have stated, compelling. Indeed, the reader will find that much of what follows in this book is heavily indebted to the remarkable groundwork laid down first in his *Drawing the Dream of the Wolves*. I would like, however, to mark a point of departure from Davis's work on the basis that his claims remain grounded in the assumption that Freud's uses of the Wolf Man's case history were directed in the first instance against Adler and Jung. Davis notes that the "*Nachträglichkeit* of writing" in the case history mirrors the defer-

Fig. 1. The drawing of the dream of the wolves (Freud 1918, 30).

ral of certainty both in Freud's analysis and in the patient's infantile neurosis. Yet he tends to focus on the construction of an uncertain past primarily in terms of a present through which sense is made of the past. Using diagrams, Davis illustrates how the structures of *Nachträglichkeit* in "the Wolf Man's childhood" (35), in "Freud's analysis of the Wolf Man" (37), in "the writing of Freud's case history of the Wolf Man" (49), and in "reading Freud's case history of the Wolf Man" (50) are identical. We should note that the picture preceding the first of Davis's diagrams is a reproduction of the drawing of the dream of the wolves (32). Before he draws the reader into sharing *his* convictions about what lies concealed behind the wolf dream, Davis establishes the principle that graphic similarity between images equates to similarity in structure and meaning. As a result, the reader is drawn in some sense into the *Nachträglichkeit* of the relation between these diagrams and the visual sources that Davis locates for the drawing of the dream of the wolves.

While these diagrams lend crucial visual support to Davis's explanations, they also make it a lot easier for the reader to overlook some

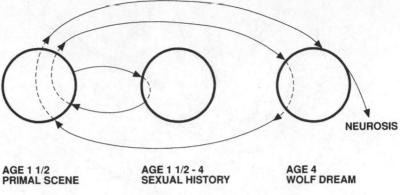

AGE 1 1/2
PRIMAL SCENE

AGE 1 1/2 - 4
SEXUAL HISTORY

AGE 4
WOLF DREAM

Fig. 2. "General structure of *Nachträglichkeit* in the Wolf Man's childhood" (Davis 1995, 35).

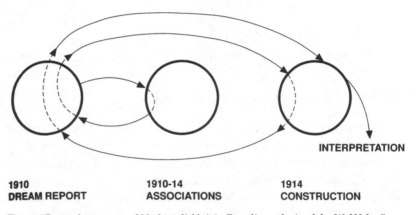

1910
DREAM REPORT

1910-14
ASSOCIATIONS

1914
CONSTRUCTION

Fig. 3. "General structure of *Nachträglichkeit* in Freud's analysis of the Wolf Man" (Davis 1995, 37).

possible alternative accounts of the relations between the various structures they depict. Concerned with depicting the general structure of *Nachträglichkeit* across several events surrounding the text of "From the History of an Infantile Neurosis," all of these diagrams loop from a primal scene shrouded in uncertainty, through a number of associations, toward the present moment when, and in terms of which, sense is made of the past. Freud's conviction is thus rendered as a primal scene (of which the dream interpretation made present sense in the course of the analysis), enabling a lucid account of the

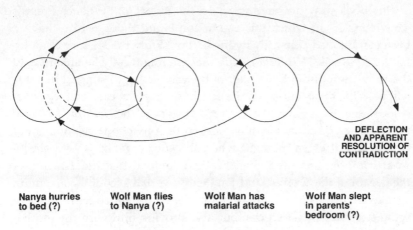

Fig. 4. "Example of the structure of *Nachträglichkeit* in the writing of Freud's case history of the Wolf Man" (Davis 1995, 49).

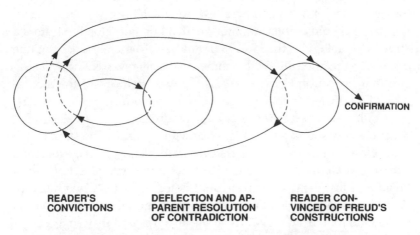

Fig. 5. "General structure of *Nachträglichkeit* in reading Freud's case history of the Wolf Man" (Davis 1995, 50).

way in which the analysis itself—or, at least, Freud's account of it in the case history—provide an example of the structure it describes. One effect of the diagrams, however, is to close off any thought of this conviction that does not anticipate the uses made of the case history in 1914. In other words, the only history we give to Freud's conviction is that which is recorded in the case history.

This book provides an answer to the question, "Whence Freud's 'conviction'?," in which this conviction is not thought of as having been conditioned primarily by the text of "From the History of an Infantile Neurosis." While it is true that we might only be able to read the conviction through the filter of the case history, I suggest that it is still possible to speculate on the condition that the case history *represents*. Rather than think of it as a primal scene to the *Nachträglichkeit* of the text, I suggest that we think of Freud's conviction as a moment of certainty in itself, a moment when the subject realizes with clarity what has been obscured. Specifically, I contend that the drawing of the dream of the wolves, and Pankeiev's verbal account, conspire in 1910 to trigger a series of associations for Freud which make sense of some significant past scenes, but also provide him with the mechanisms for working them through. In other words, we need not look at the events of 1910 only through the later text which describes them. Instead, we might look at how these events condition both the text *and* the rivalries with Adler and Jung toward which the text is supposedly directed. I should emphasize, though, that I do not intend to restore a "true" chronology to the Wolf Man analysis, to merely supplant one cause-effect relationship with another that is its reverse. Rather, I suggest that the concept of *Nachträglichkeit* was itself one of the mechanisms Freud used to make sense of, and to work through, some aspects of his own past in terms of the wolf dream.

Let me now sound a warning, since with this last suggestion I have come close to echoing claims that the case history of the Wolf Man had little at all to do with Sergei Pankeiev and everything to do with Freud and his research interests. As I noted earlier, Offenkrantz and Tobin have claimed that Freud maintained special research interests in the Wolf Man from very early in the analysis, and they suggest that the duality of these interests generated problems in what they call the "therapeutic alliance" (1973). In short, the patient's suspicions that the analyst was using the analysis to pursue other interests directly affected the analytic situation. Grounded in the belief that there is such a thing as a classic analytic situation, Offenkrantz and Tobin describe the ways in which the Wolf Man's reactions to Freud were related to the transference, yet they do not consider whether the analysand might also have used the analysis to pursue interests other than those laid down according to the classic analytic situation. Nicolas Abraham and Maria Torok's *The Wolf Man's Magic Word: A Cryptonymy* is pertinent here, since they regard Freud's continued interest in the young Russian to be a sign not only that the analyst did not see the wolf dream as a validation of his theories—he had already accumulated enough evidence from elsewhere—but that he was plagued by his ongoing failure to adequately treat the patient ([1976] 1986). Rather than attribute this failure to any shortcomings in Freud's practices, interpretations, or theory, Abraham and Torok turn to the Wolf Man, claiming—as Nicholas Rand summarizes in his introduction—that "the Wolf Man is himself only when he creates himself as an enigma" (lix). When I stated that the concept of *Nachträglichkeit* was one way that Freud made sense of his experiences, I also noted that this process took place within the terms laid down by the patient's account of the wolf dream. In this regard, I think it is crucial that we do not undervalue the role played by the Wolf Man in either the analysis or the case history. If rivalry is essential to psychoanalysis, Freud would not withhold the text that most successfully presents his case against Adler and Jung unless he also stood to gain over another rival by doing so. I will argue that between 1910 and 1914 Freud's other main rival for the control of psychoanalysis was none other than the Wolf Man.

There can be no doubt that Freud did have some kind of vested interest in the case of the young Russian, for he not only waived the fee for the analysis when his patient fell on hard times but also gave Pankeiev and his wife financial support. In fact, the pair had only married after Freud had consented to the union. As I indicated already, this interest of Freud's must initially have had little to do with the later battles against Adler and Jung. I also suggest that it is not enough to characterize this interest as an effect of the countertransference, although this may be a better place to begin than the notion of the therapeutic alliance within a classic analytic situation. Patrick Mahony has observed that Freud's argumentation reveals a personal investment in the case. Key aspects of the primal scene are reflected in biographical details from the analyst's own life. For example, until the age of three Freud had also (like the Wolf Man) shared his parents' bedroom (1984, 103–4).

Yet before we start listing the biographical materials from Freud's life which are mirrored in his reconstruction of the Wolf Man's childhood, we must first consider the mirror itself. This is to say that we should understand the process of reflection as much as the reflected material itself when discussing the presence of what we know to be the "facts" of Freud's life in his account of the life of his "patient." If we characterize this mirror as a function of the countertransference, we are at least recognizing that Freud is not simply superimposing his own history on the case history, in the same way that, as we shall see, he included autobiographical material as if it were the facts of somebody else's life in *The Psychopathology of Everyday Life* (1901). Countertransference may be defined in the most basic terms as the unconscious processes brought about in the analyst by the analysand's transference. Thus, if Freud erases Pankeiev in the sense that he writes his own history over the patient's, this erasure has at least been conditioned in some degree by Pankeiev's transference in the analysis.

Keeping these effects of the countertransference at the forefront, we can recall that we are still talking about the particular case history upon which so much of the future of the institution of psychoanalysis has subsequently hinged. The epigraph with which I have chosen to frame this chapter suggests that this institutional dimension of the analytic relationship is tied to the problem of what it means to write one's self: autobiography. In "To Speculate—On 'Freud,' " Derrida identifies the dynamic of an autobiographical writing at work in Freud's account of the *fort/da* game in *Beyond the Pleasure Principle* (*Post Card* 1987). After witnessing his grandson Ernst throwing away a spool and crying "fort" (gone) then pulling it back to a cry of "da" (here), Freud supposed that the child was gaining control of his mother's disappearance through a substitutive object. For Derrida, Freud's use of the *fort/da* example enables him to gain control over both the concept of the pleasure principle and the family members on whose example he elaborates this concept. Even as he relates the work of the pleasure principle or the figure of Oedipus in Ernst's game, Freud is also *related to* these figures, as Sophie's father, as Ernst's grandfather, and as a rival and double through his intense affection for Heinerle. Thus, Freud *relates* "Freud"—he is the spectator/speculator portraying himself in the role of a protagonist, alongside his blood relations, through the text of a relation:

The story that is related, however, seems to put into *"abyme"* the writing of the relation (let us say the history, *Historie*, of the relation, and even the history, *Geschichte*, of the relater relating it). Therefore the related is related to the relating. The site of the legible, like the origin of writing, is carried away with itself. ([1980] 1987, 304)

The account of *fort/da* is overlaid by a number of scenes, each of which relates to Freud just as Freud relates them to us.

Yet these scenes, by promising access at once to Freud (through the immediacy of blood ties) and to Oedipus (through *fort/da*, which brings us back to the Pleasure Principle—just as it offers to take us beyond the same—by way of the familial), write over the fact of their having been written. Rather than reinscribing the legibility of these scenes, Derrida suggests that the very condition of legibility (the possibility of accounting in general) is something upon which psychoanalysis already speculates. The relation between "what Freud says and what Freud does, what *Beyond* . . . treats (its objects, hypotheses and laws, its problems) *and* its writing procedure [*démarche*], its performances and operations" ([1980] 1987, 390–91), prompts the following problematic:

> What happens when acts or performances . . . form part of the objects
> they designate? When they can give themselves as example of that
> which they speak or write? There is certainly no gain in self-reflexive
> transparency, on the contrary. An accounting is no longer possible, an ac-
> count can no longer be rendered, nor a simple report or *compte rendu*
> given. (in Weber 1984, 38)[2]

The account of *fort/da* is thus no account at all because the "Freud" who relates *fort/da* is nominally inseparable from the "Freud" who forms part of the movement (which is always designated as a relation) that is described. In other words, the role played by the narrator-protagonist *within* the Oedipal relations suggests a particular investment—an Oedipal one—in both the events or movements described *and* in the description itself.

The same applies, by definition, to all psychoanalytic accounts, which form part of that upon which they speculate. Yet speculation

---

[2] I have used Samuel Weber's translation of this passage, reproduced in "The Debts of Deconstruction and Other, Related Assumptions" (1984), rather than Alan Bass's English translation (Derrida [1980] 1987) of *La carte postale* (Derrida 1980). In the translation by Bass, subtle resonances of the phrase "*compte rendu*"—as the closure of an account or a balance sheet—are closed off in favor of greater concision: "A reckoning is no longer possible, nor is an account" (391).

by psychoanalysis upon itself does not produce a gain in self-reflexivity. On the contrary, this speculation upon oneself—which is also, by extension, speculation upon "selfhood" in general—is unable to fix upon a "self" on which to ground anything like self-reflection or an account of oneself. An account cannot be rendered, insofar as closure is impossible, but this does not mean that speculation spirals in on itself to the point of perfect irrelevance by virtue of being incapable of touching upon anything except itself. Psychoanalysis *"en abyme,"* in this perpetual reflection, is not an abyssal void—as Derrida's *abyme* is sometimes taken to mean—but a thing *perpetuated*, beyond itself, beyond closure, beyond the presence of a here and now, and beyond the final balance of an account rendered ("a *compte rendu*"). To return to the question which frames this chapter, we note that autobiographical writing establishes the conditions for the birth of psychoanalysis—the conditions by which it may be perpetuated—because autobiography *is the mode of speculation* of psychoanalysis.

The discussion is complicated, of course, by the use of the term "autobiography" to describe the moment of speculation surrounding the self. As Robert Smith suggests in *Derrida and Autobiography*, the term is conventionally used to designate an account written (*graphe*) by an individual of his or her (*auto*) life (*bios*); that is, self-reflexive and unspeculative (1995). Derrida's intervention alerts us to beware the implication that writing could either contain the life or establish the autonomy of the subject. We find instead that autonomy and life are already complicated by virtue of having been written. Subject to the logic of the trace, which can be the only way to account for (or the only way to mark) the presence of an *auto* and of a *bios* in writing, autonomy and life are also inscribed with their own erasure: alterity and death. Yet the deconstructive intervention also suggests that all writing may be autobiographical in some degree. In "Autobiography as De-facement," Paul de Man refers to just such an "autobiographical moment" constituting the subject of any text (1979, 921). This moment involves two subjects of a text—akin to what students of Lacan call the enunciating subject and the subject of enunciation—determining themselves "by mutual reflexive substitution" (921). A "specular structure" is interiorized by the text in substituting one subject for another, but it also reveals itself in reflection *per se*:

> The specular moment . . . reveals the tropological structure that underlies all cognitions, including knowledge of self. The interest of autobiogra-

phy, then, is not that it reveals reliable self-knowledge—it does not—but that it demonstrates in a striking way the impossibility of closure and of totalization (that is the impossibility of coming into being) of all textual systems made up of tropological substitutions. (922)

How, then, is the autobiographical dimension of psychoanalysis any different from that of all texts, such that Derrida would want to focus on the specular structure of Freudian texts in particular, so often and at such length? I have noted that the specular moment of autobiography is foregrounded by psychoanalysis as its mode of speculation, as a way of perpetuating itself. Yet we must be clear on this point, and identify the very mechanism for perpetuation within the autobiographical dimension of psychoanalysis.

In his essay in memory of Paul de Man, Derrida cleverly uses one substitution (a reading of Francis Ponge's "Fable") as a way to read de Man's reading approaches, but another substitution intercedes. He suggests that the mirror broken in the last line of "Fable" reflects upon specularity and, therefore, upon tropological substitution and the relation of the self to the other:

Fable tells of allegory, of one word's move to cross over to the other, to the other side of the mirror . . . [as it] puts into action the question of reference, of the specularity of language or of literature, and the possibility of stating the other or speaking to the other (1989, 31).

Ponge's mirror is silvered in Derrida's reading with the language of de Man, yet even this substitution is infused with that of another who remains unnamed in this text:

The issue is unmistakably that of death, of this moment of mourning when the breaking of the mirror is the most necessary and also the most difficult. The most difficult because everything we say or do or cry, however outstretched toward the other we may be, remains within us. A part of us is wounded and it is with ourselves that we are conversing in the travail of mourning and of Erinnerung [memory] . . . the breaking of the mirror is still more necessary, because at the instant of death, the limit of narcissistic reappropriation becomes terribly sharp. . . . The narcissistic wound enlarges infinitely for want of being able to be narcissistic any longer, for no longer even finding appeasement in that *Erinnerung* we call the work of mourning. (31)

The language here is Freud's, yet in this respect it goes beyond Freud's work, since it describes the formation of the crypt, a structure that Freud never recognized.[3] Derrida reveals the phantom of Nicolas Abraham, more so perhaps for the fact that this name is never mentioned. The appearance of this phantom in Derrida's discourse foregrounds the mechanism for perpetuating psychoanalysis, by which I mean death. Even as he has been asked to write an essay in memory of Paul de Man, Derrida turns to the subject of death, and there, haunting him still, is the death of another—Abraham, who died in 1975—whose work on death and on mourning has been so often echoed in his own.

We have already ascertained that death is in some degree the absence present (or, perhaps, the absence of presence) in the autobiographical dimension of all writing, yet in most writing, and even in the most self-reflexive kinds, death must be elided and the illusion of autonomy maintained. Yet in Derrida's fascination with psychoanalysis, he finds that many of its key concepts name what Robert Smith calls "life death" (1995, 172).[4] In *The Post Card*, he reads *Beyond the Pleasure Principle* as a text providing the example for what it describes, and the death of one of the principal characters in the *fort/da* game (Freud's daughter Sophie) while this text was written is tied closely by an Oedipal thread to the naming of the death drive. The absence of the child's mother had guaranteed her presence in the game, whereas the absence of the analyst's daughter now guarantees her presence in the theory. Yet we can look further than the death drive for psychoanalytic concepts which name death. In his essay on de Man, Derrida names as Psyche the *elle* (she) who breaks her mirror in the last line of Ponge's "Fable":

[3] Readers of Derrida's "Foreword: *Fors*: The Anglish Words of Nicolas Abraham and Maria Torok" (1986)—his introduction to Abraham and Torok's *Wolf Man's Magic Word: A Cryptonymy*—will recognize the metaphor of the broken plane—the sharpness of its angles, for example—to describe the result of failed mourning.

[4] Derrida's phrase is generally rendered as "life/death," though I repeat Smith's expression here because it will allow us to move expeditiously, rather than to reiterate the problematic of the dividing line which is an integral part of Derrida's argument in postulating this phrase. In what follows, I will use "life death" rather than "life/death" and will cite Smith's understanding of the term in order to give the term currency here.

The she, in this fable, I shall call Psyche. You know that Psyche, who was loved by Cupid, disappears when she sees Eros, the rising sun. You are familiar with the fable of Psyche painted by Raphael and found in the Farnese villa. Of Psyche it is also said that she lost her husband for giving in to her wish to contemplate him when that had been forbidden to her. But in French a psyche, a homonym and common noun, is also a large double mirror installed on a rotating stand. (1989, 38)

Derrida establishes expectation and familiarity: "You know that"; "You are familiar with the fable"; "Of Psyche it is also said that." At home with Psyche and its multiple associations, we no doubt also know that psyche is identified by Homer with life itself, or by Plato with that which is divine and animated in the body, or that as the derivative designating the relation of body to spirit it is the base from which "psychoanalysis" and the other psychologies are formed.

In his reading of "Fable," Derrida concentrates on what it means for the fabled Psyche to say that she broke the mirror, an object which ostensibly bears her name. In the realm of expectation and familiarity that he opens out, we must also recognize that the mirror Psyche breaks is synonymous with the relation of mind to spirit designated by her name and synonymous, therefore, with life itself. The breaking of the mirror can be equated with the instant of death and the opening of a narcissistic wound because the mirror, the "she" who breaks the mirror, and life itself are one. The mirror through which Freud reflects himself in the Wolf Man case history may be equated in just this way with the instant of death, since the moment of writing himself is always reflected through another. Psyche herself can never be one with the mirror in which she sees her reflection, since the mirror foregrounds the problematic of "the subject's two selves," suggesting "the impossibility of seeing oneself and touching oneself at the same time" (1989, 39). Set apart from herself, Psyche is thus self and other at once, and the mirror will always already be broken. Death and alterity remain in the moment of reflection, leaving us to conclude that with the first part of the name psychoanalysis gives to itself, it names its crucial investment in this life death of the intersubjective relation.

It is not enough, of course, that psychoanalysis should name this life death with the name it chooses for itself. Psychoanalysis also names a body of concepts which attempt to give an account of perpetuation and death, just as they seek to perpetuate psychoanalysis. I refer here to that body of concepts with which Freud tried to explain how material from our past is retained and how it impacts upon our present experience. In "Freud and the Scene of Writing," Derrida demonstrates that Freud was concerned throughout his publishing career—from the *Project for a Scientific Psychology* (1895) to the "Note upon the Mystic Writing-Pad" (1925)—with defining a "writing machine" by which we may explain memory, repression, and representation in general (1978). What interests Derrida most in this writing machine is the degree to which it foreshadows "a beyond and a beneath" of metaphysics even as the terms that describe the machine are derived within that tradition (228). The key to the break is the performativity of Freud's writing, which means that it forms a part of the object that it describes. Rather than employing a *metaphor* of a nonphonetic writing, Freud *"performed for us the scene of writing"* (229—the emphasis is Derrida's). Freud performs the "effect of deferral," which is known as *Verspätung* (delay) in *The Interpretation of Dreams*, and *Nachträglichkeit* in "From the History of an Infantile Neurosis" and elsewhere (203).

Derrida insists that despite its appearance, "the deconstruction of logocentrism is not a psychoanalysis of philosophy," yet he confesses that Freud's attempt to escape his metaphysical moorings consists in anticipating the *différance* complicating any notion of presence (196). There is no autonomous subject not merely because the subject is arrived at intersubjectively—though this is important—but because the here-and-now grounding of a subject's presence is always an effect of deferral. The principal term here is the memory-trace (*Erinnerungspur*), since it is only as a consequence of any kind of retention that we can think of deferral. Yet as Derrida explains, the trace or *Spur* is as much a reminder of the subject's absence and a promise of erasure as it is a marker of a here-and-now:

> Trace is the erasure of selfhood, of one's own presence, and is constituted by the threat or anguish of its irremediable disappearance, of the disappearance of its disappearance. An unerasable trace is not a trace, it is a full presence, an immobile and incorruptible substance, a son of God, a sign of Parousia and not a seed, that is, a mortal germ. This erasure is death itself, and it is within this horizon that we must conceive not only the "present," but also what Freud doubtless believed to be the

indelibility of certain traces in the unconscious, where "nothing ends, nothing happens, nothing is forgotten." (230)

Deferral is thus both life itself and its erasure, since it withholds death only by holding out a promise of death. More important, by performing for us the scene of writing, Freud not only names deferral—*Nachträglichkeit*—but also performs this deferral that marks both life and death in his writing.[5] It is with this performance, and with the question of the performativity of psychoanalytic writing in general, that we must be concerned here.

Rewriting Life-Writing: A Methodology

We are confronted then with life death at the core of psychoanalysis, and with the suggestion raised after Derrida by Robert Smith that, "incredibly, life has an essential link with writing; a thought of writing and the trace is 'the only condition on which' life death can be thought out—it is the *sine qua non* of life as death" (1995, 172). Making a link between life and writing conditioned on a thought of the trace has an important consequence for our attempt to describe the improvisational quality of psychoanalytic writing: however much we seek to link the lives of Freud and Pankeiev to the writing of the case history and other texts, we cannot cast these "lives" in our own writing by way of traditional biography. Whereas traditional notions of autobiography elide the alterity and death which make anything like an autobiography possible, traditional notions of biography compound the problem, by insisting upon the ideal of a dispassionate or objective alterity, in which it will be possible to represent the life of one individual from the standpoint of another. As the theory of the trace of alterity and of death within representations—and as the practice of this theory—psychoanalysis would seem to be particularly resistant to a biography that does not consider that the standpoint of the other

---

[5] In *Life and Death in Psychoanalysis* (1976), Jean Laplanche provides more detailed readings of texts in which Freud names concepts touching upon death, as these texts demonstrate within their structure the very processes and erasures they describe. For another account of the way in which death and its understanding support the institution of psychoanalysis, see Philippe Lacoue-Labarthe's "The Scene is Primal," in *The Subject of Philosophy* ([1979] 1993).

is not a position one adopts dispassionately, that such a position is an effect of alterity and, indeed, of representation. With this in mind, I propose that we redefine the relation between life and writing which informs our approach to biography, by taking psychoanalysis into consideration, from which we shall arrive at a methodology for writing a biography capable of taking the improvisational quality of analytic writings into account.

My starting point for this redefinition is, perhaps appropriately, an anecdote that cuts simultaneously across details of Freud's life and psychoanalytic explanations of motivation, through the contours of a biography of Freud. Joan Riviere recounts her mentor's response after she related to him a particular psychoanalytic explanation that occurred to her: "Write it, write it, put it down in black and white; that's the way to deal with it; you get it out of your system" (1973, 354). For Riviere, the significance of this remark is to be found in what she might build up logically from them, to form a picture of the man, based on understanding Freud's words *not as a response* but as a statement about his own methods:

> I didn't feel this prescription meant much to me, and it fell by the way. It must obviously have been true for him, however, and I remembered it. In later years, as I acquired more knowledge and understanding of him and his work, and especially under the stimulus of his biography, I came more and more to realize the underlying importance in him of the creative side of his work—his work must have meant to him a structure he was building and creating. He almost says so once or twice. This idea then linked up in my mind with his former remark to me: "Get it out, produce it, make something of it—*outside you*, that is; give it an existence independently of you." (354)

A statement about analysis is here not subjected to the scrutiny of psychoanalysis in the strictest sense, as we might expect from someone who has received her training directly from the master. Instead, Riviere resorts to biography or, to be more precise, a sort of hybrid: psycho-biography. To understand why this is the case, we need only to observe that the statement she submits to scrutiny is not only a statement made *about analysis* but one made about analysis *by Freud*. François Roustang has argued convincingly that to be a disciple of Freud is to be enmeshed within an unresolved transference to Freud, the significance being that a disciple cannot analyze the master without resolving this transference relation (1982). The dilemma facing the disciple is this: how to resolve the transference while maintaining fidelity to the truth of Freud's words; how, in other words, to analyze the master without questioning the master about psychoanalysis? The dilemma arises, of course, only because Freud's speculations on analysis are caught up in the autobiographical dimension of his writing. To resolve the problem, in what has become a standard procedure since Ernest Jones's *Life and Work of Sigmund Freud* (1974), Riviere divests Freud's speculations of their autobiographical dimension, and submits these extracted details to a form of scrutiny which need not strictly be called analysis, since it no longer speculates upon analysis: *biography*.

In this movement from autobiography to biography, of course, the "auto-" drops out, as if the commandment, "Write it, . . . you get it out of your system," can be taken to mean that analytic writing is separable from (get it out of) the analyst. Riviere takes this statement, under the "stimulus" of her biographical enterprise, to mean "give it an existence independently of you." Yet the compromise, "that's the way to deal with it," already intervenes, suggesting that the analytic explanation is somehow also *inside* the analyst, as something that must be dealt with or *worked through* for oneself. Roustang suggests that the value for analysts of the theory of analysis and the figure of Freud is that they act as a *"garde-fou,"* a guard against madness or, specifically, the delirium to which (according to the theory of analysis) we are all prone (1982, 33). Explanations of the sort proffered by Riviere are thus indispensable to analysts as an aspect of their own normative psychic activity, the sense they have or make of themselves. From the standpoint of Riviere the biographer, however, Freud's words bear witness to an act of creation which does not fold back onto its creator—note that the emphasis placed on *"outside you"* in the passage that I have reproduced above is Riviere's—and which is not extended to include the person to whom they were spoken. It is as if Riviere had taken the standpoint of the biographer all along, suggesting that Freud's "prescription" was not really meant for her, but was worth remembering only insofar as it was "true for him."

By using the standpoint of the biographer to resolve one's transference, however, a disciple of Freud's risks dissolving the transference altogether, since Freud always made it very clear to those near to him that he maintained little regard for biographers. Even before he opened his clinical practice in 1886, Freud demonstrated a willingness to foil those who would one day write his biography—this from a letter to his betrothed Martha Bernays, on 28 April 1885:

> I have just carried out one resolution which one group of people, as yet unborn and fated to misfortune, will feel acutely. Since you can't guess whom I mean I will tell you: they are my biographers. I have destroyed all my diaries of the past fourteen years, with letters, scientific notes and the manuscripts of my publications. . . . Let the biographers chafe; we won't make it too easy for them. (qtd. in Jones 1974, 26–27)

Over fifty years later, in a letter honoring Freud's eightieth birthday, Arnold Zweig asked permission to write his biography. The reply was unequivocal: "I am far too fond of you to permit such a thing. Anyone who writes a biography is committed to lies, concealments, hypocrisy, flattery, and even to hiding his own lack of understanding, for biographical truth does not exist" (qtd. in Marcus 1984, 209). With this in mind, it is small wonder that the title of what was translated into English as *An Autobiographical Study* (1925) was *Selbstdarstellung* (self-portrait), not "Selbstbiographie," since Freud must scarcely have wished to be labeled his own first biographer. Of course, with this last claim we run the risk of just the sort of embellishment that Freud warns against, collapsing into the lineaments of a single "biographical truth" three texts from different contexts: the first is a letter from a young neurologist to his betrothed; the second is a reply to a close friend from an aging psychoanalyst, certain that death is near; and the third is an essay that Freud wrote at a time when he was passing on his greatest creation to a new generation of analysts, an essay in which the development of psychoanalysis is portrayed both in terms of the life of its founder and as an institution that would survive beyond his death.

In what is a generally scathing attack on the biographical practices of the Freud archivists, Steven Marcus points out that Freud was probably right in his assessment to Zweig. A quick survey of biographies, correspondences, and commentaries reveals that of the charges laid by Freud against biographers, at least two are regularly in evidence: by way of concealment, it seems that a great deal of available material is often omitted, though it may be relevant, and on occasions when an omission is noted, it is "utterly impossible to know what principle of deletion has been followed; and sometimes (as in the important Freud-Abraham correspondence) it is impossible to make out whether any principle has been followed at all" (1984, 212); and a lack of understanding seems to lie at the core of the biographer's enterprise when imposing an overarching "truth" onto statements. Marcus berates Marie Balmary (*Psychoanalysis Psychoanalysed: Freud and the Hidden Fault of the Father*), Ronald Clark (*Freud: The Man and the Cause*), and Paul Roazen (*Freud's Followers*), in particular, for their persistence in making "utterly decontextualized" claims from mere fragments of documents, or for making known their so-called discoveries for no other reason than that the information had not been made public before (212). A statement by Freud, or one made about Freud, is often taken as being indicative of something greater or more meaningful by virtue of being an insight into what Freud was like, or else it is assumed to be important in itself, simply as a statement by or about Freud—in either case, the conversion to biographical truth strips a statement of its context.

While I agree that biography needs to be rigorous, I suggest that it is possible to be too concerned with the immediate context in which individual statements are made. By placing more emphasis on context, Marcus seems to suggest that biographical truth may be elusive whereas historiographical truth is not. I do not intend to be drawn into an argument against the general merits of historicism, although I will repeat here what Rainer Nägele has written on the incompatibility of historicism with the psychoanalytic notion of time:

> In an unpublished manuscript recently sent to me for evaluation, I read the astounding assertion that both Freud and Heidegger are atemporal thinkers. To deny the thought of time to two thinkers who gave it a very special place in their works indicates a problem with temporality at the very core of the rhetoric of historicism. Paradoxical as it may sound, one thing historicism cannot think of is *time*. . . . Historicism, even in its more modern forms, even sometimes under the claim of "dialectics," can only think of things, of facts, but not of that which transforms *facere* into *factum*. (1987, 173)

Perhaps Nägele had been too harsh with the person whose manuscript he was asked to evaluate: Was it not Freud after all who claimed that the unconscious knows nothing of time? Are not repetition-compulsion, the pleasure principle, *eros* and *thanatos*, or even the Oedipal relation, like the principle of constancy on which they are based, evidence of the resistance of psychic processes to time? The answer is, in short, yes . . . and no. The unconscious knows nothing of time, yet these concepts do provide evidence of the resistance *to time* in that they describe ways in which effects of the unconscious are experienced or resisted *in time*. There can be no repetition, no cathecting of affect, no constancy, without at least a first and then a second instance between which something is repeated or remains constant. The concept of *Nachträglichkeit* marks Freud's attempt to explain this sense of a first and second instance of repetition as deferral. Cautionary directives to adhere only to the immediate context in which statements are made fail to recognize this possibility that deferred effects are also at work whenever statements are made.

To write biographies of Freud and Pankeiev—that is, rather, to write the multiple text of a countertransferential relation which speculates on the life and writing of both: a hetero-biography—we need a thought of the trace and of deferral more than we need to think only in terms of what is most immediate. We are not, strictly speaking, writing a psychoanalysis of the relation between Freud and Pankeiev, nor are we necessarily deconstructing this relation, but we must be able to respond to this relation in its own terms. As we have seen, Freud foreshadows a Derridean problematic of the trace, most explicitly, in the concept of *Nachträglichkeit* structuring his explanation of the wolf dream and his relations with his patient. The problem is of course that biographical writing as it is understood by Freud is unable to respond to the problematic of the trace or the concept of deferred effect, since this form of writing clings to the futile hope of a full presence, claiming to write a life without the promise of its erasure. This potential limitation of biography should not, however, dissuade us from attempting to expand the concept of biography and its usefulness.

As a guide to how we might do this, I shall enlist the notion of "self-fashioning" as it is developed by Stephen Greenblatt in *Renaissance Self-Fashioning: From More to Shakespeare* (1980). Using Clifford Geertz's definition of culture as a set of control mechanisms for the governing of behavior, Greenblatt explains that self-fashioning, the shaping of one's own identity as well as those of others, may be described as the Renaissance version of these control mechanisms, "the cultural system of meanings that creates specific individuals by governing the passage from abstract potential to concrete historical embodiment" (1980, 3–4). For Geertz, such systems of meanings can be identified through "thick description" of collective cultural practices. For Greenblatt, thick description can be harnessed to literary criticism in the form of cultural poetics, recognizing that some texts and practices resonate more acutely than others the making of a system of meanings in a given time and place, seeming to us to "drive themselves toward the most sensitive regions of their culture, to express and even, by design, to embody its dominant satisfactions and anxieties" (6–7).[6]

Greenblatt's resonant examples of Renaissance self-fashioning are culminated in Shakespeare, whose mode of self-fashioning is called "improvisation," the character of which is the appearance of the impromptu for what is "a calculated mask, the product of careful preparation" (227). Improvisation is the highest form of self-fashioning in the Renaissance because it not only "resonates" with that culture's system of meanings, but also manipulates this system and then projects its mask, a product of careful preparation, onto others as if it were a reflection of themselves. Already, we can see how psychoanalytic systems of representation, fashioned in the cauldron of the countertransference, might be understood as modes of improvisation. An understanding of psychoanalytic writing as improvisation allows us to picture a mode of writing in which the self can be fashioned precisely through the abandonment of a stable point of self-reference. Using the terms we have used already, improvisation speculates upon selfhood by writing oneself through the contrivance of a mask that is projected onto another.

Yet I do not pretend that this description of Shakespearean improvisation can simply be mapped directly onto the institution of psychoanalysis.[7] What is needed is a mode of reading improvisation that

---

[6] In *The Interpretation of Cultures* and elsewhere, Geertz outlines this methodology grounded in the semiotic conception of culture as a "stratified hierarchy of meaningful structures" that determine the behaviors of individuals rather than as the sum total of these behaviors (1975, 7). He argues that "being there" is impossible for a culturally removed observer, but claims that thick description of a culture is enabled by reading these meaningful structures in cultural products. Stephen Greenblatt's cultural poetics (or New Historicism, as it is more commonly known) is directly indebted to Geertz. See also "The Touch of the Real" (1997) for Greenblatt's account of his debt to Geertz.

[7] In "Psychoanalysis and Renaissance Culture," Greenblatt argues that Freud's "deeply inadequate attempts to explicate the art of Leonardo, Michelangelo, and Shakespeare" indicate that "psychoanalysis is at once the fulfillment and effacement of specifically Renaissance insights" (1992, 131). Within his argument, Greenblatt notes that the mask understood as defense mechanism, "a veneer hiding the authentic self beneath," and as identity itself, "a theatrical mask secured by authority," are

takes into account the advent of psychoanalysis itself, updating our understanding of Renaissance masks to include the idea of defense mechanisms. William Beatty Warner provides a useful starting point for this in *Chance and the Text of Experience: Freud, Nietzsche, and Shakespeare's Hamlet* (1986). His stated goal is to "lift the ban on biographical reading that has been one of the implicit corollaries and practical effects of most critical theory since the New Criticism" (28). This return to biography is qualified by an effort to re-theorize the field of biographical study:

> Because in the "life" there is no innocent state of being apart for the person, and because for the "writing" there is no condition of standing apart in the mode of pure consciousness to express an idea, life and writing are always already inscribed in the traces of a complex historical formation I will call "life-writing." Life-writing often seems to be written to, for, with, and/or against another person. (29)

Warner is aware that one of the more common pitfalls facing traditional biography is that it concentrates on an autonomous biographical subject, upon which it expects to be able to ground all details of the "life" in the "thought" of the genius. Yet this concept of "life-writing," separated out from the generic confines of the mode of writing that sometimes carries the same name, is deployed as a way of unsettling this ground, such that life and thought are seen as intermeshed in a form of a "bio-graphy" that is made up from "letters, journals, published works and those acts which have left some written trace. Not an after-the-fact-reconstruction by a historically removed commentator, this original 'bio-graphy' composes (and decomposes) the biographical subject" (30).

Warner's methodology seems implicitly indebted to Greenblatt's cultural poetics: both read established or canonical texts against a montage of less recognized texts—"those acts which have left some written trace"—to identify the formations underlying them all; both suggest that this reading procedure is a reaction against the corollaries and/or effects of critical theory since New Criticism; and both in-

---

divergent modes of thought—the point at which Freud differs from Shakespeare, for example (143).

sist that this procedure represents something other than an "after-the-fact-reconstruction." For this reason, I am inclined to think that Warner's "life-writing" is not in itself sufficient for our purposes here—not quite. The reader may have noticed that in the passages I have reproduced, the term "trace" is used in a way that is incompatible with the Derridean problematic in which trace is understood as erasure. For Warner, "trace" is a marker of presence and "always already"—in spite of the problematic to which this phrase, simply echoed by him, refers—of permanence.[8] Warner's traces enable us to situate the agency whose "acts" are responsible for the historical text, removing all question of "after-the-fact-reconstruction." Thus, Warner's version of New Historicism appears grounded in the traditional biographical practice exemplified in Riviere's interest only with what was "true for him" in Freud's words.

These practical effects aside, the concept of life-writing remains extremely useful for reading psychoanalytic writing if we can adhere more closely than Warner does to his stricture that life-writing is "written to, for, with, and/or against another person," by restoring to the subject its intersubjective and intertextual moorings. We recognize then that life-writing involves this necessary movement toward the other, thereby erasing the autonomous subject of traditional biography. Such an erasure marks life-writing as life death. With our understanding of biography reconfigured to include this relation of life to writing as a relation of life-to-death, informed appropriately by a thought of the trace as erasure, we can write the multiple biography of Freud and Pankeiev through reading the texts that surround the Wolf Man case history and others. We shall be equipped to treat these texts and the shadowy figure of the Wolf Man as a site of improvisation, upon which ongoing rivalries are played out, and not as the remains or "written traces" of a life. We shall be prepared to consider that none of these texts stands alone or merely comments on the others, since what is at stake in life-writing is something that exceeds the narrow confines of a single text. In short, we shall consider the ways in which numerous texts (includ-

---

[8] Given that Warner relies on Derrida's problematization of concepts such as chance or the subject of experience in "My Chances/*Mes Chances*: A Rendezvous with Some Epicurean Stereophonies" (1984), it seems quite remarkable that he has neglected the important point that Derrida makes in the same essay about the mark as "precisely *re-markable* from one context to another," that is, in terms of trace or deferral (16).

ing the Wolf Man's case history) participate in an ongoing narrative constituting the life-writing of Freud and Pankeiev in the birth (the institution) of psychoanalysis.

Julius from Anna within the Formation of a False Crypt

The birth of psychoanalysis, like everything else that psychoanalysis describes or does, was preceded by another birth. The death of the father, to which event many have attributed the birth of psychoanalysis, was preceded by another death. To be more precise, these preceding events are multiple, since in the course of Freud's lifetime these births and deaths were experienced anew, and in so many different ways, time and again. With the concept of *Nachträglichkeit*, Freud found a way to make sense of this multiplicity of events, these births and deaths. In a sense, *Nachträglichkeit* is his word for life death, enabling him to arrive at a solution for the problematic of the wolf dream even as he resolved the problematic of his own uncertain past. As we shall see, Pankeiev found himself at the center of some remarkable (remarkable) coincidences that made him indispensable as the foil to a burden which Freud must have carried within him since before he could remember. We shall see, then, that however much we attribute the account of the wolf dream and the drawing to the Wolf Man, they are also key autobiographical texts within the life that Freud was writing for himself.

Let us mark our beginning with the wolf dream, as Freud relates it (apparently verbatim) in "The Occurrence in Dreams of Material from Fairy Tales," the essay that was reprinted in full in section four, "The Dream and the Primal Scene," of "From the History of an Infantile Neurosis":

> I dreamt that it was night and that I was lying in my bed. (My bed stood with its foot towards the window; in front of the window there was a row of old walnut trees. I know it was winter when I had the dream, and night-time.) Suddenly the window opened of its own accord, and I was terrified to see that some white wolves were sitting on the big walnut tree in front of the window. There were six or seven of them. The wolves were quite white, and looked more like foxes or sheep-dogs, for they had big tails like foxes and they had their ears pricked like dogs when they

pay attention to something. In great terror, evidently of being eaten up by the wolves, I screamed and woke up. (1918, 29)

Even if we are to share Freud's "conviction" that the causes of the Wolf Man's infantile neurosis lay concealed behind this dream, we might still take some pause at the idea that the manifest content of this dream is sufficient to justify Freud's intense interest in the Wolf Man's case. We know that the wolf dream was first recounted in the analysis, by Pankeiev's own account, "near the beginning of my analysis, to the best of my recollection within a month or two after the start" (Wolf Man 1957, 450). We also know from letters by Freud that around the time that he took the patient into analysis in early February 1910, he was aiming to reduce his practice to enable him to devote time to the essay on Leonardo da Vinci in which he had been interested for several years.[9] With the case of Leonardo, Freud was interested in the way in which the great artist's masterpieces represented a sublimation of latent homosexuality. We can just imagine how he must have looked forward to his first sessions with the young Russian if either Leonid Drosnes or Moshe Wulff had mentioned Pankeiev's artistic inclinations when they also told Freud about his new patient's symptomatic behaviors, chief among which was the inability to effect a bowel movement until after an enema had been administered by a male attendant.

Certainly it seems that early in 1910, Pankeiev's arrival on the analytic couch was timed perfectly to coincide with Freud's most immediate research interest, but we cannot claim that Freud's interest in his new patient was incidental. Whitney Davis notes that the Russian was certainly familiar with Freud and with many of the battle lines that had been drawn around psychoanalysis, as he informed Freud in their first session that he had already consulted some of Freud's detractors, such as Emil Kraepelin (Davis 1995, 28), and we know from Freud's letter to Jung on 30 May 1910 that Pankeiev had been to see Hofrat Adolf Albrecht Friedländer, and had confirmed Freud's opinion of the man as a "professional liar and hypocrite, wolf in sheep's

[9] A letter from Freud to Sándor Ferenczi, written 8 February 1910, states that he has "taken on a new patient from Odessa, a very rich Russian with compulsive feelings" (in Davis 1995, 22–23). Freud also wrote to Karl Abraham on February 24, 1910, that "I am now writing Leonardo *at odd times* [in English in the original]; from next week onwards there will be a decrease in my practice, and then at last I shall be able to get on with it" (Freud and Abraham 1965, 87).

clothing" (Freud and Jung 1974, 324). It may be no surprise to find Freud echoing the language of the Wolf Man in correspondence less than four months into the analysis, since Pankeiev may well have used his knowledge of psychoanalysis to attract Freud's attention to his case in the first instance (Davis 1995, 24–25). Davis suggests the initial transference related by Freud—"Jewish swindler, he would like to use me from behind and shit on my head" (in Denis, 1995, 25)—so overtly exemplified "primitive lusts and scatological language" that it may have been constructed deliberately by the Wolf Man to interest his new analyst (26). It is also likely, of course, that Freud will have encouraged Pankeiev's interests if the young Russian had mentioned to Freud what he later wrote in his own memoirs about his childhood interests:

> My sister and I both liked to draw. At first we used to draw trees, and I found Anna's way of drawing the little round leaves particularly attractive and interesting. But not wanting to imitate her, I soon gave up tree-drawing. I began trying to draw horses true to nature, but unfortunately every horse I drew looked more like a dog or a wolf than like a real horse. I succeeded better with human beings, and drew, for instance, a "drunkard," a "miser," and similar characters. (in Gardiner 1973, 24)

I will return to this passage later, when I explore the Wolf Man's recollection of the wolf dream to Freud, but for the moment I shall consider some further implications of this suggestion that the Wolf Man's art was a function of his rivalry with his sister.

Roy R. Grinker has described Freud's "great zest for details in associations and dreams," in some analytic practices that also indicate his emphasis on the visual:

> When names of places were mentioned he would go into the library and ask to be shown the place on the map, which he would then study. He had to understand thoroughly locations and relationships of houses and rooms, frequently asking that diagrams be drawn. (1973, 182)

Freud's analytic attention to visual details may be explained by his awareness that what the eye sees is not necessarily commensurate with what the unconscious is capable of apprehending. During the first two months of Pankeiev's treatment, while working on the

Leonardo paper, Freud also produced the short essay, "The Psycho-analytic View of Psychogenic Disturbance of Vision," in which he claims that the dynamic unconscious often "sees" with clarity what conscious perception—grounded in merely "descriptive" faculties—obscures (1910c, 212–13).[10] The essay can also be read as Freud's claim, at a time when the demands of his writing seemed to be in competition with his practice, that the work of psychoanalysis exceeds the descriptive discourse expected by journals and other forums in which its proponents attempt to explain their work to the scientific community. What Freud saw when he saw the drawing of the dream of the wolves, in other words, may be something more than what he describes for us in the case history. To gain some idea of what this might have been, I suggest that we may need to look further than Davis does in his already remarkably detailed attempts at contextualizing Freud's reception of the drawing. Whereas Davis sought to highlight the cultural and scientific sources shaping the drawing and its reception, I suggest that we consider these same sources and others in their autobiographical (that is, in their heterothanatographical) dimension.

There can be no doubt of course that the *immediate* context for Freud's reception of the drawing of the wolf dream includes research interests and the tensions between various factions within the institution of psychoanalysis. If we take the Wolf Man's own recollection as an accurate guide to dating the account of the dream—"within a month or two after the start" of the analysis—then we may narrow the possibilities to between late March and mid-April. Freud's practice and his research would have been competing for his attention in late March with the Second International Psychoanalytic Congress in Nuremberg—at which the International Psychoanalytic Association was formed—on 30 and 31 March. As Freud claims to have taken an interest in the wolf dream from the moment that it was recollected in the analysis, we must assume that he had less to worry him outside of his practice at the time. We might consider that this was soon after 12 April, after the proofs of the Leonardo essay and the short paper on

[10] The essay can be dated almost precisely, for it is mentioned in two letters—to Ferenczi and Jung—dated 12 April 1910. To Jung, Freud explains that his week "has been taken from me by an obligation, a contribution to a special number of a medical journal in honour of Konigstein (60th birthday)," which suggests that the essay was written to order in the preceding week (Freud and Jung 1974, 306).

psychogenic disturbance of vision had been sent to their respective publishers. Since 12 April 1910 was a Tuesday, we might pinpoint the event sometime before the end of the same week, to between 13 and 15 April. Without access to Freud's analytic notes, of course, such attempts to contextualize so precisely the recollection of the wolf dream can only remain speculative, casting doubt on the historical truth claims we make. Yet with further speculation, we shall realize that this date does provide another context for the recollection of the wolf dream.

In the days approaching 15 April, Freud would have in some degree, consciously or otherwise, anticipated the anniversary of what may be the earliest significant event of his childhood. It was on this date in Freiberg in 1858, that Julius Freud, the second child of Jakob and Amalie Freud, and younger brother to Sigismund (Freud's given name) by less than eighteen months, died. Sigismund was not yet two years old, still in that stage of a child's development he would later call "prehistoric," during which time the images and sounds that form the basic material of the unconscious are recorded. Freud's early family relations were unusual, given that in Freiberg during the first three years of his life his immediate family consisted not only of his parents, but also of two half-brothers from Jakob's first marriage (Emanuel and Philipp, both much closer in age to Amalie than she was to Jakob), and a nephew and niece (John and Pauline, the children of Emanuel and Maria Freud). While these people, along with Freud's nanny, form the nucleus of the *dramatis personae* for the analyses in *The Interpretation of Dreams* (1900), *The Psychopathology of Everyday Life* (1901), and other writings, the figure of Julius, this tragically fated first younger sibling, remains surprisingly absent. Indeed, the only record of Julius's existence in all of Freud's writings is in the letter to Wilhelm Fliess of 3 October 1897, in which the earliest revelations are made from his self-analysis about the "ugly, elderly but clever" nanny, the arousal of libido toward the mother on the journey from Leipzig to Vienna, the "companion in my misdeeds" John, and his niece Pauline (1985, 268).[11] None of the protagonists are named in this letter, yet with the exception of Julius their names are all recorded

[11] Except where otherwise noted, references to Freud's correspondence with Fliess are taken from Jeffrey Moussaieff Masson's *The Complete Letters of Sigmund Freud to Wilhelm Fliess: 1887–1904* (Freud 1985).

by Freud elsewhere, which must lead us to register here the significance of a name that Freud would never submit to writing.

How are we to register this significance of a proper name that would never be re-marked by the person for whom it remained indelibly etched in the mystic writing-pad of his psyche? Freud recalls that he "greeted my one-year-younger brother (who died after a few months) with adverse wishes and genuine childhood jealousy; and that his death left the germ of [self-]reproaches in me," and he adds that "this nephew and this younger brother have determined, then, what is neurotic, but also what is intense, in all my friendships, but also their depth" (1985, 268). Yet this germinal character is erased from the published record of Freud's self-analysis, and should have been erased from the personal correspondence as well, since he determined that his letters to Fliess were to be destroyed.[12] It is as if Freud tried to wish Julius away all over again, and we may wonder if by 1910, fifty-two years after the death of his brother, he was over the guilt he confessed to Fliess. To investigate this possibility, I want to continue this apparent digression away from the events of 1910 to pursue the figure of this absence in Freud's life-writing. Specifically, I want to trace the erasure of Julius (and to identify these traces *as an erasure*) at precisely those points in Freud's writings when the event of his brother's death seems to re-mark itself in its significance.

First, we might look at the letter that mentions the event of Julius's death and Freud's jealousy and guilt without inscribing the name of Julius onto the contours of this event. Are we to assume that it is his guilt over feelings of jealousy toward the ill-fated infant that caused Freud to erase Julius from the written record? This is unlikely in light of the numerous confessions in his writings to other wishes of which he was also guilty, such as incest and parricide, the keys to the Oedipal relation. When Freud wrote to Fliess, he had not yet fully theorized these childhood experiences of jealousy and guilt, or their relation to the Oedipal conflict. Indeed, it was only in the next letter to Fliess on 15 October 1897 that Freud first expressed his insights into the universality of the Oedipal conflict (1985, 270–73). This next letter

---

[12] Jeffrey Masson records the remarkable adventure by which Marie Bonaparte and Anna Freud, among others, salvaged the letters against Freud's determination that they should be destroyed (Freud 1985, 1–13). We have already seen Freud's willingness to destroy personal documents in order to foil his potential biographers.

adds another important figure to the cast in Freud's early Oedipal drama: the second sibling Anna, in his reconstruction of the closed cupboard memory and the association of the disappearance of his nanny with the birth of Anna. Freud's rivalry with his first sister has been well documented, not least of all by Anna Freud Bernays herself, who tells us that no matter how crowded their apartment in Glockengasse became with the arrival of further children, "Sigmund always had a room to himself," and that despite the girls' wishes to take piano lessons, Freud's appeals to have the instrument removed meant that the piano "disappeared and along with it all opportunities for his sisters to become musicians" (1973, 141–42). Although Anna reminisces with apparent fondness, the jealousy behind her words is still evident, and we are probably not surprised by Ernest Jones's assertion that Freud "never liked" Anna either (1974, 39). It is of course likely that young Sigismund had transferred his infantile jealousies from Julius onto the deceased brother's initial replacement. Yet I want to suggest a somewhat more complex explanation, which will bring the whole question of Freud's stated guilt more into accordance with what Freud himself would later write about the origin of the sense of guilt—based on the ideas he seemed to develop in his analysis of the Wolf Man—and with expansions that others have subsequently made on these ideas.

In "Mourning and Melancholia," which was written between 15 March and 4 May 1915 but not published until 1917, Freud elaborates in more detail upon a set of issues that he had first gestured toward in correspondence to Fliess on 31 May 1897, in which he described melancholia as self-reproach for hostile impulses against parents. In this later essay, he explains the psychic processes that may distinguish melancholia from the normative work of mourning, insofar as in mourning "it is the world which has become poor and empty; in melancholia it is the ego itself" (1917, 246). This essay explores the process whereby the libido of the melancholic does not withdraw from an object of loss by displacing it onto another object, as in mourning, but withdraws "into the ego," where it can safely "establish an *identification* of the ego with the abandoned object" (249). Freud also paved the way for the notion of the super-ego—the psychic function chiefly responsible for guilt feelings—in "Mourning and Melancholia," by describing the splitting of the ego, which makes melancholia possible, as the splitting off *from* the ego of a "critical agency" that demonstrates its independence elsewhere (247). In *The Ego and the Id*, Freud further developed this concept of a super-ego as an identification, the first of the cathexes abandoned by the id, that will inevitably behave "as a special agency in the ego and stand apart from the ego" (1923, 48). Returning to the question of melancholia, Freud then explains that what holds sway in the super-ego is "a pure culture of the death instinct, and in fact it often succeeds in driving the ego into death, if the latter does not fend off its tyrant in time by the change round into mania" (53). On the matter of Freud's self-reproaches or guilt, he states that the super-ego (which is responsible for feelings of guilt) is characterized by its placement *vis-à-vis* the id. Derived from the earliest object-cathexes of the id, this super-ego is thus considered in direct relation "with the phylogenetic acquisitions of the id," making it "a reincarnation of former ego-structures which have left their precipitates behind in the id" (48). Thus, the super-ego is a result of and, therefore, emerges *after* the early object-cathexes characteristic of the libidinal-oral phase.

We note that at the time of his brother's birth, in October 1857, the infant Freud was nearly eighteen months old, and that Anna was born before he had turned three.[13] Paul C. Vitz argues that it is unlikely the infant Freud will have had much maternal care from his mother, since she was pregnant for 18 of the first 32 months of his life and was in all likelihood not even in Freiberg when she gave birth to Julius: Amalie's younger brother (also named Julius) died one month before her son, in Vienna, and she may have been visiting him there at the time that Julius was born, which also explains the name she chose for her second child (1988, 7). Vitz emphasizes, although he probably overstates, the importance of Freud's Catholic nanny, Theresa or "Resi" Wittek, on his early development, arguing that she had secretly baptized him, an event for which the dream reconstruction of being washed in reddish water serves as a screen memory, and that her religious influence determined many of Freud's later views.[14] This evidence certainly

---

[13] The dates that I use here are those given by Max Schur (1972) and Paul Vitz (1988).

[14] Vitz's hypothesis is based in part on the fact that in Freud's letter to Fliess on the "Schafskopf" dream, the dream account is followed soon after by the recollection of being washed in reddish water, suggesting that he had condensed the two memories: having been told that he was "washed in the blood of the lamb" and an occasion on which he saw water in which the nanny had washed herself (1988, 20–22). Max Schur suggests instead that the episode in question condenses several memories of which

suggests that Freud's earliest relations with his mother were ambivalent at best. A key term in Vitz's argument is the name *"Amme,"* meaning "wet nurse," by which Freud referred to Wittek (7). He notes also that as Wittek spoke in Czech, she would have referred to herself as "Nana," the Czech name for a nanny—also representing a common variant of the names "Anna" or "Anne" (30). We see, then, that there was a potential for the words by which the mother Amalie (Amalie, mama, or any other similar variant by which other adults may have called her), nanny Wittek (Amme, Nana), and then the third child Anna were known, to have caused confusion for young Sigismund. If he was not already in enough difficulties in his early object relations due to the infrequent availability of his mother, linguistic confusion of mama-Amme-Nana-Anna words will have made his progression through the libidinal-oral phase of object (then word) acquisition immeasurably more difficult. Sigismund will also have progressed through this phase and entered into the Oedipal conflict, formative of the super-ego and the sense of guilt, *after* the death of Julius, but around the same time as the arrival of Anna, the dismissal of the nanny, and the family's move to Vienna.[15]

In *Freud: Living and Dying*, Max Schur proposed that the substratum ascribed to the phylogenetic heritage in "From the History of an Infantile Neurosis" might also be "the time covered by infantile amnesia, the time before language is acquired, before the links between percepts and word representation are finally established" (1972, 131). This "prehistoric" period remains an ongoing problem for psychoanalysis, since what is recalled as the "events" of this period might be real memories, the content of screen memories, condensations, or merely fantasy constructions. Some of these concerns are raised by Freud in his interpretation of the wolf dream, and explained with the concept of *Nachträglichkeit*. Using Freud's explanations, Schur contends not only that Freud did not transfer infantile feelings of jealousy for Julius onto Anna, but that the opposite applies: the feelings he professed to have directed toward Julius were in reality those that he

---

we do have knowledge, including the injury that required stitches under the left side of his chin, sometime between the ages of two and three, which must have involved bleeding and the washing off of blood (1972, 127).

[15] Vitz shows that the date of the nanny's dismissal, as given to Freud by his mother and as repeated by Jones—shortly after Anna's birth on 31 December 1858— is most likely a fabrication, as the nanny was still working for the Freuds until about a month before their departure from Freiberg in June 1859 (1988, 12–16).

later felt for Anna, displaced backward into his infancy (341). Schur does not expand upon this in his reading of Freud's self-analysis, but I think that we need to take it further here, as it raises the question of Freud's guilt in as much as Anna, unlike the earlier sibling that she replaced, did not die. Let us consider instead that if Sigismund had wished his sister away like he claims to have done with Julius, he will have seen his wishes realized in an unthinkable event: he wishes Anna away, but it is the other Anna (his Amme-Nana) who disappears. In what may have seemed to him to be a consequence of wishes aimed toward the sister, through the medium of homonymic confusion—that is, confusion of two distinct word-things—Sigismund thus loses the surrogate mother-object. This loss is then followed soon after by the physical removal of Sigismund and his most immediate family grouping to a city for which he would continue to express his dislike throughout his life: Vienna.[16]

Sigismund's rivalry with the sister Anna produces the most unexpected of results, for which he could have considered himself responsible. Indeed, it is easy to imagine that Freud's wish to remove the sister-Anna produced behavior in him that led to the nanny-Anna's dismissal: his feelings could have been unwittingly redirected toward the nanny, resulting in behavior (such as the theft described later by his mother, or some other act) that subsequently turned the parents against Wittek.[17] Note that the sense of guilt, as Freud later explained it, is more accurately labeled a "need for punishment," since it involves a self-reproach associated with having hated the parents in the earliest object-cathexes (1924, 166). Yet when Freud writes about the sense of guilt in these later essays, he is writing about psychic conditions in adult mental life—melancholia, obsessional neurosis, masochism and so on—which he explains with reference to the formation of the super-ego in childhood. In "Mourning and Melancholia," the essay that signals the beginnings of the concept of the super-ego, he had described conditions *in early childhood* which produce the

[16] Note that Freud's dislike for Vienna may be expressed in the conjunction of the Roman number "vi" (six) with the unstable name "Anna." The importance of Rome and of the number six in connection with Anna associations will become increasingly apparent throughout the present work.

[17] Vitz suggests that instead of suspicion of theft, the nanny was dismissed because of her attempts to have Sigismund converted to Catholicism, a secret that he perhaps unwittingly betrayed by preaching sermons to his family after attending church services with his nanny (1988).

splitting of the ego as a normative function of libidinal-oral development. This essay is of special relevance here, since its role in the
broader project to which it is a contribution—*Papers on Meta-Psychol-
ogy* (1915)—may be as a sequel to "From the History of an Infantile
Neurosis." Although this essay was published in 1917, before the
publication of the case history, it was written several months after
completion of the case history, and its observations on the relevance
of the libidinal-oral phase to the mechanism of introjection—which
Freud still calls "identification" here[18]—can be linked to the promi-
nence already given to this phase in Freud's reconstruction of the primal scene in the case history.

The work of Abraham and Torok will prove useful in developing
this connection here, since their rewriting of the Wolf Man's case history, framed by the elaboration of the concept of the crypt, is
grounded by their investigations into the normal function of introjection during the libidinal-oral phase. In "Mourning *or* Melancholia: Introjection *versus* Incorporation" (in *The Shell and the Kernel*) they include within the definition of the term "introjection" the processes
whereby the infant realizes that the objects taken inside the ego must
remain physically absent, producing an emptiness of the mouth
which is only remedied by the formation of words (1994, 128–29).
What they then call the "fantasy of incorporation" is what happens
when normative introjection fails due to loss of an object that has been
"narcissistically indispensable," a loss that cannot, therefore, be communicated: the object is taken into the ego in the form of the fantasy of
the reality of that object, as a denial of both the loss of the object *and*
the emptiness of the mouth (129). They stress, then, that "the crucial
aspect of these fantasies of incorporation is not their reference to a
cannibalistic stage of development, but rather their annulment of fig-
urative language" (132). The result of such annulment is the establishment of an intrapsychic tomb or a "crypt" within the ego, wherein the
object of loss is maintained as if no such loss was incurred. This crypt
intercedes in normative word-formation because its function is to
maintain that secret which rendered the lost object indispensable, a
secret in which the subject is implicated. It performs this function,

[18] Strachey notes that the term is used in "Mourning and Melancholia" with reference to the "preliminary stage of object-choice," for which the term "introjection"
would be used at several points in 1921 in *Group Psychology and the Analysis of the Ego*
(Freud 1917, 241).

specifically, by rendering words which pertain to the secret unspeakable, and more generally (as a mechanism for achieving its specific goal), by blocking the pathway between the unconscious and its exterior—that is, it blocks the *metaphorics* of word-formation.

It would of course be a mistake to assume that the figure of the crypt arises from the autobiographical dimension of "Mourning and Melancholia" and "From the History of an Infantile Neurosis," if we were to proceed to suggest that Freud's life-writing in these texts gives rise to a theory of the crypt even though the crypt is not theorized in them. The subject of Abraham's and Torok's analysis remains the Wolf Man, as he has been presented in (or insofar as he is present to) psychoanalysis, and they make it clear from the beginning that *this* analysis has been conducted in parallel with those carried out by Freud and Ruth Mack Brunswick. By revising the case history which they view as the "break" between the "first or second topography— the early or later Freud," they explicitly state their aim: "to bring back a more unified view of psychoanalysis" (1986, 2). One implication of this approach is that it is in the case history, in particular, that we may situate both the rupture in the continuity of psychoanalysis—this "infantile neurosis" which sowed the "seeds of doubt in Freud's first views" (2)—*and* the source from which a synthesizing unity may be restored to psychoanalysis. Indeed, the reader will find that by the end of this book, I will identify a similarly synthetic function in the improvisational dimension of the case history. Another implication of Abraham's and Torok's approach, of more immediate concern, is that there is no suggestion that Freud was personally subject to this cryptophoria, which threatened to remain enigmatically beyond his frames of reference. Freud cannot be reproached for his inability to treat the Wolf Man, since he had no access to the crypt.

With this in mind, we should clarify our account of young Sigismund's troubled object-relations by adding that the child had obviously registered his own responsibility for the loss of the nanny in order to have developed self-reproaches, from which we can conclude that no crypt would have been necessary to keep the object of the nanny alive. If we can use Abraham's and Torok's work to rule out the thought of a crypt as a key factor in Freud's own psychic development and therefore, by extension, as a core of all psychoanalytic concepts, we can also turn the same reasoning upon itself, to ask how they could imagine the father of analysis failing to recognize a cryptic topography at work in his analysis with the Wolf Man, since they deduce the existence of the crypt from the very same writings with which Freud expressed this failure? This gap in their reasoning is of course incalculable, unless it is sustained by a division between analysis and writing—that is, between practice and theory. Their goal is not division, however, and their cryptonymic method is clearly an attempt to cast analysis in its own modes of expression—to psychoanalyze psychoanalysis in and through psychoanalytic writing. The gap in their reasoning arises, then, not from the division of analysis and writing but from being too close, in a sense, to the problem. In short, by walking a mile in Freud's shoes, or by conducting analysis in parallel with Freud, Abraham and Torok ensure that the one figure that remains beyond their purview is Freud himself. The reasons for this are methodologically sound—sidestepping the transference to Freud (a problem that we have already discussed here) and allowing themselves to present a picture of the master from the perspective of the Wolf Man (the master, that is, insofar as he is present to the analysand)—yet the effect is, as we can see, a gap in the formulation of a theory of the crypt.

If we are to continue to explore the conditions for deferral in "From the History of an Infantile Neurosis," it will be necessary to redress this gap in reasoning the crypt. It seems to me that this may be done by reversing the direction in which the theory of the crypt arises, turning it back toward the autobiographical dimension of both analysis and writing. Freud was unable to treat the Wolf Man because this patient was present in analysis only *as an enigma* (this is the effect of *this* crypt), a problem that Freud could not admit yet which left the most suggestive traces in the case history and elsewhere. If the effects of this crypt presented themselves in analysis only on the side of the Wolf Man, then nothing would seem to prevent the analyst from recognizing the absences in the Wolf Man's testimony (in the same way that Abraham and Torok recognize them), unless of course the analyst was being blinded to these particular absences by a crypt-like structure on the side of analysis. To be precise, what is needed for Freud to have been unable to recognize the Wolf Man's crypt—yet for the crypt's enforced silences to have left sufficient traces in his writing for another pair of analysts to look therein and see this crypt—is for his own life and writing (his life-writing) to have been obstructed by a figure of absence not unlike the Wolf Man's crypt except insofar as this "false" crypt was its exact opposite, and included the Wolf Man's magic words within its own list of words whose meaning must be kept secret.

This false crypt emerges, I suggest, alongside the earliest reaction-formations of Sigismund's embryonic super-ego, as the responsibility that he felt over Amme-Nana's disappearance is displaced onto the sibling that sister-Anna replaced. In the figure of Julius, as Freud would have learned at some stage in his childhood, he had an available target for the backward displacement of both his rivalry with a younger sibling and his feelings of responsibility for the loss of an important object. As Freud's mother Amalie must have remembered the loss of both her brother and her son on the anniversaries of their deaths, on March 15 and April 15, the months immediately prior to Sigismund's birthday on May 6 will have been quite somber in his first few years in Vienna. The figure of death will have loomed large over the stories told within the family in these months, and it will have been associated with the name of Julius. The consequences of the displacement of feelings of rivalry and the sense of responsibility for loss onto this figure of death will have been not unlike the fantasy of incorporation, but it will have introduced erasure into the expansion of the ego, since it replaces an object of loss with yet another object of loss, and not with an object of plenitude. In place of the crypt—which keeps the lost object alive, but cannot allow the words to be spoken which justify keeping this object alive—a pseudo-cryptic gap in the ego will have been opened out, *which introjects death*.

Another consequence of this displacement will have been the condensation of two distinct and opposing object-relations: death-wishes toward the rival and mourning of the object of loss. These relations will have been condensed to form a single figure, producing an ambivalence that characterized all of Freud's closest friendships in later life. In his interpretation of the *non vixit* dream in *The Interpretation of Dreams*, Freud casts his older nephew John in the role of the originator of this ambivalence:

> Until the end of my third year we had been inseparable. We had loved each other and fought with each other; and this childhood relationship . . . had a determining influence on all my subsequent relations with contemporaries. Since that time my nephew John has had many re-incarnations which revived now one side and now another of his personality, unalterably fixed as it was in my unconscious memory. (1900, 424)

In the letter to Fliess, however, Freud had given this designation equally to John and to Julius. Does this mean that the *non vixit* dream has found no room for Julius, thereby raising doubts about Freud's earlier claim for the significance of his younger brother?

There is a strong reason to believe this is not the case. The key to Freud's interpretation is a reference via the Latin phrase *non vixit* to Brutus's speech of self-justification in Shakespeare's *Julius Caesar*, though Freud also notes, almost as an aside, that he had himself once played the part of Brutus alongside his nephew John in a performance of Friedrich Schiller's *Die Räuber* (*The Robbers*). Max Schur notes that the analogy made in reference to the Schiller play is clearly directed toward Julius instead of John, since *The Robbers* depicts an intense sibling rivalry, with the elder left contemplating fratricide: as an analogy, Schiller has Caesar's ghost appear to Brutus after the battle of Philippi, whereupon Brutus justifies himself with the words, "Where Brutus lives, Caesar must die" (1972, 166). To Freud, such an allusion must have been clear, if not in 1870 when he played the role of Brutus, then at least in 1900 as he wrote his interpretation of the dream: Where I live, Julius must die.[19]

Paradoxically, the very words which point us in the direction of Julius are also the words that explain why he is never named in the interpretation of the dream, save for the one reference in a letter to Fliess. Where Brutus lives, Caesar must die: where I, Sigismund, live, Julius must die—Freud's ego requires that Julius remain dead, so it carries the dead infant within itself as a guarantee, and can never allow this object to be replaced with the formation of the words which speak of the object directly. The mouth must be made to believe that it is already full, even if what fills it is a death. We may begin to see another hypothesis developing, though it is one to which I shall return

[19] William McGrath unravels numerous associations arising from the *non vixit* dream and Schiller's play, such as in Freud's multilayered identification with the main protagonists, whose last name is Moor (Freud was known in his infancy as his mother's "Little Moor" because of his black hair), as well as in references to the Battle of Philippi (Freud's battles with his half-brother Philipp, for example, in the screen memory of the young Freud crying before a closed cupboard), the competition for the love of a woman named Amalia, and the presence of a Pastor Moser who reveals to Karl Moor the meaning of his terrifying dream, linked here to the Julius Mosen parapraxis discussed by Freud in *The Psychopathology of Everyday Life*, and Freud's Moses identification (McGrath 1987, 291–92). To McGrath's detailed analysis, I can add only that Michelangelo's Moses, which so fascinated Freud, was commissioned for the tomb of Pope Julius II—"Julius must die"—a link apparently overlooked.

only briefly: the cancer of the mouth to which Freud succumbed in his later life may well be related to this need to keep the mouth full with a death. To follow the point through, however, we shall need to look more closely at another name that Freud erased in later life—his given name Sigismund—for as I shall argue in the next chapter this name will have served as another of the texts onto which the erasure of Julius was marked. For now, though, I will draw some brief conclusions about the reference to Julius in the letters to Fliess in October 1897. First, note that the month in which Freud made his revelations was the anniversary of the *birth* of his younger brother. By re-marking this birth and the other associations that accompanied this recollection, Freud seems at least on an unconscious level to be registering the transferral of his feelings of ambivalence toward Julius *onto Fliess*, at the same time as he attempts to throw his correspondent off the scent of the key events to which these ambivalent feelings refer. In addition, the names of the protagonists are withheld at the moment of revelation, marking a refusal to explain the contiguity of these associations through the similarity in name of the mother, the nanny, and the sister. To name the nanny would be to name the mother and the sister, the effect of which would be to fill the mouth which, by the ego's reckoning, is already full. Rather than lock them away in a crypt, where Freud's secret could be held in perpetuity, though, his ego opens out onto a false incorporation and a false crypt, which feign both mourning and self-reproach, thereby paving the way for the repetition of ambivalence.

CHAPTER TWO

Corresponding with Revenants

In no way can the subject relate to the phantom as his or her own repressed experience, not even as an experience by incorporation. The
phantom which returns to haunt bears witness to the existence of
the dead buried within the other.

(Abraham and Torok [1987] 1994, 175)

The Burden of Irresponsibility, between Julius and Sig(is)mund

Despite a rigorous examination of Freud's *non vixit* dream analysis as
life-writing in *The Interpretation of Dreams*, William Beatty Warner
passes over the clues that have pointed us in the direction of Julius
Freud. What remains of use to us here, however, is that—true to his
aim to read life-writing as "written to, for, with, and/or against another person" (1986, 29)—he targets Fliess and the correspondence
between Freud and Fliess as the personal and textual foci for the
dream interpretation. In short, the self-analysis that is made possible
by the death of the father is realized through the correspondence. The
father and the correspondent signify as if they were one, so to overcome the father's mastery, Freud must do away with the surrogate father who hears his confessions: Fliess. Since Warner's reading is
grounded in the figure of the father at the core of the super-ego, it is
unlikely that ambivalence derived from conflicts in early libidinal-
oral acquisition will be considered. We would of course be wrong to
dismiss the death of Freud's father as a factor in his self-analysis, but
we can no longer think of his response to this death as the work of
mourning (nor, strictly speaking, as the work of melancholia) since
the displacement of an early object-loss onto a death has rendered all
further object-loss problematic. We can put this problem to work in
the reading of the correspondence-cum-self-analysis as life-writing if
we add that the self-analysis inscribes the first death, which cannot let

itself be worked through, even as it works through the death of the father. The trace of the first death is inscribed only as a non-inscription or an erasure in the self-analysis, and in the working-through of the death of the father. We must suspect, then, that Freud's self-analysis challenged the false crypt to relinquish its secrets, but at the same time furnished it with a new mechanism for maintaining these secrets. The material thrown up by the analysis in the wake of the father would have seemed like the questions leading down the road to the false crypt if they didn't look so much like answers on the road to the unconscious. By playing the self-analysis off against Fliess-the-father, Freud recasts his ambivalence toward Julius and conceals even more deeply the primary (though later) relations that were in their turn recast as this ambivalence toward Julius.

By introducing the thought of a false crypt into the Freud-Fliess relationship, we also prompt a question about the correspondence. The false crypt which situates itself like an unerasable trace between the ego and its other—an erasure that behaves within the self like full presence, a successfully incorporated object—renders suspect the idea that what Freud was doing in the letters to Fliess was *corresponding*. Whether we take "corresponding" to mean being in agreement or conformity and/or exchanging letters, it is dependent in the first instance on the verb "to respond," which even as an intransitive verb indicates a movement toward another, since a response is by definition a response-*to* and presupposes an invitation to respond. After Heidegger, the invitation to respond and the response-to have been tied directly to notions of responsibility by displacing the idea that responsibility is an accounting of Being to itself before another. As Rodolphe Gasché summarizes, for Heidegger, "responsibility is primarily a response to which one commits oneself, or pledges oneself in return" (1994, 228). Every response—indeed, the condition of responding in general, that is, *responsibility*—responds *to* this pledge and, as Derrida adduces in *Of Spirit: Heidegger and the Question*, is therefore also "of this pledge" (in Gasché 1994, 229). The important thing here is that Heidegger's rethinking of responsibility recasts it in advance, and in the consent to which one pledges oneself before any other event, as a function of the entry into language. There is nothing in the response to which one pledges oneself, or in the general condition of responsibility, that occurs outside of the conditions for the possibility of language.

As young Sigismund displaces his sense of responsibility for the disappearance of the nanny onto the already-dead Julius, he introduces an irruption into the condition of responsibility insofar as this displacement registers in the acquisition of language. The resulting gap in the ego, which I have described as a false crypt, impedes responsible relations with the other not by keeping the lost object alive but by keeping it dead, filling the mouth and the language that it acquires with the death of the other. Under these conditions, nothing like a response is possible unless it has at first, irresponsibly, been directed toward the *death* of the other. We shall see later how this aspect of the false crypt will impact upon Freud's relation with the Wolf Man and with his rivals in the institution of psychoanalysis, but let us register for now that in his correspondence nothing like a "response-*to*" can take place. Since the correspondence will always be predicated on the death of the other it cannot, therefore, presuppose the invitation from the other to respond. Instead of a response-to, Freud's correspondence functions as life-writing that continually redefines self and other in terms of the interior polylogue of the false crypt, and not as a responsible movement toward the other.

The same mode of self-redefinition can be traced in the letters that Freud wrote to correspondents other than Fliess. One of his earliest known correspondences was with Eduard Silberstein. The pair had been close friends at the Leopoldstädter Communal-Realgymnasium in Vienna between 1870 and 1873, and as they were apart from each other during holidays, they began a correspondence which continued, after Freud went on to the University of Vienna, until around 1880. In *Freud's Discovery of Psychoanalysis: The Politics of Hysteria*, William McGrath charts the academic directions taken by Freud and the intellectual influences to which he was exposed at the University, by clarifying what Freud wrote in his letters to Silberstein about his activities (1987). McGrath highlights the philosophical and political leanings Freud developed even as his interests began to be directed toward marine biology and medical science, and he foregrounds the hitherto underestimated influence of Franz Brentano on Freud's early thought. In a more recent study, Madelon Sprengnether uses a detailed reading of the Silberstein letters (together with the letters to Martha Bernays) to demonstrate the degree to which Freud's writing in his letters constitutes "a profound labour of self-construction" (1998, 142). While McGrath reads these letters as evidence (in a more biographical sense), Sprengnether treats the same material as a performance of Freud's "life," without which the factual biographical material is meaningless. What I will do here is provide a further reading of the life constructed in the Silberstein letters. In the sense that I shall read the gaps in meaning rather than providing a detailed reading of the content of these letters, I will produce claims that supplement those made by both McGrath and Sprengnether. My aim, in other words, is to read these letters and the relationship to which they give expression from the viewpoint of what they do not tell us (at least not directly, in so many words) about Freud's self-construction— that is, his inability to respond-to, and the cultivation of ambivalence.

Freud and Silberstein taught themselves Spanish while at the Gymnasium, so as to read the works of Cervantes in their original language. In their correspondence and, as all evidence suggests, in private personal interactions, the pair adopted the names of the canine protagonists in *El coloquio de los perros* (*The Colloquy of Dogs*)—Freud was Cipion and Silberstein was Berganza—and they named their private community the "Academia Castellana." John E. Gedo and Ernest S. Wolf have suggested that it may be no coincidence that Freud chose Cipion, since we already know of Freud's strong identification with Hannibal and his anxieties about the city of Rome. In its Latin form, Cipion is Scipione, which might refer to Scipio Africanus the Elder, the Roman commander who had defeated Hannibal—Freud must have been aware of this derivation when he signed one letter "Cipion, *non imperador romano*" (1976b, 98n6). Freud's choice thus "betrays that his openly declared identification with Hannibal was ambivalent at best and more probably stood as a thin screen hiding his partisanship for Rome" (98n8).

In addition to Gedo and Wolf's observation, we may note that the identification with the Cipion-Scipio figure was not the first occasion on which Freud had associated Hannibal with images of dogs. Among the visual sources that Whitney Davis finds for Freud's interpretation of the wolf dream are a pair of illustrations from the picturebook that Martin Freud described as one of his father's childhood favorites: Friedrich von Tschudi's *Das Thierleben der Alpenwelt* (*Animal Life in the Alpine World*, 1865). In the first of these, a pair of dogs chase a wolf away from a village, an image which, as Davis suggests, is recast by Freud as "Sigmund the wolf-hero—as a wolf-dog *doctor*, the attentive listener who will save the patient from the consequences of his childhood trauma by chasing away the terrible wolf-parents"

Fig. 6. Illustration from Friedrich von Tschudi, *Animal Life in the Alpine World*, 1865 (Davis 1995, 201).

Fig. 7. Illustration from Friedrich von Tschudi, *Animal Life in the Alpine World*, 1865 (Davis 1995, 203).

(1995, 202).[1] The second image depicts "an Alpine rescue dog, striding out with one foot with its ears pricked, saving a little boy lost in the snowy mountains" (200). Davis takes this description of the image to point out similarities between the dog in the illustration and the description of the picture of a wolf that had so frightened the Wolf Man in his childhood: "striding out with one foot, with its claws stretched out and its ears pricked" (qtd. 200). As a result, he disregards the structure on which the top half of the picture centers—a structure that can be identified, not least of all by reference to the type of dog below it in the picture, as the Hospice St. Bernard.[2] The Hospice stands along the Great St. Bernard pass, the path Hannibal is said to have taken on the last leg of his ill-fated Italian campaign.[3] In Cipion-Scipio, the conqueror of Carthage *and* the attentive canine listener, Freud was to rediscover those symbolic associations that Tschudi's illustration had suggested to him some seven years earlier.

Though we can explain Freud's choice of the name Cipion, we might wonder to what extent Silberstein would have made Berganza—whose life serves to provide the exemplary novel with its moral—his pseudonym of choice. As Freud was in the year above Silberstein, it seems more likely that the younger of the colleagues will simply have acquiesced to the wishes of his senior partner. Indeed, for Silberstein, the chance to play the role of Berganza would not have been without its advantages, since it is the errant dog who discovers that the pair must be twins, which allows him to rise above his junior status and become Freud's equal. The same episode does, of course, also provide Freud with a chance to play out what is to become a familiar scene of negation, as Cipion claims their kinship is a hoax played on them by the witch who was "foolish, cunning, and malicious—if I may be pardoned for speaking that way of our mother, or

---

[1] Davis points to the very obvious graphic association that Freud is most likely to have made between the Wolf Man's initial transference—"Jewish swindler, he would like to use me from behind and shit on my head" (in 1995, 24)—and the positioning of the animals within this picture, wherein the closest of the dogs is clearly coming at the wolf *from behind* (202).

[2] I would like to thank Anna Bemrose for bringing this important detail to my attention.

[3] See, for example, Sir Gavin de Beer's calculations of Hannibal's trajectory, based on many historical accounts, in *Hannibal: The Struggle for Power in the Mediterranean* (1969). Of the many possible paths that Hannibal might have taken over the Alps on his journey, that provided by the Great St. Bernard pass is one of the few that fits in with all of the accounts of his march (159–61).

rather your mother, for I will not have her for mine" (in Gedo and Wolf 1976b, 101). By choosing Cipion, Freud also takes on the role of prototype for what would later become the psychoanalyst, as he moralizes about the harm done to individuals by deficiencies in their early caretakers, and since his role with relation to Berganza is, in Gedo and Wolf's description, equal to the role of the analyst: "that of listening to a life's story and making occasional comments to facilitate the flow of the material" (111). If we consider that the correspondence with Silberstein-as-Berganza is a model for the later development of psychoanalysis, in the same way as the Fliess letters, then we must also note that at the core of this model the would-be-analyst renounces the analysand-as-other.

In the Silberstein correspondence, this renunciation is realized by a displacement onto the characters with whose names the pair replace their own signatures. Silberstein and Freud are, in a sense, erased from their correspondence by deleting their own given names. Peter Gay has described how Freud's history as a nomenclator—from choosing the name Alexander for his youngest brother, through to the selection of the names of his six children—is tied to his prolonged "detachment from identifications and object choices imposed on him by his fate of being born Jacob Freud's son, and a substitution of identifications and objects freely chosen" (1990, 73). By adopting the name Cipion, Freud experiments not only with the association which enables him to renounce the mother and the brother in one stroke, but also to renounce the name of the father, by casting off the name given by the father. Freud also experimented during the period of his studies at the Gymnasium with formally adopting the German form of his name, Sigmund, for his signature. On the reasons for this change, as Gay rightly suggests, we can only speculate, since Freud never explained his reasons for dropping the middle syllable from his given name. Gay repeats Ronald Clark's claim that the name was shortened because Sigismund, "widespread among Jews, served as a favorite butt in anti-Semitic jokes" (55). Yet we should note that "Sigismund" would have carried symbolic weight for Freud since, as Paul C. Vitz suggests, the name was given to him in honor of Saint Sigismund, patron saint of Bohemia, whose feast is only five days before Freud's birthday:

The original Sigismund was a Burgundian King of the Franks in the sixth century. His first wife, by whom he had a son, Sigeric, died, and the king remarried. The new queen had a falling-out with Sigeric, her step-son, and she moved against Sigeric by telling King Sigismund that his son plotted to kill him and usurp the kingdom. The king, incited by the queen, had his son killed: The youth was throttled while he slept. (Vitz 1988, 42)

By abandoning his name, Freud seems to elide the Oedipal associations that are tied to it. This happens, of course, well before he would make his crucial discoveries on the general relevance of the Oedipal drama, and we must note that the name given by the father to Freud is also the name of the father who had his son killed at the incitement of the second wife. The name given by the father is in this instance a warning against the threat of parricide, though it recasts the son of Jakob's second wife in the role of the father who puts the son to death.[4] By abandoning this name, then, Freud symbolically removes himself from the Oedipal drama *and* carries out the abandonment of the father (symbolic parricide) against which the name serves as a warning.

We might also suggest that the abandonment of the given name is an effect of the false crypt centered on Julius. As a scholar, Sigismund taught himself Spanish in order to read the works of Cervantes in their original language, which suggests that he would not have stopped at only reading *Don Quixote* and *The Colloquy of Dogs*, works whose influence on him are now well documented. Indeed, it seems ridiculous to think that he would not also have read the work whose title bears the likeness of his name, *Persiles y Sigismunda*. When we consider Freud's affinities with Rome, we note that he will have identified with the female protagonist who bears the likeness of his name, as she and her lover Persiles seek a union that can only be realized in Rome. However, Sigismund will also have noticed that in Book IV of the *Persiles* Sigismunda, in the guise of her lover's sister Auristela,

---

[4] Max Schur suggests that Freud may have suspected that Amalie was in fact his father's third wife, even though the second wife Rebecca was almost certainly kept as a secret among the adults (1972). The silence of the adults also means that we do not know why Rebecca was considered a taboo subject. Marie Balmary emphasizes the role of the second wife in the development of psychoanalysis, on the basis that the silence that came to be associated with her name impressed itself unconsciously upon Freud's imagination (in Sprengnether 1990, 15). The importance of the role of the second wife in the history attached to Sigismund's name may have indeed served at some level as a device for erasing her from the family history, and Freud never indicated any conscious awareness of her existence.

must overcome one final obstacle on the verge of realizing her goal, after the witch Julia casts a spell causing the heroine to deteriorate "until she comes to resemble death itself" (El Saffar 1984, 165). This depiction of his namesake's being reduced to a living death as a consequence of rivalrous jealousies, and by a witch whose name was uncannily like that of his dead brother, reverses the roles played out in the false crypt. The roles are reversed using the very names that the crypt is supposed to keep secret within the mouth. The name Sigismund is therefore a symbolic threat to the body of the son, but also a "real" threat, in the sense that the real is only ever constituted psychically, to the ego.

This threat to the ego, in the form of the words whose dead object supposedly fills the mouth, is overcome by a further displacement which will, tragically, attach Freud's name inexorably to an object that would be what post-Freudians might call "transitional" were it not acting as a barrier separating the ego from its outside. The name "Sigmund" can be translated as "cig-mouth," and we might suspect that Freud acquired his addiction to smoking at around the same time that he experimented with the change of name—in later life, he thought nothing of offering a cigarette to his seventeen-year-old nephew Harry, which we may take to mean that Freud had been smoking by the same age, before 1873 (Harry Freud 1973, 313). It would of course be absurd to suggest that Freud's adoption of the name Sigmund— fifty years before his cancer was first recognized by Felix Deutsch—is in any direct way an early "cause" of his cancer. Yet we can observe the associative attachment of his own name to the habit which, in all likelihood, produced the cancer that took from him much of the quality of the last twenty years of his life. If he required that his mouth be filled with the death of his brother, in order to maintain the psychic formation that nevertheless determined his sense of himself, Freud could never undo his attachment to smoking without further threatening his ego with a return of the scenario from which it had apparently gone to such lengths to remove itself.

The Silberstein letters foreshadow much of the (falsely) cryptic strategy used later in the Fliess letters. Following in Sprengnether's path, I have concentrated upon those strategies of displacement that Freud used in his relationship with Silberstein to redefine his relation to the events and personae of his infancy. Yet the work of Gedo and Wolf or of McGrath also suggests that Freud's early correspondence foreshadows the method he used in later life for developing his metapsychology in correspondence. From Gedo and Wolf, we see that Freud gestures toward a prototypical analytic relation in his use of the names Berganza and Cipion, and in McGrath's reading of the letters, we see that Freud's later thinking flows out from directions taken in his thought during the time he was writing letters to Silberstein. In other correspondence, Freud actively redefined himself and his relations to others in ways that are irresponsible (in the sense that I have been describing here) *and* constitutive of psychoanalysis. For example, the letters written to Emil Fluss at about the same time as those to Silberstein work through the failed relation with Fluss's sister Gisela by casting the love object in the role of the "ichthyosaura." McGrath points out that this code name is a pun on the name Fluss (a word meaning "river"), suggesting that the beloved is seen as a river creature (1987, 89), yet Gedo and Wolf suggest that this "ichthyosaur" is the libidinal object whose acquisition Freud would later characterize with the abbreviated "ich" (ego) and that these letters demonstrate narcissistic reworkings of incidents in Freud's adolescence (Gedo and Wolf 1976a, 74–86).[5]

Might we gain something by submitting Freud's use of this term "ichthyosaura" to a cryptanalysis, in the same way that Conrad Stein's "archaeopteryx" is read by Abraham, in "Psychoanalysis Lithographica," as the secret of a "cryptorchia" (Abraham and Torok 1994, 218)? If we were dealing with a crypt, then this would seem to be a valid course to take, but we have seen that the strategies employed in Freud's correspondence point more to the formation of a *false* crypt. Rather than attempt to read the "ichthyosaurus communes" as an attempt to block metaphorics, then, we should be willing to find in it the workings of a metaphorics that lead us into a crypt only *as if it were* attempting to block metaphorics. In other words, the trick of the false crypt is in creating a secret and in strategies of concealment that feign unreadability after the manner of a crypt, so as to keep the ego from acknowledging its assumed complicity in a greater loss. Recalling that the term "ichthyosaura" names the love object from whom Freud concealed his love, we recognize that the term itself refers to— that is, it *reveals*—a concealment. We are of course mistaken if we

[5] Similarly, in *Object-Choice (All You Need is Love)* (1994), Klaus Theweleit reads Freud's courtship letters to Martha Bernays as a sort of test-case for the analytic relation. See also the next note.

think, as Ernest Freud suggests in his introduction to the Freud-Fluss correspondence, that this term "ichthyosaur" is Freud's invention (in Gedo and Wolf 1976a, 76n2), which leads us all too easily to think of the term as a construct or a cryptonym. Yet as Gedo and Wolf note, the term actually refers to "an extinct fish-lizard of the Jurassic period" and Freud's use of it reflects his preference at that time for "metaphorical allusions derived from geology and paleontology" (76n2). This reference to Gisela Fluss as an "ichthyosaur" is an overt deployment of a metaphorical relation which, as McGrath points out, ties the subject of sexuality to sea creatures, the importance of which is that Freud's early scientific successes were acquired through his studies into the nervous and reproductive systems of eels (1987, 132).

We may also wish to consider that if the "ichthyosaur" functions as a metaphor by way of allusion, then Freud's use of the metaphor is determined, narcissistically, in part by ambition, since allusion is a testimony to erudition. His vacillations throughout his teenage years over the choice of a career path are well documented, but we may observe that the one path from which he never deviated, even as he pondered options, was that of the scholar. As we have seen, his success with study was encouraged by his parents, who clearly set the eldest of their children above the others within the Freud household. Though he often lamented that scholarship and, later, his clinical research would never be a financially rewarding career path, the young Freud was aware of the prestige that could be acquired through scholarly pursuits. By using a term that is both a pun on Fluss's name and an allusion to his own scientific research, he cleverly works through his failure to declare his intentions to Gisela during his stay with her family. In "Screen Memories" (1899), Freud lists a memory supposedly provided by a "man of university education, aged thirty-eight"—though there is no doubt that the material is autobiographical—in which two boys (John and Sigismund) snatch a bunch of yellow flowers (dandelions) from a little girl (Pauline), an incident that culminates in all three children's receiving delicious bread from a peasant woman (309–11). Closer analysis of the memory revealed that it screened the "first calf-love" (Gisela) that he had "kept completely secret" (313). The memory screens both Freud's inability to follow sexual desire through to its fruition ("to deflower" his calf-love) and his failure to secure for himself the comfortable future that a union with Fluss would have guaranteed (315). The screen memory emerges later, when Freud was "a slave to my books," "struggling" for his "daily bread," at which time he was too distracted by his studies to settle down and marry his cousin, as his father had planned (314–15). By using the "ichthyosaur" in his correspondence, Freud subordinates the object of his secret love to the objects of his research, enabling his studies to absorb questions of marriage and ambition.[6]

In both the correspondence *and* "Screen Memories," the metaphorics of the "ichthyosaur" and Freud's "calf-love" point us toward the drama being played out in the false crypt. To follow them along this path, we begin by observing the keys to unlocking the material hidden behind the memory of the dandelions: the color of the flowers and a trip to the Alps. Though the dandelions in the screen memory were not the same shade of yellow as the dress Gisela Fluss wore at their first meeting, Freud recalls that "I saw how certain flowers which have light coloring in the lowlands take on darker shades at high altitudes," and that there is "a flower which is very similar to the dandelion but which is dark yellow and would exactly agree in color with the dress of the girl I was so fond of" (1899, 314). What Freud does not follow up in this crucial part of his own self-analysis is the use of the word *goldlack* (wallflower) in his first description of the difference between the color of Fluss's dress and that of dandelions. After the manner of a crypt, the use of this term transgresses the boundaries between languages, since one of the text's key English phrases is only present in the form of a German word, and it is a function of this transgression that the key phrase will only be concealed by translation—Strachey's version renders the word faithfully, and without comment, as "wallflowers" (314). Strachey's failure to comment upon the term is more striking for the fact that the German term voices the theme of poverty—that is, "gold-lack"—that Freud is discussing in the text *at that very moment.*

I suggest, however, that it is precisely this immediacy that renders any further comment potentially damaging to Freud, since the theme that he is explicating at that very moment in his text echoes the relations that fed off (and were feeding into) his self-analysis. "Screen Memories" was written sometime very early in 1899, as a letter to

---

[6] Klaus Theweleit reads Freud's choice of Martha Bernays as the choice of an object whose familial ties to academics and scholars mirror his own scholarly ambitions. Uncle Jacob Bernays was a professor of philology who "had devoted particular attention to Aristotle's concept of catharsis" (1994, 44).

Fliess of 3 January suggests (Freud 1985, 338–39). He claims in the letter that from a portion of his self-analysis he has confirmed that fantasies are projected back into early childhood from later periods, an argument that is made throughout "Screen Memories." Yet Freud withholds the details of the self-analysis from Fliess, suggesting that writing the details out would take "half a sheet," so he holds further discussion on these matters over until their congress at Easter.[7] As he withholds material until their Easter congress, Freud is also potentially threatening to withhold the material altogether, since he could recall that their previous Easter congress had failed to eventuate. Moreover, a glance at Freud's letters to Fliess around the time of the previous Easter is particularly revealing. In the letter of 3 April 1898, Freud laments that the congress would not happen, and adds that he will not take an alternative journey to "our beautiful Italy again this year," as "earnings were bad" (1985, 307)—gold-lack, indeed! When he next writes, less than two weeks later, he describes the trip to Italy, through the Alps, that he has just taken in the company of his brother Alexander and which he "took in a grumpy mood, but from which I returned refreshed" (308). The closing statements in the first of these letters and the opening statements of the second appear, when placed together in this way, rather like the argument posed in "Screen Memories," in which the difficulty posed by poverty (or gold-lack, the wallflowers) is overcome with a revealing trip to the Alps. In other words, the argument that Freud makes in "Screen Memories" echoes the attempt in his correspondence to begin to exclude Fliess from his life.

Freud's denial of the autobiographical source of "Screen Memories" conceals this link between the essay and his letters to Fliess, thus pushing his correspondent into the background. As I have suggested, the attempt to exclude the correspondent from their correspondence is typical of Freud's inability to respond-to, and of the way in which his life-writing more directly addresses the false crypt than any external dialogue. It is not surprising, then, that the language Freud uses to

[7] To be precise, Freud states that the explanation of the mechanisms involved would take "half a sheet," which Jeffrey Masson notes is equivalent to half of a "signature" of sixteen pages (Freud 1985, 339n2). If we add the suggestion that the explanation of the mechanisms involved is only one half of the story, and that the "elucidations of the story of my early years"—which he also holds over until the congress—comprise the other half, then the whole discussion would take a full sheet of sixteen pages. Not surprisingly, this is the same as the number of pages that "Screen Memories" filled when it appeared in print later that year.

push Fliess into the background derives from this cryptic drama. The frustration of the gold-lack is not simply one of thwarted ambition in Freud's career, in his calf-love, or in his analysis of the yellow flowers, but of a failure to match up to maternal expectations. As an infant, Freud was "mein Goldener Sigi" to his mother (Shengold 1993, 100). As he grew, the golden hair that brought this affectionate title upon him began to darken, a process that Freud sees repeated by those flowers in the Alps which "take on darker shades" as the altitude increases. By raising the wallflower, or gold-lack, only to immediately dismiss its relevance, Freud points to this golden expectation of his infancy. Note, however, that he dismisses the gold-*lack*, suggesting that he believes himself to still be his mother's "Goldener Sigi" somewhere beneath the darker shades of his maturity. At base, then, the dismissal of the gold-lack is also an affirmation that he remains, over his sibling rivals, his mother's favorite.[8]

Freud places a great deal of importance in "Screen Memories" on the suggestion that his patient (himself) first made his "acquaintance of the Alps" while undertaking the studies which distracted him from carrying out his father's plans. Though his first personal acquaintance with the Alps may have happened during his studies, Freud had, we must remember, already been familiarized with images of the alpine landscape from his childhood picturebook. What Freud does not tell the reader is that the Alps function not only as an immediate context for the formation of the screen memory, but as one of the associative devices linking this screen to his childhood and, as we have now seen, to events surrounding the composition of "Screen Memories." Given this claim, we might ask how the series of determinations centered on the Alps leads Freud to revisit the failed calf-love for Gisela Fluss, the "ichthyosaur." We have seen that the use of this term can be read as an allusion to Freud's scholarly achievements, and in particular I suggest that the use of this term is at least in part an allusion to one of the important German texts on marine biology: *Untersuchungen uber die Fauna Peruana* by Johann Jacob von Tschudi, published in 1845. The erudite researcher into marine biology can hardly have been ignorant of Tschudi's text, nor could the scholar have

---

[8] There may also be verbal echoes of the "brother" in Freud's use of the term "bread-and-butter" (*Broterwerb*) to make sense of the image of the bread in the screen memory (1899, 315).

missed that the surname of the author of this important "Ichthyolo-gie" was the same as that of the author of *Das Thierleben der Alpenwelt* (*Animal Life in the Alpine World*), the treasured picture book that he had acquired as one of his first prizes for academic excellence. Thus, in a way that may be overdetermined, yet which remains unstated in Freud's essay or his correspondence, past and present merge ab-solutely, making it impossible to say which has determined which.

This indeterminacy is, of course, as the false crypt would have it be, since it also becomes very difficult to look past Freud's stated guilt over the death of Julius. Need we add, then, that when Freud writes to Fliess on 14 April about his trip to Italy, he is writing on the day before the anniversary of his brother's death, and that his description of the passage through the range specifically names the "Julian Alps" (1985, 308)? If we are drawn toward such details, it is because Freud's state-ment of guilt opens for us a doorway to the false crypt, wherein all roads lead to Rome, and not to the unconscious. As we have seen here, Freud's correspondence and essays intersect with each other and with innumerable other sources—literary and scientific—to form a complex network of images and associations that we are calling his life-writing. We have also seen that this life-writing takes its language from the false crypt, which insists that the mouth is full and no ges-ture or movement toward the other is necessary. What we are for the sake of convention calling Freud's correspondence is thus, in effect, nothing at all like a correspondence, since it excludes the correspon-dent from its parameters. To put this another way, when Freud writes "to" Fliess, for example, he *writes* Fliess, in the same way that he writes himself, according to the language provided by the false crypt. Thus, we see how Freud's life-writing takes the form of an improvisa-tion for which any external *or internalized* material provides a source to be manipulated, so as to preserve the structure of the false crypt.

"Guilt; or, the Anniversary"—The False Crypt in Freud's Life-Writing

I have been arguing that Freud's simplified assessment of his guilt over the death of his brother is compromised by the definitions of guilt that he was to make later, in the face of his challenging analysis with the Wolf Man. Yet such an argument runs a risk of unscrupulously conflating two distinct phases in the development of Freud's metapsychology, making the earlier Freud answerable, as it were, to the later Freud. I contend, however, that the development of the metapsychology is a part of an ongoing process of self-definition, contributing to Freud's life-writing, which makes the clear distinction between an earlier or later phase untenable. Specifically, with regard to the question of Freud's guilt, we are not merely impressing a later *definition* of guilt onto an earlier *confession* of guilt. Instead, we consider that Freud *continually* addressed guilt in and through his life-writing, and that the later definition of guilt emerges as he reconfigures his own past in the terms thrown up by the analysis with the Wolf Man. I suggest that at around the time that Freud took Pankeiev into analysis, the drama that had been playing itself out in the false crypt was prominent among the conflicts raging against the ego of the analyst, but also that the wolf dream provided Freud both with his conviction about the Wolf Man's infantile neurosis and the terms by which he would be able to work through his own infantile drama. To return to an issue that I raised earlier, I will argue here that what Freud saw with clarity—what his conscious perception had obscured but his unconscious or, rather, his false crypt had observed—when he saw the drawing of the dream of the wolves was the key to unlocking secrets from his own past.

I have already suggested that the anniversary of his brother's death seems to have been important for Freud, but it remains to be shown here that he demonstrated what we might call an anniversary reaction. Perhaps the earliest such reaction that we can date with some precision is the "severe cardiac misery" of which Freud complains in a letter to Fliess dated 19 April 1894 (1985, 67). He states that this discomfort "lessened during the past two days," and that "the last few days have undoubtedly brought relief," which places the attack no later than 15 or 16 April (67, 68). In addition to his physical symptoms, Freud complains of having undergone "a feeling of depression, which took the form of visions of death and departure in place of the usual frenzy of activity" (67). He suggests that the abstinence from smoking that Fliess had enforced upon him contributed to this "lypemanic mood," leading to the first time that Freud expressed what would later become his outright mistrust: "This time I am especially suspicious of you, because this heart affair of mine is the only one in which

I have heard you make contradictory statements" (67–68).[9] Though these cardiac symptoms were to recur at irregular intervals in the years that followed, the visions of death and departure which accompanied them in April 1894 would return at more predictable intervals. However, as we shall see, the regularity of the *Todesangst* (anxiety based on fears of the imminence of the death of oneself or of an acquaintance) may be directly attributable to Freud's concern for what Fliess called "critical periods," and to the sense of guilt that stemmed from the drama in the false crypt, rather than being attributable to a strict repetition compulsion.

Two years after he first complained to Fliess of visions of death and departure, Freud complained again of "attacks of fears of dying, such as today, although Tilgner's cardiac death is most likely more responsible for this than the date," in the letter of 16 April 1896 (1985, 181). This "date" (*Termin*) is a reference not to the day and month of the calendar year, but to a point in time upon which a particular event is anticipated, calculated in this case according to Fliess's theory of critical periods. Freud confesses immediately before registering his complaint that he is making "daily notes about my health, so that they can be used to check special dates" (181). These special dates were determined according to the hypothesis that before birth—that is, from conception and other prenatal events—the patterns of the lives of all human beings, down to the likely date of their death, is shaped by the interweaving of the terminal dates of two "critical" periods: "the menstrual process of the twenty-eight day type," and "a twenty-three day cycle, to which people of all ages and both sexes are subject" (in Schur 1972, 94). Freud later claimed ignorance of the complexities of Fliess's hypothesis—"I lack any mathematical talent whatsoever and have no memory for numbers and measurements" (1985, 450)—although he was for quite some time heavily involved in substantiating the critical periods. Indeed, as Leonard Shengold suggests, this admission of ignorance represents a last attempt by Freud to stave off the end of the correspondence, washing his own hands of Fliess's numerological fantasies in the same movement by which he defers to his correspondent's mathematical knowledge (Shengold 1993, 82–3).

[9] Jeffrey Masson notes that the "lypemanic mood" ("*lypemanische*"), which is a state of "morbid depression," is incorrectly given in *Anfänge* as *hypomanische*, explaining the translation of the phrase in *Origins of Psychoanalysis* as a "hypomaniac state" (Freud 1985, 69n1).

Freud repeats the admission of his ignorance in such matters, just as he again demonstrates his mathematical abilities, in a letter to Abraham in 1924. This letter mimics his letters to Fliess so closely that, according to Shengold, it demonstrates both Freud's continued identification with Fliess through "longing to be taken care of by his old doctor" now that he is confronting his cancer and a warning to Abraham to be cautious in his own growing dependence on Freud's old nemesis (82). We could add that the continued identification with Fliess is a functional one, since it enables Freud to redeploy in his later correspondence the same strategies of exclusion that doomed his relationship with Fliess. His deferral to Fliess was always compromised in advance, and the resulting ambivalence, carried over into the later correspondence, both closed Abraham out *and* unwittingly played on the transference by pointing the younger analyst in the direction of Freud's old surgeon.

The strategic character of Freud's admissions of ignorance becomes obvious when we also reflect upon the times he demonstrated his propensity to use complex numerical calculations. As early as the Silberstein correspondence, Freud elaborated what John Gedo and Ernest S. Wolf describe as a "beautiful numerological fantasy" (Gedo and Wolf 1976a, 72). Later, in the letters to Fliess, Freud collected data to substantiate the periodicity theory, but also performed many complex calculations, often attempting to relate Fliess's theories to his own. For example, in the letter of 6 December 1896, in an attempt to calculate the age groups during which "repressed memories relate to what was actively current" in the case of each of the three groups of sexual psychoneuroses, Freud tied the ages to "multiples of the 28–day female period," and even stated his suspicion "that the distinction between neurasthenia and anxiety neurosis, which I detected clinically, is related to the existence of the two 23–day and 28–day substances" (1954, 179). The editors of this first Freud-Fliess correspondence (Eric Mosbacher and James Strachey) note that Freud abandoned this suspicion, which they describe as "the climax of his efforts to connect Fliess's views with his own," soon afterward (179n2). It is more instructive to look at some of the material that the editors did not include when they published this letter:

> I am trying to introduce the notion that it is a male 23–day substance the release of which produces pleasure in both sexes, and a 28–day substance the release of which is experienced as unpleasure.

I then note that I can account for all psychic periods as multiples of 23–day periods (π) if I include in the calculation the period of gestation (276 days = 12π).

$$3 \times 12\,\pi = 1\,^{1}/_{2}\ \text{years}$$
$$6 \times 12\,\pi = 3\,^{3}/_{4}\ \text{years}$$
$$12 \times 12\,\pi = 8\ \text{years} \ldots$$

This would mean that psychic development occurs according to 23 [-day] periods, which would summate to multiples of 3, 6, 12, . . . 24, in which case the duodecimal system would become effective. (Freud 1985, 211)

When Freud admitted his ignorance of mathematics some years later, did he expect that Fliess would have failed to remember such obvious displays of arithmetic skill? To the contrary, he expected nothing *from* Fliess. The admission of ignorance performs what can only be called a forgetting of its own, by which the letter writes only to the moment and with no sense of respondence.

Examples of such mathematical gymnastics also occur in the *Psychopathology of Everyday Life* (1901), precisely at that point, in the final chapter, when Freud begins to mark a distinction between determinism and superstition. The first example is taken directly from the correspondence with Fliess. In the letter of 27 August 1899, he had explained that "nothing in the mind is arbitrary or undetermined," and had used the example of his claim in the same letter that the final proofs of the *Psychopathology* had contained "2467 mistakes" to make the point (1901, 242). The number emerged, according to Freud, after he had read that a "General E. M.," whose career he at one stage wished to emulate, was retired (242–43). By taking his age at the time that he had formulated this wish (24), and his age at the time of writing the letter to Fliess (43), he established that the number 2467 expressed both a triumph at the end of the General's career and a strong wish that he himself should have another "twenty-four years' work" (243).[10] In the second example, added in 1907, Freud recounts the case of a "perfectly healthy" man who had been inspired by the *Psychopathology* to test the determination of seemingly arbitrary numbers

---

[10] Might we consider this wish to have been in some degree self-fulfilling? Note that Freud first complained of his cancer, which was already at a highly advanced stage and undoubtedly will have been causing him discomfort prior to his initial complaint, in April 1923, some twenty-four years after he had expressed this wish, and only a few weeks short of his sixty-seventh birthday.

by choosing the number 1734. It then occurred to the man that he apparently divided his life into "portions of 17 years," and that "34 is the last year of youth," for which reason the man, who had only recently celebrated his thirty-fourth birthday, had been feeling miserable (243–44). It is not difficult to show that this is a thinly veiled autobiographical reference, since in 1907 Freud celebrated his fifty-first birthday (51 being the next number in the same sequence). We can refer to *The Interpretation of Dreams* to find Freud expressing fears that 51 had occurred in a dream in connection with the death of a colleague, and observing that "51 is the age which seems to be a particularly dangerous one to men" (1900, 438). Later in the same book, he returns to the same "absurd dream" and his fear of "51 years being the limit of my life," and then returns immediately to the *non vixit* dream, which we have already tied directly to his revelations about Julius (513). What we glimpse momentarily in *The Interpretation of Dreams* is this connection between Freud's *Todesangst* and the death of his younger brother. This connection is diffused in 1907 through Freud's avoidance of the number to which it ultimately refers: his own age. We note, of course, that Freud's concern over his age in 1907 is evidence of the residual influence on him of Fliess's ideas, since the critical age of 51 is calculated by adding the two critical periods: 28 + 23.

For Freud, as Max Schur observes, seventeen would have seemed like a perfectly "good" number to which to attach significance. From his earliest years, he was exposed to Jewish superstitions "linked to the Bible or to the use of the Hebrew alphabet, as an orthographic and a numerical system" (1972, 25). An example of this is the attachment of a particular meaning to a number, determined by the numerical equivalents of the Hebrew letters in a word, such that the numerical values of the letters in the Hebrew word for "life" add up to eighteen, while the values of the word for "good" add up to seventeen. Schur explains that when Freud selected the seventeenth as the date for his engagement to Martha Bernays, he told his betrothed that the number was one that he had, as a boy, chosen in a lottery designed to reveal a person's character, which for Freud revealed the word *Beständigkeit* (faithfulness) (1972, 25). As Schur suggests, the superstition was probably behind Freud's choice of that number ("good") in the first place. As he later reached his fifty-first birthday, Freud's association with Fliess had long since been severed, yet the idea that the number 51 should be an especially critical one will have been particularly difficult for Freud to revise in the light of the significance that he had attached to its largest divisor. What is of particular importance is that in the case listed in the *Psychopathology*, Freud conceals the one number that would allow us to read the entry as autobiographical *and* to identify the residual influence of Fliess's periodicity theory. He performs calculations that skirt the number fifty-one, yet refrains from including it: "$1734 \div 17 = 102; 102 \div 17 = 6$. I then divided the number into 17 and 34" (1901, 243). He divides the number by its first portion, 17, to produce 102 and 6, yet does not divide it by its second, 34, to produce 51 and $1\frac{1}{2}$.[11]

In addition to showing how the figures relate to each other arithmetically, Freud attaches significance to each of them by taking the corresponding number of the work in the Reclam Universal Library. He begins by stating that number 102 in the collection is "Kotzebue's play *Menschenhass und Reue* [*Misanthropy and Remorse*]," and finds the significance of the reference in the fact that his "present psychical state is one of misanthropy and remorse" (1901, 244). In the other cases, he finds that the numbers 6 and 34 correspond to plays by Adolf Müllner (*Die Schuld* and *Der Kaliber*), and the number 17 to Shakespeare's *Macbeth* (244–45). As for the last of these, the supposedly thirty-four-year-old man records his inability to bring the reference to mind. Upon discovering the source, he points out that although he had read it closely he could think of very little about it at that moment, save for the following: "murderer, Lady Macbeth, witches, 'fair is foul' and that at one time I had found Schiller's version of *Macbeth* very fine" (245). From these few thoughts he concludes that there is "no doubt then that I wished to forget the play," yet he does not provide an analysis of the reasons for forgetting. In what we have observed, however, there are sufficient clues to suggest that references to parricide, to witches, and to versions of Shakespeare's plays by Schiller also parallel other references to the death of Julius.

Yet, more significantly, in what Freud does *not* recollect about *Macbeth* we find an affirmation of what we have also seen about the relation between his ambition and his assessment of his own personal guilt. He does *not* recollect that a key motivation in Shakespeare's

[11] The latter number, $1\frac{1}{2}$, approximates Freud's age at the time of Julius's death (before his second birthday) and, later, will become a recurring figure throughout his analysis of the wolf dream.

play is the degree to which ambition and the fall of the ambitious are fuelled by prophesies. Ernest Jones records the events by which the future greatness of his biographical subject had been supposedly foretold:

> He was born in a caul, an event which was believed to have ensured him future happiness and fame. And when one day an old woman whom the young mother encountered by chance in a pastry shop fortified this by informing her that she had brought a great man into the world, the proud and happy mother believed firmly in the prediction. (1974, 33–4)

His mother's "Goldener Sigi" later dismissed such prophecies as a common event, yet Freud also attributed his ambition in some degree to his father's exclamation: "The boy will come to nothing" (in Shengold 1993, 13). Shengold demonstrates the efforts by which the negative image provided by Freud's father was countered with positively inflected ego ideals, yet we might add that attempts by Freud to prove his father wrong were also by their very nature attempts to prove his mother and the prophetess *right*. It is for this reason that Freud's expressed guilt is so ambiguous, since the removal of the rival for his mother's affections will indeed have been the only way to ensure that his mother's hopes for her firstborn could be realized.

The other screen memory that, as we have seen, ties Freud's ambition to events in his earliest childhood—the one which incorporates both early childhood memories and the memory of Freud's "calf-love" for Gisela Fluss—is also packed into this listing of numbers and works. The informant points out that number 34 refers to *Der Kaliber*, and that the title reminded him of a rhyming game he once played with his "(six-year-old son) Ali," in which he had rhymed his son's name with *"Kali,"* meaning "potassium" (1901, 244). He notes that his son is no longer the sweet boy he had been on that occasion, with the phrase *"ka (kein) lieber Ali,"* which is pronounced *"Kaliber Ali."* We may note that of Freud's sons, the one with a name closest to Ali is Oliver ("Ollie") and that the year in which he was six is the same as that in which Freud embarked upon his self-analysis and recorded some of his revelations in letters to Fliess: 1897. We can also note that this reflection upon the resonances of the term *Kaliber* in the phrase "*ka lieber*" might have evoked reflections that Freud had, *at the same time*, been casting upon his "calf-love"—literally, a "*Kalb-Liebe.*" Thus, the references to *Macbeth* and to *Der Kaliber* are determined in some degree by association to the link made between Freud's scholarly ambition and the guilt that he claimed to have felt over the death of his younger brother.

Yet it is only in reference to the number that does not strictly belong to the series to which Freud's age belongs that he can even hint at this association. The numbers 17 and 34 provide the series culminating in the unspoken number 51, yet it is in reference to the multiplier 6 that he voices both guilt *and* ambition: "No. 6 in the U.L. (I know a whole quantity of its numbers by heart) is Müllner's *Die Schuld* [*Guilt*]. The thought plagues me constantly that the guilt is mine for my failure to become what I could have been with my abilities" (1901, 244). Observe the telling shift in tense in this sentence: though his "failure to become" is measurable directly in relation to what "could have been," the thought presently "plagues" him that the guilt for this past failure *is* his. In 1907, Freud confronted what he had for some time been expecting to be his final year of life, which is why I think these reflections upon his "failure to become what I could have been" is cast so irretrievably in the past as a potential or, perhaps, a prophecy that has not—and, therefore, will not—be realized.[12] It is on this point that I want to turn again to Freud's reference to Tilgner in his letter to Fliess on 16 April 1896. In Max Schur's reading of this letter, Freud's neurotic identification with Tilgner is taken as the key determinant in the onset of another cardiac episode, the basis for this identification (apart from the obvious fact that Tilgner died from precisely the sort of cardiac episode of which Freud complained) being the news related in Tilgner's obituary which parallels some aspects of Freud's own life and his fears of dying before his potential is realized (Schur 1972). Tilgner had died less than a week before he was to have unveiled, in the presence of the Emperor, his *magnum opus*, a statue of Mozart that was to stand between the Vienna Opera House and the Albertina Museum. As Schur points out, Freud had in the letters which preceded this one detailed the works he would complete if he

[12] In *Freud: Living and Dying*, Max Schur details Freud's fear of his death throughout 1907, and the impact this fear had upon the development of his theory of guilt (1972; see especially 225–54).

could have but a few more years in which to write (1972, 102). Between 1896 and 1907, then, the only shift we see in Freud's attitude toward his death is ostensibly one in tense, entailing the shift from hoping that he *would* live long enough to realize his potential to expecting that he *has* not realized his potential in what time he has had of life.

Of particular interest to our study of relations between Freud's lifewriting and the institution of psychoanalysis, however, is that a defining moment in the history of this institution is recorded in the letter of 16 April 1896. Freud mentions to Fliess that he is enclosing "the French publication," by which he is referring to *"L'hérédité et l'étiologie des névroses"* ("Heredity and the Etiology of the Neuroses"), the paper containing the first published instance of the name of the theory and method that he would invest in his future success: psychoanalysis (1985, 181, 171n2). He adds that he is expecting "any day" the arrival of the "German," to which Masson has appended "[translation]," suggesting that what Freud is expecting is a translation of the French publication he has just mentioned. An equally valid proposition, I suggest, is that Freud refers not to a German translation of the French paper but to the publication in German of *"Weitere Bemerkungen über die Abwehr-Neuropsychosen"* ("Further Remarks on the Neuro-Psychoses of Defense"), in which the term "psychoanalysis" is also used, and which had been sent off to its publisher on the same day as the French paper—5 February 1896 (Freud 1896b, 159). If we agree that Freud's identification with Tilgner is motivated by the sculptor's death prior to the unveiling of his masterpiece, we may also suspect that a more immediate association for Freud is not the work that he is intending to write in years to come, but that work which he has already completed and which is still to be unveiled to his public. The French paper has passed into history as the first published appearance of the term "psychoanalysis," yet the delay before the release of the German paper will have been the source of some anxiety for Freud. Only with the release of this work, after all, could he be confident that German readers would be exposed to his latest neologism and, most importantly, that his claim over rights to name the method that he and Josef Breuer had recorded in *Studies on Hysteria* would have been announced to the German public *and* to Breuer:

> In some passages in a book which has since appeared by Dr. J. Breuer and myself (*Studies on Hysteria*) I have been able to elucidate, and to il-

lustrate from clinical observations, the sense in which this psychical process of "defence" or "repression" is to be understood. There, too, some information is to be found about the laborious but completely reliable method of psycho-analysis used by me in making these investigations—investigations which also constitute a therapeutic procedure. (1896b, 162)

With the use of the term "psycho-analysis," then, Freud marks the line of demarcation separating the investigation upon which he pinned the success of his metapsychology from Breuer's. Confronted with the untimely end of the sculptor Tilgner, however, he would have reflected anxiously upon the possibility that his own demise might occur before this demarcation was unveiled before the German public—without which his own individual ambitions must falter.

Are we not overlooking some of the more important things that can be said about the letter of 16 April, however, if we pursue Freud's identification with Tilgner without considering that his dismissal of the "date" and even his professed identification can be read as functioning strategically, in the same way as we have been reading other letters in Freud's correspondence? Schur's portrait of a neurotic identification with Tilgner, and the material that I have added here to this portrait, is a valid one, but it is, I think, a portrait that risks taking Freud's confessions to Fliess too literally. This dismissal of the "date" as a factor in his cardiac episode is, of course, an early form of the distancing of his own theories from Fliess's which characterizes the later letters, in its suggestion that not all of Freud's episodes can be explained with the periodicity theory. However, this dismissal of the "date" also warns the reader against thinking too much of another "date" or *Termin;* that is, the date of the letter understood as an anniversary. As Schur will himself find much to say about the death of Freud's brother—it was his work that led me to consider the impact of Julius's death upon Freud's life[13]—I find it remarkable that he so readily heeds Freud's warning, failing to point out that Tilgner's death neatly coincided with the anniversary of Julius's death. To be precise, the sculptor died on the morning after this anniversary, though we

[13] While Schur's book is clearly the stimulus for many of my suspicions about the role of Julius's death, he was not the first to include Julius among the residues discussed in relation to Freud's dreams. Four years before the publication of *Freud: Living and Dying,* Alexander Grinstein had published *On Sigmund Freud's Dreams* (1968), in which Freud's infantile jealousy toward his brother is listed as a key determinant in many of the dream images that Freud records in his self-analyses.

might find a more precise parallel exists between their deaths by comparing these with the date on which Easter Sunday fell in the relevant years: in 1858, it was celebrated on 4 April, while in 1896 it was 5 April. This means that, relative to Easter Sunday, Julius and Tilgner both died on the second Thursday following the day of the Resurrection—too precise a match for the ever-evolving false crypt to have failed to attach some significance to it.

I have been chary until now of raising the issue of any connection between the date of Julius's death and the Easter celebrations, since it has seemed to me that for the first five years of Freud's life, during which time he established the death of his brother as a convenient earlier event on which to displace his feelings for Anna, there was never a sufficient correspondence between dates to warrant drawing any direct association from them. This is to say that from 1858 to 1861 there was never less than a week separating Easter Sunday from the anniversary of his brother's death, suggesting the unlikelihood that Freud would have made any direct connections between the Easter celebration and the solemn remembrances of Julius's death by his mother.[14]

Yet I raise the issue here because with the death of Tilgner we find a particular reason why Freud might have linked the Resurrection to the anniversary of his brother's death. Schur notes that according to Tilgner's obituary, which was Freud's source for his identification, the sculptor had on the afternoon of 15 April given final instructions for engraving a few bars from *Don Giovanni* onto the base of his Mozart (1972, 103). Schur also notes that as *Don Giovanni* was a particular favorite of Freud's, he would have recognized that the bars to be engraved on the monument were from the final scene, in which the protagonist dies under the impact of witnessing the ghost of the Commandere whom he had murdered. Again, surprisingly, Schur fails to recognize in this association the "revenant theme" that he later identifies in his analysis of the *non vixit* dream (158). The revenant theme refers to the emergence of repressed material in dreams, particularly in the form of a haunting or spectral figure, or indirect references to such haunting, as in the appearance of the ghost of Julius Caesar before Brutus in Schiller's *Robbers*. If we recall that Freud

[14] Given the move to Vienna and the arrival of more children in these years, it also seems unlikely that his mother will have maintained any overt remembrance of the death of her second child any later than about 1861.

began his analysis of the *non vixit* dream in October 1896, at around the time that he realized that Fliess's date of birth was almost the same as Julius's, and that he experienced his cardiac episode and identification with Tilgner—another "revenant theme"—on the anniversary of Julius's death, we recognize the precision with which he was resurrecting and reliving the death of his brother in his life and correspondence during his self-analysis.

Yet the theme of the Resurrection involves more than the question of the return of the dead. The particularly striking feature of the Resurrection, as it is remembered in the Easter festival, is that it serves as a reminder to the followers of Jesus Christ that he has died for their sins.[15] Easter is, in other words, an annual reminder of the guilt and the mortality of those who celebrate it. Freud's cardiac episode in 1896 reflects just these concerns, prompting me to speculate further that *if we could* trace a history of the false crypt, we might find that the displacement of feelings toward Anna (the sister-nanny-mother) onto Julius occurs toward the end of the libidinal-oral stage, but also that the particular dynamic of the false crypt (anniversary reactions and a heightened sense of mortality) develops at a later time, when the anniversary of Julius's death is closer to Easter Sunday. Though there are no instances of a correspondence between these dates in Freud's early childhood, we find that between his ninth and twenty-eighth years the date of Easter Sunday falls within two days of 15 April—between 13 and 17 April—on no less than seven occasions: 1865, 1870, 1873, 1876, 1879, 1881, and 1884. In other words, there are many occasions on which the language of the false crypt could extend to include the then-contiguous themes associated with the Resurrection. In any case, I am not concerned with dating this particular development precisely; rather, my intention is to point out the frequency with which such correspondences might arise and to suggest, therefore, that frequency or repetition may be significant, not as the *sign* of an anniversary reaction, but as one of the *determinants* of such a reaction.

The reader may recall that I have been oscillating between the Tilgner reference in 1896, after one of Freud's cardiac episodes, and the addition of an analysis of the number 1734 to the 1907 edition of *The Psychopathology of Everyday Life* (that is, in the year that Freud

---

[15] Paul Vitz's account of Freud's Christian influences also includes an explanation of what he calls Freud's "Easter-Pentecost complex" (1988, 15).

reached the critical age of 51) to show that in the years between these two texts, Freud's perception of his mortality had shifted from a fear that he might die before his expected success could be realized, to an expectation that his death would mark the certainty of his failure to achieve the success he could have achieved with his abilities. I took this ambivalent expression of guilt and ambition in 1907 as a cue to return to the letter of 16 April 1896, prompting the suggestion that Freud's anxieties about his mortality were associated in the false crypt, via a developing Easter complex, with the anniversary reaction triggered by the date of Julius's death. Yet we have seen only a few details or possible references to Julius likely to support the claim that the anxieties expressed in 1907 are connected with this anniversary reaction.

However, I only pursued these parallels between the letter of 16 April 1896 and the 1907 text after finding that the latter suppressed themes of guilt and ambition in recollecting *Macbeth*, a text whose action relies heavily on these themes. In something else that Freud fails to reveal, we find the theme of the anniversary insinuating itself. What he fails to reveal is simply anything about the various plays that he lists except for their name and number in the Reclam Universal Library. On Müllner's *Die Schuld*, in particular, we are given the word *Schuld* (guilt) only to refer to the informant's guilt over his failure to succeed. Freud does not say that Müllner's tragedy—more precisely, a *Trauerspiel*, since the tragedy in the German tradition conventionally revolves around bereavement—concerns the lot of Count Oerindur, who is haunted on the anniversary of a death for which his ancestors are to be considered responsible—a legacy of *Schuld* (blame and debt, as well as guilt) that it is his fate to inherit. By associating the guilt arising from unfulfilled ambition with Müllner's *Schuld*, Freud indirectly points us to the connection between this ambition and the guilt that he had expressed over the death of his younger brother. He also points to the *anniversary* of this death as a catalyst for the renewal of the legacy of *Schuld*.

In his fifty-first year, as in his fortieth, Freud maintained this almost obsessional accumulation of identifications and associations whose value lay in the degree to which they progressively legitimated the stories told in the false crypt. A function of the false crypt, however, is precisely to smooth over the traces of accumulation or progression, to treat material *as if it were* unconscious, knowing nothing of time. We glimpsed here the signs of this smoothing in two texts separated by more than a decade, in parallels that might have seemed like a mere repetition or reworking—not even a variation on a theme but more of the same—were it not that we recognized from the outset that these texts are marked by a shift in tense. Yet it is difficult to describe this shift in tense as a progressive movement in something like a history of the false crypt, since acquisitions made by the false crypt are admitted only insofar as they can be made to fit its internal schema well enough that it will not have to admit to having externalized itself through the emptiness of the mouth. Accordingly, no new object is incorporated-introjected into the false crypt unless it can be made to seem like it has been there already—unless, that is, it enriches the originary plenitude with which the false crypt purportedly fills out the subject's ego. I have been looking closely here at Freud's identification with Tilgner in 1896 and his use of *Schuld* in additions to the 1907 edition of *The Psychopathology of Everyday Life*, but I want to stress that what we have been looking at are examples of a life-writing whose language is *symptomatic* of a crypt-like structure in the ego, and not wholly coterminous with that structure. We have tied Freud's Tilgner identification to the anniversary of his brother's death, and we have located expressions of anniversary reactions in the use of *Schuld* eleven years later, yet we have also seen that the themes of guilt, mortality, and anniversary were adopted by the false crypt at some earlier stage that may be impossible to locate with any degree of precision.

Are we saying, then, that these structures of association are both overdetermined *and* indeterminate? As these structures are symptomatic of a crypt-like formation that feigns to block metaphorics (to preserve a lost object), yet which relies on metaphorics to perpetuate the displacement of a (falsely) lost object onto the site of another loss that the ego must not admit, the answer is, quite simply, yes. Such a claim cannot be made, however, without recognizing that it compromises the structure of what we have been calling an identification. I have already pointed out that the identification with Tilgner functioned strategically to close the letters to Fliess off from their respondent. As such closure is symptomatic of the false crypt's denial of the mouth's emptiness, it would seem also to block any form of internalization, especially identification (in which the object of representation is kept intact—hence, its exteriority is still recognized—and internal structures are reorganized around this object).

Thus, we may be describing what Melanie Klein called projective identification, whereby internal impulses are projected onto an external object and assumed to then be directed back toward oneself. What Klein describes with this concept is an exteriorizing principle for identification, rather than simply an interiorizing process or an adoption for oneself of characteristics of some external object. A projective identification is an internal process which presumes the exteriority of that which is interior. Alternatively, we could reinforce the point that the form of identification we have been describing in the formation of the Tilgner association is triggered in the first instance by an irruption in the primary process, somewhere between perception and preconsciousness, which I have elected to label as a false crypt. In the case of the crypt proper, *this* crypt defined by Abraham and Torok specifically in the case of the Wolf Man, there can be no such thing as identification: projections from the safety of the cryptic enclave are all there is.

Yet in the case of the false crypt, something altogether opposite takes place. We could attempt to argue whether the false crypt is enabling identifications in the form of internalizing processes or introjections, or if it enables identifications, in the Kleinian sense, in the form of projections, but it is not altogether clear that we may arrive at a satisfactory conclusion. This apparent indeterminacy with respect to the directions of the false crypt may be an inevitable consequence of the conditions for the discovery of the Wolf Man's crypt concealed behind the words used in the case history. When they describe this cryptic enclave, Abraham and Torok are referring to a blockage in what Abraham describes elsewhere as the "somato-psychic" mediating between the interior of the unconscious and its exterior (1994, 86–87). The somato-psychic relation can be understood psychoanalytically as a relation between neither "the body proper" nor "the habitudes of the Ego," since both soma and psyche "mean" nothing to psychoanalysis except inasmuch as they represent the terminal poles embedded within each other, between which drives (understood as "representative") mediate. The ego is cast here not as the psyche proper but its outermost layer, a topographical model according to which the crypt situates itself between the innermost (unconscious) kernel and that portion of the ego which is projected toward the exterior.

Whereas the crypt proper remains nestled within this enclave, the false crypt is forced to function on behalf of the somato-psychic relation so as not to draw attention to itself absolutely. The false crypt therefore functions simultaneously in the direction of both introjection and projection, since the sense of there being any direction at all is one of the effects of the somato-psychic relation rather than one of its conditions. The far more serious threat of absolute exposure is countered by allowing for extensions beyond the site of the enclave. In the case of Tilgner's death, on the anniversary of Julius's death, the false crypt confronted such a threat; the date of the event signified Tilgner as a revenant of Julius, but the name of the deceased sounded the *Tilgen* or the erasure of the *Schuld* which the ego associated with this anniversary: *Tilgen* means to expiate, to pay off a debt, or simply to erase.

If the false crypt extended beyond its enclave to identify directly with Tilgner's death—or, more precisely, to identify with the *record* of this death in his obituary, as objects or word-things—then it might have found for itself a magic word in the form of this death whose name sounds erasure. Yet this magic word also threatened the false crypt since the particular erasure it sounds is that of the *Schuld* which now functioned as guarantor of the infantile scene that the false crypt had locked away inside the ego. Of course, the false crypt does not merely extend itself beyond the safety of its enclave within the ego. The false crypt is not a fixture whose dimensions can be determined with any degree of certainty, no matter how much we seem to need to rely on spatial or topographical language to alert ourselves to its presence (or the absence which it allows to be substituted for the plenitude of the mouth). As a surrogate for the somato-psychic relation which determines any sense of exteriority and interiority, the false crypt will effectively reorient the inside and outside of itself, enabling this "Tilgen," which sounds the erasure of the indispensable *Schuld* to pass directly to the interior without passage of any kind. This is to say that it will bypass the mouth already filled with erasure, by literally projecting the new material inside: a magic word indeed.

The Primal Horde Stirs: Rivalries with Adler and Jung

We have seen that from within the insularity of the Fliess letters, Freud indulged in an identification and a symptomatic language, both of which gestured to the "false" scene of infantile jealousy and recrimination. Of course the letters often functioned as practice for (and examples to be used in) Freud's public writing. The language of the false crypt thereby proliferates, turning his self-analysis and the metapsychology that it generates into a game of hide-and-seek in which the analyst knows not what he seeks, and in which but a trace of Julius has been left behind every door. Yet it is a game that Anna (the sister-nanny-mother)—the object of Freud's jealousy and guilt (perhaps, that is, of his "misanthropy and remorse")—has refused, in advance, to play. We are not surprised, then, to find that the absence of Julius resonates through Freud's life-writing in his letters and essays—he is never named as such, but a word here and a date there abound. By conceiving of Freud's writing as life-writing, we thus establish a crucial point to keep in mind when discussing Freud's earliest responses to Pankeiev in what Offenkrantz and Tobin called the "therapeutic alliance": even if we wished to think of Freud's approach to his patient as that of a researcher to his main research interest, we must recognize that these interests have already been shaped in some degree by the symptomatic language of the false crypt, or at the very least by the complex personal history driving Freud's scholarly ambitions.

Another important corollary that arises from these claims concerns the question of Freud's rivalries with Jung and Adler: if his interest in the Wolf Man is understood in terms of his attempt to rebuke his two chief dissenters, then our aim here must be to attempt to understand how these rivalries are enacted, as in the letters to Fliess, in life-writing *and* in language and behavior that are symptomatic of a false crypt. It is not surprising that of the many men and women who developed close affiliations with Freud, Jung and Adler are the two whose relationships with Freud are readily compared with that of Fliess. During the last year of his personal acquaintance with Adler, Freud himself described their relationship with just such a comparison: on 3 December 1910, he complains to Jung that Adler "awakens the memory of Fliess, but an octave lower. The same paranoia" (1974, 376); and to Ferenczi he writes on 16 December that "Adler is a little Fliess . . . just as paranoid" (in Fiebert 1997, 243). We may note that this comparison is not made as a suggestion that Freud felt with Adler the same intensely ambiguous attachment that he previously felt with Fliess. Rather, this "Fliess" with whom he compares Adler in December 1910 is the delusional malcontent he addressed when, on 27 July 1904, he wrote the last letter that would pass between them:

You are not alone in regretting—I do too—that this incident in which you reproach me has reawakened a long-dormant correspondence. It is not my fault, however, if you find the time and the inclination to exchange letters with me again only on the occasion of such petty incidents. The fact is that in the past few years—"Everyday Life" is the dividing line—you have no longer showed an interest in me or my family or my work. By now I have gotten over it and have little desire for it any longer; I am not reproaching you and ask you not to reply to this point. (1985, 467)

We have already seen examples of the way in which, in his half of the correspondence, Freud excluded Fliess from the role of respondent. Perhaps it is no mere coincidence that Freud locates *The Psychopathology of Everyday Life* as "the dividing line" in the decline of his relationship with Fliess, since this work represented the completion of a number of contradictory messages that he had been sending Fliess. We have seen that the mathematical gymnastics Freud displayed in the final chapter contradict his own denials to Fliess that he possessed such skill, and we have seen that the first example is taken directly from the correspondence, as if the letters were always only rehearsals for the published work.[16] In spite of himself, then, Freud's comparison of Adler with Fliess suggests that the former was a target for similar strategies of exclusion, and perhaps a similar (though less intense) ambivalence, based in part on a continued identification with his former mentor and tormentor.

The comparison may be traced with some degree of certainty to at least as early as 1907, when Adler published *A Study of Organ Inferiority* after presenting a paper on his ideas to the Wednesday Psychological Society on 6 March. Martin S. Fiebert points out that Adler "acknowledges Freud's influence on his thinking but presents his own framework for understanding the development of neurosis" (1997, 244). In what would become a familiar pattern in Freud's relations with Adler, he expressed dissatisfaction not in so many words, but the latter must have been made to feel unwelcome during the months

---

[16] Certainly Freud used the early correspondence to present drafts of material to Fliess. The difference in the later correspondence is that Freud does not present the material as drafts eliciting responses from his colleague and peer, but as examples proving theories for which he expects no rebuttal, and he provides no clear indication that the material used in the correspondence will appear soon after in general circulation.

that followed, because at the end of the year he wanted to leave the Society. On 31 January 1908, Freud wrote to Adler, persuading him to reconsider, and stating to the "strongest thinker of the small group" that changes would be made within the group "to accommodate your desires" (Fiebert 1997, 244). Though Freud was clearly sensitive in 1907 to the threat of ruptures from within his fledgling institution, he also seems to have been willing to play favorites among the people whom he considered to be his pupils. His relationship with Adler at this time already seemed to be taking on all of the signs of ambivalence that he had practiced with others and perfected in the letters to Fliess. It may be no coincidence, then, that Freud attributes to Adler the material that is added on "chance numbers" to the 1907 edition of *The Psychopathology of Everyday Life* (1901, 243).

As we have already stated that this material is autobiographical, we must ask why Adler, of all of Freud's disciples, is listed as the source. At one level, we may state that the attribution of autobiographical material to Adler is a form of favor in that it may privilege him as a confidant and the keeper of his master's legacy. Another way to state the matter may be to suggest that Freud favors the disciple that he feels may be closest to rebellion, in expectation that dissension can be contained and controlled from within the institution. Both Adler and Jung were described by Freud at one stage or another in terms that suggested their minds and work were at one with his own, and each of them was elevated to high office within the institution of psychoanalysis (as we shall discuss shortly) at precisely the time that they seemed the two most likely to tear the institution apart. In addition to reading Freud's favor as an attempt to control dissent, however, we might also consider that the particular favors he bestowed were in some degree a way to position his disciples as rivals within his own internal drama. If we look at the autobiographical material attributed to Adler, for example, we see that its themes—achievement, ambition, failure, and guilt—extend beyond the childhood material with which it is associated toward Freud's concerns for his greatest creation at a time when he is convinced that he is nearing his death.

Adler may indeed be a source for the autobiographical material— but only because he was the one who, in 1907, was the root of Freud's gravest concerns for the future of psychoanalysis. For Freud, these concerns in the present were also linked with the sins of his past, with Adler in the role of the brother as the object of love and hatred. Fiebert points out that Adler had himself endured "a lifelong rivalry with his older brother, who was named Sigmund" (1997, 264–65). Adler's refusal to play the part of the obedient, subordinate pupil is thus unfairly characterized if dismissed as paranoia, as it was by Freud. We may suspect of course that Adler used Freud as a substitute for his brother, and that he used his departure from psychoanalysis as a symbolic departure from his restrictive family ties.[17] Yet we must not forget that Freud cultivated Adler's paranoia by behaving toward him with the same degree of ambivalence that he had displayed in other doomed friendships.

In the material added to *The Psychopathology of Everyday Life*, Freud seems to honor Adler by attributing to his pupil material drawn from his own experience, as if to elevate the pupil to the status of confidant or even analyst to the master. The honor is a dubious one, since the series of associations brought to light by the number 1734 are left incomplete, and Freud records his "regret" at Adler's discretion in not detailing the significance of the associations (1901, 244). He goes even further, though, as he attributes to Adler the suggestion that this "perfectly healthy man" did not succeed in synthesizing his ideas (244). In other words, the analysis that he attributes to Adler is a failed one. Even in bestowing honor, then, Freud taints honor, which he exacerbates by concealing the autobiographical status of the added material: we cannot read that Adler has been presented as analyst to the master because this is not the master's story; instead, this pupil is a (failed) analyst to an otherwise perfectly healthy individual.

Fiebert provides further factors behind the enmity that developed between Adler and Freud, citing Freud's admission to Joseph Wortis that the scientific differences had not been of principal importance in any of the dissensions affecting psychoanalysis: "it is usually some other kind of animosity, jealousy or revenge, that gives the impulse to enmity. The scientific differences come later" (in Fiebert 1997, 264). In addition to sibling substitutions, Fiebert points to Freud's conflict with the older Viktor Adler as a factor shaping his attitudes toward Alfred. Freud had "both admired and seriously quarreled [with]"

[17] Fiebert notes his suspicion that Adler's conversion to Christianity in 1904 "both annoyed and troubled Freud" (1997, 265). He notes that Adler came from a community that "de-emphasized its Jewish heritage," although we may suspect that this conversion was a rejection of that heritage emphasized by Sigmund, that is, by Freud the rival brother-substitute (267n9).

Viktor, a well-known socialist, while he was a student at the Gymnasium (265). Ambivalence turned into animosity during one argument in which the pair insulted each other and, as Jones claims, "there was even for a moment some talk of a duel" (in Fiebert, 265). There can be no doubt that the incident remained significant for Freud, as it figures in the Count Thun dream in *The Interpretation of Dreams* (1900, 213). Fiebert also points out that Freud's apartment in Bergasse 19, "which he impulsively rented in 1891, was formerly occupied by Viktor Adler" (1997, 265). With this, he concludes that one might "suspect that some of Freud's ambivalence and irritation toward Viktor Adler may have been transferred to Alfred" (265). Alfred was, like Viktor, committed to socialism, and he developed a close friendship with Leon Trotsky, yet Freud thought that Trotsky's involvement with Adler at the Viennese Cafe Central was inappropriate since, as he later told Joseph Wortis, "Communism and Psychoanalysis go ill together" (in Fiebert, 265n1).

While I agree with Fiebert that Freud transferred some of his feelings for the older Adler onto the younger, I think that these associations between the two Adlers need not be considered *in addition* to the sibling substitution, for they form an integral link in the same chain. Freud suggests in his interpretation of the Count Thun dream that Viktor's insult was to claim that, like the prodigal son, Freud would return meekly to his father's house, meaning that he would renounce the ideals of those activists with whom he was associating at the time (1901, 213). While the insult obviously refers to the reward that the prodigal son receives on his return, and to the lack of punishment for his disobedience, the parable highlights the theme of fratricidal conflict. William McGrath takes up this point, claiming that in the material called upon in the dream the quarrel with Adler symbolized Freud's break with the "brother band," which had been forced upon him by the impossible dilemma that he confronted: "his liberal sentiments were outraged by the autocratic style of government, and his impulse to rebellion was undercut by knowledge of the fratricidal consequences of revolt" (1987, 271). There are two key assumptions in Freud's interpretation of the Count Thun dream that are of importance to us here: he considers fratricidal conflict to be a key motivation behind political action—or, for that matter, behind any form of social action (a theme to which he will return in developing the theory of the primal horde)—and he considers Viktor Adler to be included among his brother substitutes. If Freud transfers his ambivalence and irritation toward Viktor onto Alfred, it is not only because the name and political affiliation of the two Adlers serve as catalysts for the displacement. They also function as a shield behind which another form of displacement (a brother substitution) hides—or, in the case of the false crypt, a shield behind which the brother substition can be *seen* to have been hiding.

In the two years after Adler's threat to resign from the group, his relationship with Freud seemed to stabilize. Fiebert even suggests that a greater degree of personal contact was achieved in 1909, with Freud inviting Adler to dinner in his wife's absence (1997, 245). Yet in the middle of 1909 (June 18), Freud had also admitted in a letter to Jung that Adler would inevitably be lost to them: "he won't desert in the immediate future, but neither will he participate as we should like him to. We must hold him as long as possible" (in Fiebert 1997, 245). Then, in the first few months of 1910 (the period with which we are particularly interested here), Freud's ambivalence intensified. He wrote to Jung in February that Adler was to be the only one whose contribution to the *Jahrbuch* "can be accepted without censorship, though not without criticism," but after Adler's paper on psychosexual hermaphroditism was delivered Freud complained to Ferenczi that Adler's conception of the genesis of neuroses was "a bad speculation!" (in Fiebert, 246). He also wrote to Jung on 6 March, asking that the Nuremberg conference not begin with "heretical papers like Adler's" (in Fiebert, 246). At the conference, he handed Jung the presidency of the International Psychoanalytic Association, thereby effectively shifting the base of power in psychoanalysis away from Vienna and angering his long-serving Viennese supporters. Within two weeks of the conference, however, Freud was to cede the presidency of the Vienna Psychoanalytic Society to Adler, to ease their dissent, though he wrote to Jung on 12 April that the Viennese group was "very much shaken, and for the present I am satisfied with the outcome of my statesmanship" (in Fiebert, 247). In the days leading up to the anniversary of his brother's death, and at about the time he was to form his conviction that the secret to the Wolf Man's neurosis lay with the wolf dream, then, Freud was clearly locked into the political struggle with Adler for control of psychoanalysis. As we have seen, however, this political struggle and the struggle of ideas through which it expressed itself were expressions of the fratricidal conflict in which Freud and Adler were pitted against each other.

If Freud's reception of the wolf dream is shaped in some way by concerns over Adler's dissensions—concerns which Offenkrantz and Tobin (and others) classify as research interests—then it is also clearly shaped, together with his rivalry with Adler, by his own internal psychic conflict. Yet we must recall that the break with Jung is just as frequently claimed to have contributed to Freud's attachment to the Wolf Man as a research interest. However, from what we know of the break with Adler, Jung presented himself as one of Freud's staunchest supporters during the turbulence of 1910. Indeed, the majority of accounts of the Freud-Jung relationship recognize that the break erupted suddenly sometime after Adler's defection. Jones states that 1912 "was the year when the personal relations between Freud and Jung began to be less friendly than before, and there were two painful years ahead before that separation came about" (1974, 365). Prior to their break, the pair apparently enjoyed a close friendship which at times took on the character of the relationship between a father and his son, with Freud clearly grooming the younger man to be his heir. Phyllis Grosskurth picks up on this father-son relation, suggesting that the origins of the break may be traced back to the appointment of Jung as president of the International Psychoanalytic Association or, perhaps earlier, to the moment that Freud first decided to nominate Jung as his successor: "He might have appeared to be honoring him, but Freud was in effect castrating the younger man" (1991, 40). For Grosskurth, Freud was just as keen to have Jung as a successor as he was worried that the young heir *wanted* to usurp him. This dilemma is not the same as that informed by his fratricidal conflict, yet it may be no coincidence that Freud gave such urgency to the task of nominating an heir to the institution of psychoanalysis after he celebrated his fifty-first birthday.

My own inclination is to suspect that Freud gained such an immediate and intense attachment to Jung, in part, because he was (in a sense) on the rebound. Adler had been an obvious heir but he was too much the brother, and their obvious rivalry had surfaced by the end of 1907. In despair, Freud turned his attentions to Jung. I do not of course wish to suggest that dissatisfaction with Adler was the only motivation pushing Freud toward Jung, nor might it have even been the primary motivation. One need only read the detailed accounts of the Freud-Jung relationship, including their correspondence, to realize that the attraction to Jung was a complex one and its motivations manifold.[18] I do suggest, however, that toward the end of 1907 we find substantial evidence in their correspondence of an intensification in the relationship, accompanied with an increase in material that we may relate to the false crypt and its fratricidal drama. It even seems that Jung may have unwittingly instigated this intensification. In his letter to Freud of 10 October 1907—remember here that this month saw the anniversary of the birth of Julius, in the year that Freud reached what he thought to be his most critical age—Jung records his analysis of a patient whose case is a copy of Ibsen's *Lady from the Sea*, for she lost her young daughter within two years of giving birth to a boy: "The dreams are interesting as they show that her unconscious actually wanted to *kill* not only the boy but also the beloved little girl" (Freud and Jung 1974, 93). If Freud's false crypt was not alerted by parallels with its own internal drama, it certainly could not have looked past Jung's reference to "the well-known Dr. Juliusburger," a founding member of the Berlin Society. Even a seemingly innocent question on "the story of the Fontana Trevi" may have sparked the associations with Rome (93, 94). The editor notes that, according to Anna Freud, the story refers to "Freud's having, in accordance with superstition, tossed a coin into the Fontana di Trevi and vowed to return to Rome" (94n9). With references to Rome, to the death of infants (a boy and a girl), and even in the date, Jung's letter thus contains several references that could easily have triggered material in the false crypt, especially at this quite "critical" time, when Freud was particularly sensitive to such spurs.

Unfortunately, we cannot know how Freud responded, as the two

18 In addition to the biographies by Ernest Jones, Paul Roazen, and others—most of which provide surprisingly little detail on Freud's relationship with Jung, I have found the following texts invaluable: John Kerr's *A Most Dangerous Method: The Story of Jung, Freud, and Sabina Spielrein* (1994), Samuel Rosenberg's *Why Freud Fainted* (1978), Saul Rosenzweig's *The Historic Expedition to America (1909): Freud, Jung and Hall the King-Maker* (1994), Max Schur's *Freud: Living and Dying* (1972), Leonard Shengold's *"The Boy Will Come to Nothing!" Freud's Ego Ideal and Freud as Ego Ideal* (1993), Madelon Sprengnether's *The Spectral Mother: Freud, Feminism, and Psychoanalysis* (1990), and Klaus Theweleit's *Object-Choice (All You Need is Love): On Mating Strategies & A Fragment of a Freud Biography* (1994).

letters from him to which Jung refers in his next letter (28 October 1907): "Your last two letters contain references to my laziness in writing" (94)—are missing. What we do know is that in the missing letters Freud confided something to Jung that was of a far more personal nature than anything that had previously passed between them, and I speculate that the material in question was linked to his childhood. Jung's reply to these missing letters states that he resisted writing his reply because he is hampered by a "disgusting and ridiculous" affection he has for Freud, and is worried that his colleague may have a similarly strong transference to himself: *"I therefore fear your confidence"* (emphasis in original; 95). I suggest that Freud's confidence includes childhood material because in Jung's reply, despite his confirmed resistance to exchanging confidences, he confesses that the origin of this resistance is "the fact that as a boy I was the victim of a sexual assault by a man I once worshipped" (95). *Quid pro quo,* perhaps? In any case, we can be sure of Freud's increased display of affection for Jung from the fact that the next surviving letter, dated 15 November 1907, is the first (after more than fifty had been exchanged) in which he addresses Jung as *"Lieber Freund und College"* (Dear friend and colleague). He had used the more formal *"Lieber College"* (Dear colleague) in all previous letters to Jung.[19]

Leonard Shengold has demonstrated the increasingly "Fliess-like" qualities of the Freud-Jung correspondence (1993). I only want to qualify Shengold's assessment by adding that, unlike with the Fliess correspondence, we know how Jung responded to all of Freud's strategies of exclusion. His first reference to Freud's childhood material may well have been unwitting but, as we shall see, he quickly learned to manipulate what he knew of Freud's past in his half of the correspondence. Freud's mistake, as Shengold points out, was to envisage Jung narcissistically "as a conquistador who would fight for Freud and psychoanalysis," that is, as "an extension of himself" (124). While Jung was happy to play the role of the son and heir to the father

[19] An apparent error in Jung's letter may be remarkably telling. He writes, "I honestly do try, but the evil spirit that (as you see) bedevils my pen often prevents me from writing" (Freud and Jung 1974, 95). In the original, according to the editor, the *redch* (which is meaningless) is crossed out and followed by "(!) *redlich* (!)" (which means "honestly") (95n4). The pen is not only bedeviled into error, as Freud is prompted to see, but into a particular error: the missing letters in the first nonsense word spell out the Latin number 51, the critical age that Freud was at when the letter was written!

of psychoanalysis, he clearly did not wish to be the passive Oedipus that Freud expected. Indeed, as Shengold explains, Jung's continual repudiation of the Oedipus *complex* (a word Freud had borrowed from Jung) represents his need to escape his emotional tie to the "father creator" (in Shengold, 125). The father takes the son's word and uses it for his own (castration) and the son refuses to accept that the resulting formation applies to him—in this way, the Oedipus complex can be seen not simply as a theory to explain the father-son relation, but as the very site upon which the father (Freud) and the son (Jung) enacted their rivalry.

For his part, Jung had one advantage that Fliess did not have: some knowledge of the Freud-Fliess break, and of the associations likely to trigger the memory of the break for Freud. In the months after the initial exchange of confidences, their correspondence hedges the issue of the intimate relations in which they have been involved, until March 1908, when Jung refers to "Fl." in relation to a question of paranoia, and Freud replies promptly "Do you mean Fliess by Fl.?" (Freud and Jung 1974, 136). If Jung was aware that he had touched the nerve with the initial reference, he exacerbated the situation by not answering. It was not until 11 April 1908 that he wrote again, in a short letter explaining that he had been ill with influenza, and would be "recovering as thoroughly as possible on Lago Maggiore," due to return on 16 April (136). Freud's reply indicates his state of irritation, a state that was aggravated, shall we suggest, by the fact that Jung had made himself unavailable until after the anniversary of the death of Julius. On 14 April 1908, Freud wrote a letter to be "waiting for you when you get home," in which he sharply criticized Jung for two of the three papers he has been reading:

> The first, the one you did in collaboration with Bleuler, displeases me with its hesitations and concern over the good opinion of E. Meyer; you have forbidden me to speak of the second, your long-awaited Amsterdam report; . . . Oddly enough, I have been reading in your Amsterdam paper that child hysteria does not enter this context [psychotraumatic neuroses]. (137)

Rather than referring again to Fliess, Freud simply concludes that he is "hoping to find a moment in Salzburg for a private talk with you about paranoia" (138). Jung was clearly ruffled, beginning his reply on 18 April with the claim that the last letter "upset me" and adding that "I have read a lot between the lines. I don't doubt that if only I could *talk* with you we could come to a basic understanding" (138). After attempting to explain himself, he concludes in agreement with Freud: "I too hope very much that we can snatch an hour in Salzburg for a talk on some things that are still hanging in mid-air" (139).

What interests me in particular about this exchange is the suggestion on which the correspondents agree: that the correspondence is in itself insufficient, as there are things that simply should not be put into writing. We have seen that from at least as early as his letters of courtship to Martha Bernays, Freud was acutely aware that his correspondence was every bit as public as his essays and publications, and that his biographers would be foiled if his letters were destroyed. Jung, it seems, agreed. Yet Jung also seems to have been prepared to use this public forum for their relationship to assert himself even as the castrating father tried to use it to shape in him the image of the compliant son. In March–April 1908, he discovered that Freud's own paranoia could be inflamed with the merest hint of the break with Fliess, and perhaps he took note of the timing as well. On 11 March 1909, he tested the same waters, taking it upon himself to assure Freud, "not only now but for the future, that nothing Fliess-like is going to happen" (212). Though he assures Freud that his "affection is lasting and reliable"—notwithstanding moments of "infatuation"[20]— there is an indication that Jung's assurance is not grounded in the degree to which he shall remain loyal solely to Freud; rather, nothing Fliess-like will happen because Jung has none of the Fliess-like dependence on Freud: "I have endless plans for work next year, and I look forward so much to the new era of outer (and inner) independence that is so important for me" (213). As for Freud's reaction, again, we cannot know, but not because letters are missing or removed. Jung and his wife were due to visit Freud in Vienna only one

[20] Jung's "infatuation" had only recently been tested during his affair with Sabina Spielrein, insofar as she expressed her jealousy of Jung's love for Freud. Spielrein had wanted to have Jung's son, but intended to name him Siegfried, the name of the son of Siegmund in German lore. Shengold points out that Viennese colleagues jealous of Freud's paternal attitude toward Jung often called him the blond Siegfried (1993, 115n22). The work to which most commentators have turned for details of the Jung-Freud-Spielrein triangle in the past has been Aldo Carotenuto's *A Secret Symmetry: Sabina Spielrein between Freud and Jung* (1984), although John Kerr's more recent *A Most Dangerous Method* (1994) represents the most comprehensive study to date.

week later, so Freud may have left off responding in writing with the intent to speak his mind at their meeting. Once again, however, with Jung having in all likelihood inflamed Freud, he postponed the master's opportunity for response: the next two letters record that Jung was (as it happened, unnecessarily) called to Berlin by the wife of a patient (213–14). Finally, then, Jung visited Freud between 25 and 30 March 1909. What happened when they were alone, and what they wrote in letters that follow, demands our attention at this point.

In his memoirs, Jung refers to a particular episode from his stay with Freud: as the two men were talking alone in Freud's study, a loud noise that seemed to emanate from a nearby bookcase frightened them terribly (in Schur 1972, 251). Their conversation was concerned with "precognition and parapsychology," so Jung attempted to explain to Freud that he had had a "peculiar sensation" immediately before the event, suggesting that the noise represented an example of "catalytic exteriorization phenomenon." Freud did not of course accept this explanation, so Jung predicted that another would follow soon after, and when it in fact did Freud was clearly shaken. Jung claims to have realized at once that he had shattered Freud's trust in him, and notes that they never spoke of the matter. In the letters after Jung's stay, however, the incident weighs heavily upon the minds of both. On 2 April 1909, Jung began a letter that he stopped writing after only a few lines (Freud and Jung 1974, 215). On 12 April (Easter Monday) he continued, stating that he had finally found time to himself to devote to the bicycle tour that he had been planning for some time: "On the 15th I'll wrench myself free without fail and start" (215). The letter then stumbles through some of his current analyses, including the "spiritualistic phenomena" they demonstrate, then returns to the sensitive matter at hand: "When I left Vienna I was afflicted with some *sentiments d'incomplétude* because of the last evening I spent with you. It seemed to me that my spookery struck you as altogether too stupid and perhaps unpleasant because of the Fliess analogy. (Insanity!)" (216). He is then sidetracked by a proposition that a "psychosynthesis" is every bit as viable as a "psychanalysis"—some of Jung's scientific differences with Freud begin to take clearer shape after this time—before returning to the so-called spookery, claiming that it "most happily, freed me inwardly from the oppressive sense of your paternal authority. . . . I hope I am now rid of all unnecessary encumbrances" (217).

Jung's phrasing is considerably inflammatory, but his pen is also bedeviled (to use a phrase that he was himself fond of using) into using even more subtle ways to set Freud's paranoia alight. The date on which he will depart for his tour is by now all too familiar to us, and the use of Fliess's name is also obvious. Yet in the last paragraph of the letter, Jung's tactics become more cryptic. He writes: "I have heard that Abraham with some others has issued a 'psychanalytical questionnaire.' Let's hope it's a canard" (217). This questionnaire, as the editor notes, was published by Magnus Hirschfeld in December 1908, having been discussed in an earlier form at the meeting of the Vienna Society the previous April (217n7). Jung's otherwise obscure protestation becomes, in this sense, a very direct reference to the events of the previous April, which include, as we have seen, Jung's illness and the flaring of the conflict within their correspondence. In addition to this, the phrasing "Abraham and some others" invokes recollection of the names of those who assisted in the preparation of the questionnaire. We may no longer be surprised to find that the small group in question includes Otto Juliusburger, whose name may have been one of the triggers for Freud's first confidences more than two years earlier.

If Freud had hoped that after his fifty-second year he would not be so plagued by the events of his past, he continued to find further frustration in correspondence with Jung. His reply, dated 16 April 1909, confronts this frustration in such a direct way that at least one commentator has been prompted to consider this as the most significant and problematic of all of Freud's letters. Max Schur cites the letter in connection with the obsession Freud had with the date of his own death, the *non vixit* dream (therefore, in connection with Fliess and the death of Julius), his "derealization on the Acropolis," and ultimately Freud's own mystical preoccupations (1972). Freud prefaces the letter with a touch of regret, as though there is an air of finality to what he writes: his opening line reads "I hope this letter doesn't reach you for a while. I'm sure you see what I mean" (Freud and Jung 1974, 218). If he regrets what he is about to write, then why does he bother to write it? I suggest quite simply that Freud may well have been aware that the "Fliess analogy," as Jung described the incident in the study, now held true for the whole relationship. In any case, Jung had now consigned the spookery to writing, forcing Freud's hand. In his reply, Freud goes through the motions in repeating some strategies that should now seem uncannily familiar to us. In the first half of the letter he attempts to distinguish between his analytic attitude and his narcissistically motivated objectification of Jung as the son and heir:

> It is strange that on the very same evening when I formally adopted you as eldest son and anointed you—*in partibus infidelium*—as my successor and crown prince, you should have divested me of my paternal authority, which divesting seems to have given you as much pleasure as I, on the contrary, derived from the investiture of your person. Now I am afraid of falling back into the father role with you if I tell you how I feel about the poltergeist business. But I must, because my attitude is not what you might otherwise think. I don't deny that your stories and your experiment made a deep impression on me. I decided to continue my observations after you left, and here are the results. (218)

The result, of course, is that a logical explanation existed for the continuing noises in the bookcase. Yet Freud also confesses that this analytic attitude is complicated by the effect of Jung's presence: "Accordingly, I put my fatherly horned-rimmed spectacles on again and warn my dear son to keep a cool head, for it is better not to understand something than make such great sacrifices to understanding" (218–19).

The first half of the letter mirrors some of Freud's strategies for divesting himself of responsibility for being taken in by Fliess's numerology: I never fully believed in the numbers, because I never fully understood, and besides, I was under your spell. If Jung missed this part of the analogy, however, Freud confirms it by setting up the second half of the letter as a duplication of his engagement with Fliess's numbers. This latter half of the letter outlines Freud's "conviction that I would die between the ages of 61 and 62," along with an analysis (after the manner of those in letters to Fliess and *The Psychopathology of Everyday Life*) of the determination of this conviction:

> It made its appearance in 1899. At that time two events occurred. First I wrote *The Interpretation of Dreams* . . . second, I received a new telephone number, which I still have today: 14362. It is easy to find a factor common to these two events. In 1899 . . . I was 43 years old. Thus it was plausible to suppose that the other figures signified the end of my life, hence

61 or 62. . . . The superstitious notion that I would die between the ages of 61 and 62 proves to coincide with the conviction that with *The Interpretation of Dreams* I had completed my life work, that there was nothing more for me to do and that I might just as well lie down and die. You will admit that after this substitution it no longer sounds absurd. Moreover, the hidden influence of W. Fliess was at work; the superstition erupted in the year of his attack on me. (219)

In the context of everything that we have said so far about Freud's relations with Fliess and Jung, perhaps the first thing we notice about these revelations is that Freud leaves out any mention of the critical age between 51 and 52 that had only recently concerned him. Schur points out that the critical ages were calculated along the series 41–42; 51–52; 61–62 and so on, yet he also places emphasis upon the number 51 because it is the sum of the numbers for Fliess's two critical periods (23 + 28), and also because the fifty-first birthday was the first critical age Freud reached *after* the break with Fliess, during which period Fliess's influence on him began in retrospect to seem destructive and evil (1972). We have already found good reason to suspect that Jung knew how critical Freud considered the period from his fifty-first to fifty-second birthdays. As we asked in relation to Freud's claims of ignorance to Fliess, we should also ask of his maneuverings in this letter: Did he imagine that Jung would forget? More important, perhaps, is the suggestion made by this letter that there are many things in Freud's life (in the past and the present) that Jung could not forget, precisely because he did not know.

You know nothing about me; you are a poor confidant: this seems to be the gist of Freud's revelations, especially if we recall the importance that both correspondents once placed upon talking, rather than writing, about the most intimate matters. The emphasis upon 61 and 62 allows Freud to draw attention to his telephone number—"which I still have today," (as if you did not know, my son)—but it also allows him to substitute the 6, the number of *Schuld* (that is, of guilt and the visitation of the sins of the father upon the son) for the 5 in his critical equations (do you know the meaning of the 6, my son; how well do you know my work?)[21] In the same movement by which he invokes the number that had, in *The Psychopathology of Everyday Life*, been left

[21] The reference to Freud's telephone number may also be an invitation (or a threat) for Jung to call. In Harry Freud's recollection of his uncle Sigmund, Freud "did not like the telephone and refused to use it" (1973, 313). The message to Jung seems clear:

over from his divisions of 1734 by a factor of 17, Freud also conceals the critical age at which he had made these additions to *The Psychopathology*—the same age he had been when Jung expressed the fear of his confidence. In other words, this letter of revelation improvises closure and concealment, because it attempts to wrest the initiative in their correspondence away from Jung by confiding to him (which he fears), in writing, material that is directly and cryptically tied to the life-story that the pair had discussed, and had agreed to leave out of their correspondence—yet which Jung had invoked time and again in his letters. Two of Jung's most recent letters referred to Fliess—the first claiming that nothing "Fliess-like" would happen, and the second describing what had since transpired between them with the "Fliess analogy"—but in this letter Freud reclaims "Fliess" for himself, as if to preserve the contents of the false crypt and the associations drawn from it.

In a number of ways, then, Jung's letter of 12 April and Freud's letter of 16 April are in disagreement. At least with regard to their symbolically filial relationship, the pair seemed now only prepared to agree to disagree. Jung considered that the spookery had freed him from Freud's paternal authority, while Freud had tried to divorce the "poltergeist business" from the crucial issue of paternal authority, and also claimed to have "formally" adopted his colleague as son and heir to his crown. Not surprisingly, a brief hiatus followed from this exchange, Jung was the first to revive the correspondence, a month later. We should take note that the reply came a week *after* Freud's birthday, on 12 May 1909, and in it Jung makes no attempt to refer to Freud's last letter or to his personal life, with the exception that he claims to have heard from Oskar Pfister that Freud's daughter Mathilde had been operated upon (Freud and Jung 1974, 220). Then, within two months, Jung allowed himself the luxury of confiding in Freud once again, as the fallout from his affair with Sabina Spielrein threatened to engulf him. In these letters, written in the latter half of 1909, Jung's tone is somewhat subdued, and on more than one occasion he appeals to Freud as a son to a father. For his part, Freud remains more aloof under such circumstances than one might expect. If his suspicions about Jung's ambitions were confirmed by the young analyst's willingness to adopt the role that he had formerly resisted so keenly,

---

if you phone, my son, you confirm to me that you do not know me at all; in any case, if you phone, I will refuse to speak.

he certainly kept his concerns close to his heart. After all, we have seen that as the trouble with Adler flared in 1909 and 1910, Freud often used Jung as a sounding board for his concerns—only this time it was Freud who invoked the Fliess analogy. By doing so, of course, he hinted to Jung that it was Adler, and not he, who more adequately occupied the role of the arch-revenant formerly monopolized by Fliess. As a context for Freud's reception of the wolf dream, the rivalry with Jung had by 1910 yet to manifest itself in fully articulated scientific differences, but it had provided Freud with an opportunity to work through some of the more troublesome aspects of his internalized fratricidal conflict (in preparation, perhaps, for the conflict with Adler). Freud's letters in April 1910 make no suggestion that he viewed Jung's appointment as president of the International Psychoanalytic Association with any sense of triumph or celebration. Indeed, Jung was the first to write, two weeks after the Congress, with a letter that simply covered business at hand (304). Freud's response dealt with these business affairs and, of course, the matter of Adler's disquiet (305–06). I suggest, then, that with Jung's appointment as president, Freud merely actualized what he had already done symbolically a year earlier—adopting him as son and heir. In 1910, Jung's appointment formalized a relationship of which Jung's colleagues were already jealous, which leads us to agree with Phyllis Grosskurth's assessment, that Freud was just as keen to have Jung as a successor as he was worried that the young heir wanted to usurp him and to extend it to include the gesture that guaranteed Freud's authority over both the Viennese and the Swiss. With the power to appoint and, as the world would soon see, to expel, Freud had presented himself as the castrating father to the whole of his analytic horde. The complication for the father was of course that each of the brothers within this horde seemed persistently to emerge as a revenant of Julius. These brothers were thereby destined, in their relationships with the father-creator, to only ever be already dead to him, and therefore incapable of being maintained as viable successors.

CHAPTER THREE

Assuming the Wolf Man's Burden

> A certain process of *imposition* . . . installs a peculiar indebtedness
> at the very core of psychoanalytical thinking. For *to assume assump-*
> *tions* is not merely to open oneself and one's thought out to an exte-
> riority that comes from without: it is to accommodate something
> that remains, in a certain sense, alien, strange. . . . It is to install a
> debt at the core of cognition, *owing* at the heart of *knowing*.
>
> (Weber 1984, 57)

Bearing (a) False Witness: Freud's Fateful Encounter with the Wolf Man

In previous chapters, I have suggested that the Wolf Man's verbal account of the dream of the wolves may not have been sufficient in and
of itself to prompt Freud's conviction about the relation between the
Wolf Man's dream and his infantile neurosis. Given several other factors, such as Freud's penchant for tracking visual details, his interest
at the time in Leonardo and in the psychogenic disturbance of vision,
and the possibility that Pankeiev recounted in the analysis what he
later recorded in his memoirs about his love as a child for drawing, I
also suggested that Freud relished the opportunity to witness the production of art in the repression of homosexuality. In short, he
prompted his patient to give him a drawing of the dream, or at least
received the patient's offer of a drawing with approval. Rather than
thinking of his conviction as a *consequence* of his reception of the
drawing, then, I suggest we think of it as a *condition* for the production of the drawing of the dream in the analysis, and for the selection
of details, by analyst and analysand, for recollection.

With this suggestion, we are of course directly in the realm of the
transference, or at least we would be if we were suggesting that it was
the patient whose presentation of the drawing responded to Freud's
convictions. Yet the reader may notice that I referred to Pankeiev in
the last passage only when discussing the recollection of his childhood love for drawing. It was to the Wolf Man that I attributed the

wolf dream and the verbal account of this dream in analysis. I have already recognized that the distinction is quite a slippery one to maintain, yet I make the point here precisely because I want to make a case for suggesting that in the realm of the false crypt, "Pankeiev" was no more nor less than the figure on whom Freud pinned the objective ground for the patient's childhood memories. I will argue that very early in the analysis, Freud's use of the word for his "conviction" (*Überzeugung*) encountered resistance in the patient's crypt, with the resulting reaction-formation, arrived at in the countertransference (*between the analyst and the analysand*), being what Freud called the "Wolf Man."

The first step in this direction will be to attempt to synthesize the paths that I have already taken in reading Freud's correspondence and essays as life-writing, in order to answer the question that I raised earlier: what did Freud "see" when he saw the drawing of the dream of the wolves? This is a question we may now reconfigure accordingly, to ask what Freud was looking for when he elicited this drawing from his patient. In April 1910, as we know, Freud was embroiled in a war of diplomacy with the arch-revenant Adler, which suggests that his anxiety over the internal fratricidal drama—a drama over which he had gained some degree of control in his letters to Jung—was heightened prior to the anniversary of Julius's death, in the wake of Nuremberg. Where Freud had given Jung the presidency of the IPA. From letters that Freud was writing at this time to his numerous correspondents, we can gain a clearer picture of his attitudes toward some of his disciples. His relationship with Jung was now centered around the business of presiding over the International Psychoanalytic Association, yet he also used his letters to Jung as a sounding board for his complaints about Adler, and to brag about his skills as a statesman. It is interesting to note that his letters to Sándor Ferenczi— the *"enfant terrible* of psychoanalysis," as he would later recognize himself (in Haynal 1988, 189)—employ a register that is similar to that used in the letters to Jung, perhaps foreshadowing the split that would develop much later with this favorite disciple. To Ferenczi and Jung, Freud directed the types of comments that he would soon make public against Adler and, in the process, may well have been showing them his brooding side. In his letters to Karl Abraham, Freud is generally cordial without being confidential, though the letter of 5 June does provide him with an opportunity to note (to one of Jung's most vehement detractors) that "Jung is having great difficulties in Zurich at present" (Freud and Abraham 1965, 90). Before Nuremberg and in its wake, Freud continued to exercise his will by turning the primal horde of disciples upon each other.

The two disciples who seemed to have been exempted from this treatment were Ernest Jones and Oskar Pfister. I think it fair to say that Jones was still very much enamored of Freud at this early stage of their relationship, and was fortunate to be kept at a physical distance from the dealings in continental Europe by being stationed at the time in America. On 15 April 1910, Freud wrote a letter that, for the first time in their correspondence, signals his acceptance of Jones: "Your letters prove a continuous source of satisfaction for me. . . . I am happy I did not listen to the internal voices hinting at giving you up when the odds were against you, and now I trust we will walk and work a good bit together" (Freud and Jones 1995, 51). According to the editor, Freud had walked Jones to the station after the Worcester lectures in 1909 because he wished to talk more not being convinced of the younger man's commitment (52n1). If Freuds letter refers indeed to events during the American trip in August 1909, then it is also worth our while to note that the same trip, according to Jung's recollections, marked the beginning of the end for his relationship with Freud. In Jung's account, he asked Freud, on one occasion when the pair were discussing their dreams and he asked Freud to relate some of the personal associations for a dream that had "bothered him very much." To this, Freud responded bitterly, "I could tell you more but I cannot risk my authority!" (in McGrath 1987, 280n15). I remind the reader here that Freud excluded Jung from his confidence in the letter of 16 April, earlier in that same year. Whether or not Jung understood that he was being excluded from the correspondence in the same way that Fliess had once been, he seems to have thought that they would continue to talk about intimate matters. As he stated in his memoirs, however, Freud's "sentence burned itself in my memory; and in it the end of our relationship was already foreshadowed" (Jung 1963, 158).[1]

---

[1] Jung's recollections of August 1909 include the claim that Freud had an affair with Martha's younger sister Minna Bernays, that Jung knew about the affair at the time, and that it formed the latent content of the dream that had so bothered Freud. Like other commentators, I am not as convinced as Peter Swales of the legitimacy of Jung's claim, given that it contributed to forming a negative picture of Freud's role in the break with Jung. Like William McGrath, however, I do believe that the question of the affair remains open (1987, 280n15). Indeed, Jung's recollections of August 1909

Might I suggest, then, that although there is nothing in the letter to Jones of 15 April to mark the anniversary of Julius's demise, this letter does represent a movement in Freud's troubled relations with Jung?[2] A year earlier he had attempted to close Jung out from his life-writing on the fateful anniversary, and now he marked the occasion by forming a new attachment. Yet these two letters mark both a shift in Freud's relations and the termini of a second critical period that we have failed to consider yet: that is, they mark the fifty-first and fifty-second anniversaries of the death of Freud's brother. While it would be ludicrous to suggest that Freud could believe that these anniversaries formed critical periods in the physiological sense theorized by Fliess, we have seen the continued importance Freud placed upon these numbers (and upon the idea of a critical period) in the formation of his own anxieties. Indeed, in the final instance, the question of Freud's belief is of no consequence, since we are dealing with the embeddedness of material within the false crypt. However, we must ask what association could render the period between 51 and 52 suitable for inclusion in the drama of the false crypt, that these numbers should prove so resilient in shaping Freud's anxieties. The answer rests, I think, in the Jewish practice of Gematria—taking the Hebrew alphabet as both an orthographic and a numerical system. I have already mentioned the importance Freud placed upon the number seventeen, the numerical equivalent of the Hebrew word for "good," and discussed the degree to which the presence of this number in a series of divisions can only have strengthened his concerns about the critical 51. Yet the number 52 is critical not simply because it completes the period beginning with the fifty-first anniversary, since, as Max Schur

---

confirm my claims about his willingness to taunt Freud with suggestions of a guilty past and to play upon unpleasant associations. Perhaps the most comprehensive account of Jung's allegations and their potential veracity, along with their role in the split, is John Kerr's *A Most Dangerous Method* (1994).

[2] Though Julius seems conspicuous by his absence here, do we see Anna intervening even as Freud states Jung's appointment? He writes that the group "took up Jung as president for the next two years and fixed an [yearly] annual congress which is to be the source of all the powers" (Freud and Jones 1995, 52). The editor points out that in the original the word "yearly" is crossed out and the English word "annual" is used in its place (52n5). In the next section of this book, I shall explore the crucial role played by "anna-" words in (and including) psychoanalysis, but for now we need only register that the celebration of the *anniversary* of Julius's death installs an "anna-" word at the heart of the screen material.

points out, the number is the equivalent of the Hebrew word for "dog" (1972, 25). He adds that 52 is thus a "bad number," but does not explain this reasoning. Obviously, the designation "dog" is given colloquially to despicable persons, like those whom the Bible lists as the first among those who will not enter the kingdom of heaven: "For without are dogs, and sorcerers, and whoremongers, and murderers, and idolaters, and whosoever loveth and maketh a lie" (Revelation 22:15). For Freud, as we may guess, the designation of the number 52 as "dog" will attach to it childhood and teenage associations linking images of dogs to the drama in the false crypt.

On the day after the fifty-first anniversary of Julius's death, a whole constellation of materials from the false crypt had, as we have seen, been concentrated in the letter to Jung of 16 April 1909. During the next year, as relations with Adler cooled and Freud jockeyed Jung closer to the presidency (but further from his affections), the master took a special interest in the young Russian handed into his care by Leonid Drosnes. One of the reasons for this special interest, during a period when Freud intended to reduce his hours of clinical work, was Freud's research at the time into Leonardo's art. Another, less obvious, factor, as the fifty-second anniversary of Julius's death drew nearer, may have been the name of another Russian analyst in the series of associations that could be formed around Drosnes and Pankeiev: Otto Juliusburger. The link here is Moshe Wulff, whom Pankeiev had consulted in Odessa in 1909, and who had requested to review Freud's books in December of the same year (Davis 1995, 24). A month earlier, in a letter dated 10 November 1909, Abraham had informed Freud that "a Russian doctor by the name of Wulff, who has been Juliusburger's assistant in a private mental hospital for some time, is now going to settle in Odessa" (Freud and Abraham 1965, 81–82). I have suggested that the name of Juliusburger had already acted as a primary catalyst in the rivalry-via-correspondence with Jung. We can also note here that the name may have acted as a catalyst for Freud's agreement to receive Pankeiev, since the period between the time that he had been first informed of the move by Juliusburger's former assistant to the time that he took one of Wulff's patients in Odessa into his own care—from November 1909 to January 1910— is a short one indeed.

A simple enough association, then: when Pankeiev was entrusted to Freud, he was in a sense already the Wulff-man, and this alone may have been sufficient for the false crypt to have incorporated-introjected the young Russian into its internal drama. Even if the association with Wulff did not force entry into the false crypt, however, the initial stages of the analysis will have thrown up enough material for the impenetrable barrier of the empty mouth to be compromised. Consider again what Pankeiev later recalled in his memoirs about his childhood interests:

> My sister and I both liked to draw. At first we used to draw trees, and I found Anna's way of drawing the little round leaves particularly attractive and interesting. But not wanting to imitate her, I soon gave up tree-drawing. I began trying to draw horses true to nature, but unfortunately every horse I drew looked more like a dog or a wolf than like a real horse. I succeeded better with human beings, and drew, for instance, a "drunkard," a "miser," and similar characters. (Gardiner 1973, 24)

Throughout the initial stages of the analysis, Freud also faced the approach of the fifty-second anniversary (the "dog" anniversary) of Julius's death, complicated by the less than appealing imbroglio of his relations with the arch-revenants Adler and Jung. How much more simple and accessible must the young Russian have seemed, then, with his tale of a childhood rivalry with the sister Anna, and of pictures of dogs and wolves? In the privacy of the countertransference, Freud had been given the most visibly apparent material, insofar as so many elements of Pankeiev's childhood recollections mirrored elements in Freud's own past, from which to form an identification. As we have seen, however, the formation of such an identification was a necessary evil to which the false crypt occasionally subjected itself, admitting to the emptiness of the mouth only so new material could be incorporated into the schema of the mouth's originary plenitude. The question of Freud's initial "research interest" in Pankeiev, with the suggestion that he intended from an early stage in the analysis to direct his inquiries into Pankeiev's early childhood against the dissensions from Adler and Jung, seems no longer to be as useful as this suggestion that Freud's primary interest in his patient lay in the less complicated and more direct associations with material from his own childhood that it offered him, *set apart from* the complexity of his relations with Adler and Jung.

At this point we might wish to reconsider a debate that was not settled by Freud in 1926, after Otto Rank suggested that the dream of the wolves was not a recollection from the patient's childhood, as the interpretation in "From the History of an Infantile Neurosis" requires it to be, but a reworking of day residues from the analysis sometime between 1910 and 1914. As Whitney Davis summarizes Rank's claims, the dream was reported as a childhood dream only because the Wolf Man was compliant with Freud's desire to uncover childhood material (1995, 61). Chief among the day residues was the source of the numbers of wolves in the dream account and in the drawing, derived from the different numbers of photographs of Freud's closest followers on the wall of his consulting room—a claim that Freud rejected immediately, on the grounds that at the time the dream was reported to him in the analysis there could have been in all "only two or three" pictures hanging in this room (in Davis 1995, 61). Freud refuted the assertion by soliciting a written testimony from his former patient—to which I shall return later—effectively derailing Rank's claim. As Davis points out, though, Freud did not refute Rank's *psychoanalytic* reading of the drawing as an object into which any number of wolves could have been inserted, to expand upon the number of Freud's followers:

> Freud and Ferenczi did not acknowledge that at the time he made his dream report, the Wolf Man could have built *any* number of photographs hanging in Freud's consulting room into his description or drawing of the dream as an object to offer Freud. After all, the "five" wolves in the drawing, and the "six or seven" wolves in the dream report, were explicitly described by Freud as "distortions" or "corrections" of the underlying reality—namely, in his view, the *two* parents of the patient. If two parents, then why not "two or three" photographs? (Davis 1995, 62)

Rank's claim implies that the dream from which Freud drew his evidence for infantile sexuality may only be a product of the transference. For my own part, I do not see that we must choose between the dream being a recollection from childhood (in which case Freud is right) *or* a product of the transference (in which case Freud is wrong). Instead, might we not consider the possibility that the transference provided the condition under which the dream from Pankeiev's childhood repeated itself? To add this possibility to the synthesis I have been attempting here, of course, requires a moment of reflection on how the conditions for the dream's initial iteration are to be understood.

We know a surprisingly great deal more about Pankeiev's childhood than Freud is likely to have ever learned from his patient, thanks to research that was carried out in the wake of the publication of the Wolf Man's memoirs, some three decades after Freud's death. For some researchers, the information that has come to light, including the Wolf Man's own recollections of his childhood and of his analyses with Freud and Ruth Mack Brunswick, has provided material evidence for the inadequacies of Freud's reconstruction of the Wolf Man's childhood and, in particular, the primal scene. Allen Esterson, for example, lists a number of points on which the Wolf Man ("W" in what follows) contradicted Freud's claims ("F"), so as to demonstrate how Freud had been implicitly "misinforming the reader" in his account of the dream interpretation and the analysis (1993, 69):

F: The patient was "entirely incapacitated" and "in a state of complete helplessness" at the start of the treatment. [S.E. 17:7; 23:217]

W: He was considerably improved by the time he came to Freud, and able to engage in a large number of social activities. [Gardiner 1971: 82, 83, 89; Obholtzer 1982: 40–41]

F: On the death of his sister the Wolf Man showed no sign of grief, and in fact rejoiced in being the sole heir to their father's property. [S.E. 17: 23]

W: He fell into a state of mental agony, and the event marked the onset of his serious depression. [Gardiner: 25; Obholtzer: 89]

F: The patient's intestinal trouble was functional in nature. [S.E. 17: 75–76, 80]

W: Some inappropriate medicine prescribed by a country doctor had permanently damaged the mucous membranes of his intestines, resulting in chronic bowel trouble. [Obholtzer: 47]

F: The intestinal symptoms cleared up in the course of the treatment. [S.E. 17: 76]

W: He emphatically denies Freud's claim. The trouble remained with him the rest of his life. [Obholtzer: 48]. . . .

F: In his narration of the dream the animals were wolves. [S.E. 17: 29]

W: The animals sitting in the tree "were not wolves at all but white Spitz dogs with pointed ears and bushy tails". [*Psychoanalytic Quarterly* 1957, 26: 449] (At one point in the case history Freud himself asserts as a "fact" that the animals "were actually sheep dogs". This was at a time when he needed sheep dogs for an alternative interpretation of the dream. [S.E. 17: 57–58]).

F: The Wolf Man's sister repeatedly tormented him by showing him a picture of a wolf standing upright and striding forward, which caused him to scream that he was afraid of the wolf eating him up. [S.E. 17: 29–30]

W: There was a single occasion when his sister told him she would show him a picture of a pretty little girl, only to reveal a wolf on its hind legs about to swallow Little Red Riding Hood, and his scream was in anger at his sister's teasing rather than due to a fear of the wolf. [Gardiner: 7]

(Esterson 1993, 69–70)

As this artificial dialogue demonstrates, Esterson is concerned with demonstrating the degree of disagreement between the two versions of the Wolf Man's history, under an assumption that on any given point of contradiction only one represents the "true story" (71). For Esterson, this "true" version is most likely the patient's, a conclusion he bases on the assertion that "Freud has a tendency to dissemble when it suits his purpose" (71). Such reasoning proceeds, however, from a *non sequitur*: it does *not* follow that where two versions of the same event contradict each other, if the one is not the truth then the other must be truthful. Might we not consider that the patient also has just such a tendency to dissemble? More to the point, might we not consider that the Wolf Man *is a dissimulation*, as in the enigma described by Abraham and Torok? Rather than pursue the claim that Freud is simply "misinforming the reader"—although we shall return to this issue—I want to look instead at the suggestion that the crypt had already embarked upon its own campaign of disinformation, consequent upon the initial conditions for the formation of the wolf dream and upon the dream's reiteration.

From the available research (the analyses with Freud and Ruth Mack Brunswick included) we have a wealth of material to consider here: for Freud, the latent material included the primal scene of parental coitus *a tergo* at eighteen months, the defecation during the primal scene, the seduction by the sister Anna, the Grusha scene, and being frightened by a picture from a storybook ("The Wolf and the Seven Little Goats" or "Little Red Riding Hood," depending on whether Freud's account or the Wolf Man's memoirs are to be believed, a point that I will consider shortly) shown to him by the sister. Of course, Freud's reconstructed primal scene was taken as a key factor in Brunswick's analysis—though her "Supplement" added emphasis to the "voyeurism-exhibitionism, his fears of looking and being looked at" derived from the primal scene (Blum 1980, 348)[3]— but the details of this reconstruction have in the past few decades commonly been rejected as "real" factors in the wolf dream formation. From the work of Muriel Gardiner and Karin Obholzer, each of whom communicated directly with Pankeiev, and the subsequent research produced by Abraham and Torok ([1976] 1986), Harold Blum (1980), Patrick Mahony (1984), Carlo Ginzburg (1986), Ned Lukacher (1986), George Dimock (1995), and Whitney Davis (1995)—among others, though it is upon these that I have been drawing here— Freud's inability to look beyond the case of an individual to the cultural context has, it seems, been corrected. While Blum and others had begun to raise specific objections to details of the reconstructed

---

[3] Blum notes that Brunswick denies the emergence of any new material in her treatment of the Wolf Man, since she insists that "only unresolved transference to Freud was uncovered" during her treatment of the Wolf Man's paranoia, and he adds that her analyses in the "Supplement" do not alter Freud's basic formulation (Blum 1980, 348–49). He also notes—that this treatment of an adult paranoia hinged on the Wolf Man's recollection that "after his nightmare at age four he couldn't bear to be looked at and would scream if he felt a fixed stare"—which may represent new material for the dream interpretation, as it places new emphasis on the degree to which the staring wolves project his own staring at the primal scene (349). Blum adds in a separate point that the Wolf Man assumes he must have been swaddled during his attack of malaria, "which, if true, could have been an important developmental influence and have contributed to the motionless figures in his dream" (350). Such motionlessness could also have contributed in the first instance to the fixedness of the infant's vantage in relation to the primal scene of witnessing, and henceforth to his fear of being held by a "fixed" stare.

primal scene, Mahony seems to me to have been the first to systematically interrogate the full scope of the primal scene, related latent material, *and* the uses Freud makes of these details in "From the History of an Infantile Neurosis" (see chapter three, "A Postponed Review of Several Key Episodes," in Mahony 1983, 49–73). Material from medicine and sociology demonstrate that the primal scene as Freud describes it would have been highly unlikely because little Sergei would have been swaddled, as Blum suggests, *and* he would have been kept in a separate room in their large house. Of course, Mahony uses such material to dismantle the primal scene, and his intention is not to find newer material from which to propose an alternative picture of the dream's formation. Indeed, he remains skeptical of the primal scene's validity as an explanatory device in psychoanalysis (53–54).[4]

Similarly, Carlo Ginzburg's essay "Freud, the Wolf-Man, and the Werewolves" points to a broader cultural context for the wolf dream in order to interrogate Freud's ongoing concern with the degree to which ontogenesis recapitulates phylogenesis (1986, 151–53). For Ginzburg, the presence of the "superstitious" nurse comforting the young Russian after he first dreamed of the wolves allows us to introduce material from Eastern European folklore and myth which Freud clearly overlooked. According to Slavic werewolf myths, children born on Christmas day or children born with a caul were likely also to develop powers of lycanthropy (Ginzburg 1986, 147–48). As Freud informs us in the case history, the young Russian's birth was marked by both of these signs, and it is unlikely that the patient would recall such facts about his birth unless some significance had been ascribed

---

[4] Rejection of the primal scene does not invalidate the principle of deferred effect, since the activation of a mnemic trace need not be understood as "primal." Accordingly, Mahony clarifies the notion of deferred traumatic effect without recourse to a primal scene which is not (in and of itself) traumatic (1984, 54–55). It is important to recall that the issue of the primacy of the primal scene is not one of chronology, since a mnemic trace is not imbued with a sense of time in the unconscious. To think of the primal scene as the first in a sequence of scenes is a misconception not so easily made when we recall that Freud's German term *"Urszene"* uses the ambiguous prefix *"Ur-,"* meaning that which is first in the sense of *having been* first *and* in the sense of *being* hypothetically reconstructed from subsequent material. Furthermore, if we ascribe to the primal scene its sense of prehistoricity, as Freud does, we replace the question of whether the scene need be traumatic in order to activate the mnemic trace with the questions of the roles played by heritage and heredity—questions arising from the debate over ontogeny and phylogeny—in the retention of early material prior to the splitting of the ego and the Oedipal conflict.

to them by close members of his family (or by his carers) during his childhood. For Ginzburg, it is the superstitious nurse who would have conveyed the importance of these signs, and who may even have induced the wolf dream by telling the child that, as part of the initiation into their future destiny, such magical people are visited in their dreams by apparitions of animals during infancy and adolescence (148). Ginzburg thus buys into the debate over ontogeny and phylogeny by arguing that the mythic elements of the wolf dream reside not in heredity but in the storytelling and superstitions of carers.[5]

Following Ginzburg's cue, George Dimock argues that the Wolf Man's memoirs may themselves be read as an attempt to restore to his life history several key elements passed over by Freud in "From the History of an Infantile Neurosis" (Dimock 1995). For Dimock, the memoirs resist Freud's interpretation of the wolf dream by rewriting the case history in such a way as to restore the central role to the sister Anna. Dimock's argument is different from Esterson's list of points on which the Wolf Man contradicts Freud, however, on the basis that he is not concerned with demonstrating that one is "true" and the other is therefore "false;" rather, Dimock elaborates the structure and motivation of the Wolf Man's contradiction. Adding to the mythical elements that are identified by Ginzburg, Dimock outlines another potential source for the deployment of the wolves in the wolf dream, in a complex meshing of cultural text with visual history and mnemic trace. From family photographs in the Pankeiev collection, Dimock locates two in which the large hunting party—"gentry, huntsmen, and serfs," and *including* a group comprising the adolescent Wolf Man, Anna, and their mother—are arranged around the carcasses of three wolves (64). Using these as a focal point, he aligns the account of the Russian wolf hunt from the Wolf Man's memoirs with "perhaps the most famous of all Russian texts, one that effectively portrays the

---

[5] Whitney Davis turns this same material back upon Ginzburg, arguing that Freud will have had access to werewolf and wolf mythology of his own—including the crucial legend of Sigmund and Sinfjotli—which acted as a cultural context for *his* reception of the wolf dream (1995, 192–94). Furthermore, Davis suggests that the child's terrified reaction to the threat of being eaten by the wolves is an unlikely response to the initiation rite described by Ginzburg (190–92). For my own part, I am inclined to think that the terror may be a fear of intense narcissistic retribution, given that the wolf hunts seemed to have been such a regular part of the lives of the people who inhabited the Pankeiev estate. The dream in this sense may have manifested some deep kinship conflicts between the boy who believed himself to be the becoming-wolf and the boy whose family hunted wolves as part of their subsistence.

love of a brother and sister in close proximity to wolves. I have in mind Leo Tolstoy's *War and Peace*" (65). The possibility that this great literary text provides an imaginative source for the Wolf Man's memoirs does not in any way bring into question their status as recollections, but it does remind us that recollection, like all forms of expression, distorts unconscious material as representations.

Dimock then provides two more examples of the way in which the memoirs maneouvre the sister back into the core of the young Russian's psychic life. The recollection of the drawings made by the two children also recalls the drawing of the wolf dream, insofar as it provides a potential source for the wolves and the barren tree: the wolves are what resulted from all of little Sergei's attempts to draw horses, and the tree without leaves manifests the boy's failure to imitate the little round leaves which made his sister's drawings of trees "particularly attractive and interesting" (a failure that motivated him to attempt to draw horses) (62). In the other example, as Esterson points out, the Wolf Man's memoirs contradict Freud's claim that the picture of the wolf with which the sister scared the young Russian could not have illustrated "Little Red Riding Hood" as the Wolf Man had thought, but must have illustrated "The Wolf and the Seven Little Goats," an assumption that the patient was supposed to have confirmed when he located the picture in a second-hand bookstore. In the memoirs, the Wolf Man recalls, without any reference to the case history, that his sister had promised him a picture of a "pretty little girl" but then showed him "a wolf standing on his hind legs with his jaws wide open, about to swallow little Red Riding Hood" (in Dimock 1995, 63). For Dimock, the contradiction marks an unconscious intent to relate a different story to the one settled upon by Freud, retaining the sister and her promise of the picture of a pretty little girl at its core.

For Dimock, however, these two examples fail to provide the same sort of cultural context—"a second, more nationalistic and literary frame of reference," as he describes it (63)—as that provided by finding *War and Peace* reflected in the account of the hunt. Whitney Davis, whose *Drawing the Dream of the Wolves* (1995) was written around the same time as Dimock's essay, does unearth source material with which we may broaden the frames of reference for the children's drawings and the storybook. Freud's dismissal of "Little Red Riding Hood" as a source is driven by his assumption that it "only offers an opportunity for two illustrations [of the wolf]—Little Red Riding

Hood's meeting with the wolf in the wood, and the scene in which the wolf lies in bed in the grandmother's night-cap" (qtd. in Davis 1995 64). Yet Davis contends that the "most famous version of the fairy tale, presented in Charles Perrault's *Contes* (1697), was commonly illustrated with multiple wolves" (64). For Davis, Freud's suspicion that "some other fairy tale" lay behind the dream formation was prompted more by his own "Christmas Fairy Tale"—the letter to Fliess on New Year's Day 1896, in which he postulated a theory of infantile sexuality among the etiology of defense neuroses (65–70). These suspicions prompted the compliant Wolf Man to attempt to provide visual confirmation of Freud's doubts—just as he was prompted to confirm his dream account with the drawing of the wolf dream—resulting in the location of "some other fairy tale," which just happened to be "The Wolf and the Seven Little Goats" (64–65). For reasons that will be explained in the following section, I suggest that Davis's account is correct in as much as the Wolf Man did feel obliged to locate visual confirmation, but I also think that Freud had reason to actively promote "The Wolf and the Seven Little Goats" as the preferred source, thus prompting the Wolf Man to search for *this particular fairy tale*.

Davis also explores in greater detail the relationship between the drawing of the wolf dream and the children's drawings, by investigating the Wolf Man's own artistic development, from his training as an adolescent on the estate under the guidance of an unidentified artist—Davis suggests that this may have been the Russian landscape artist Victor Borisov-Musatov (10–13)—to his maturation as a painter, almost exclusively, of "charming landscapes" (40). Just as Dimock locates a literary frame of reference for the account of the wolf hunt in the Wolf Man's memoirs, Davis locates source material for the drawing (and the later painting) of the wolf dream in art and in imagery from other cultural traditions. The work of Caspar David Friedrich, for example, is singled out by Davis as the most likely source for the image of the barren tree on a winter landscape, including the reading of the tree as a distortion of the Russian Orthodox cross, among other possible iconographic associations (52–59).

Such attempts to broaden the frames of reference for the dream formation do not necessarily drive a wedge between cultural context and individual context, and the task of locating cultural sources for latent material is not always an attempt to refute Freud's individualized case history. Indeed, the vast artistic and iconographic panorama within which Davis situates the drawing of the wolf dream, and the literary frame of reference within which Dimock situates the memoirs, bring the sister and the fractured self-image of little Sergei into focus with even greater intensity. They allow us to recast the Wolf Man's memoirs and art as a "life-writing" devoted in part to the childhood relationship between the young Russian and his sister. The next step is to recognize that, at least in some degree, the recollection of material in analysis also contributes to the Wolf Man's ongoing process of writing for himself (and his sister) a life that will have been capable of sustaining their relationship long after family, social taboos, adulthood, and even the sister's death had rendered this relationship untenable. For analysis, such a recognition means that the precise (and "primal") conditions for the formation of the wolf dream at age four are unrecoverable: it is impossible to determine which of the contexts for the dream were only *subsequently* incorporated to make sense of the material locked in the crypt. For *Freud's* analysis, Rank's interpretation of events is thus potentially viable, in that the transference and the whole of psychoanalysis may have been incorporated by the Wolf Man.

A crucial term, as I have suggested, is "conviction" (*Überzeugung*). In Mahony's estimation, this term dominates "From the History of an Infantile Neurosis," with some twenty occurrences in the first five chapters alone (1984, 112). This term characterizes the case history in two ways: in the sense that it marks the essay as polemic, an attempt to convince, unlike the "demonstrative stance" that Freud had normally adopted; and in the sense that the term's German root, *zeugen*, means "both to witness and to procreate, which are the two very actions comprising the primal scene, the witnessing of the child and the copulating of the parents" (111). Yet we must add that the term is *not* one that Freud brought to this case history only when he sought to construct his polemic against Adler and Jung, *after* the initial termination of the analysis. In the letter to Jung of 16 April 1909—to which I have referred here, in dealing with Freud's relations with Jung immediately prior to the start of Pankeiev's treatment—and in the lectures delivered at Clark University during the trip to America in the latter half of 1909, the term appears at crucial moments: to Jung, he noted having discovered within himself the conviction that he would die between the ages of 61 and 62, coinciding with the conviction that with

The Interpretation of Dreams he had completed his life work (Freud and Jung 1974, 219); and in *Five Lectures on Psycho-Analysis*, "conviction" is discussed as a positive outcome, shared by an analyst and a patient, resulting from the transference (1910, 52).[6] Mahony also points out that in writing about the Rat Man in 1909, Freud had already signaled his awareness of the lexical complexities inherent in the term's ambiguous German root by writing that a witness who testifies before a court of law "is still called '*Zeuge*' [literally, 'begetter'] in German, after the part played by the male in the act of procreation" (in Mahony 1984, 111).

These revelations enable Mahony to argue that Freud's interpretative strategies, driven by his conviction, and the content of his interpretations manifest a desire to "fill the gaps" in dreams—gaps which, for Freud, symbolize the female genitalia (110). Thus, Freud's continual use of the term "conviction" is an ongoing expression of (or wish for) potency. What this does not tell us, however, is just how Freud's sexualized conviction impacted on the young Russian whose first transference, we may recall, was to express concern that this "Jewish swindler" would use him from behind. Mahony refers to Abraham's and Torok's "startling revelation that witnessing and dreaming in Russian are essentially the same word," but he invites us only to "wonder even more about the unconscious impact of various polyglottal meanings and signifiers" circulating between Freud and Pankeiev (114).[7] With further reference to the Wolf Man's cryptonyms,

[6] In this latter instance, however, "conviction" is rendered by the term "*Übertragung*," which in itself is the term for "transference," making Freud's claim seem somewhat redundant: "transference" in an analysis brings "transference" to the patient and to the analyst. Yet Freud's use of the term indicates the degree to which the term for a psychoanalytic modality (the transference) is also descriptive of what this modality produces *in* analysis, an aspect rendered more easily in English by translating the product of the transference as "conviction." We might add that given its root, "*tragen*" (to bear), the term for the transference *and* Freud's conviction carries resonances of the "burden" that we are examining.

[7] Mahony seems reluctant to give too much credit to Abraham and Torok here. Indeed, he fails to give a page reference for their "startling revelation." He also marks this reluctance in an earlier chapter, where he summarizes their work in some detail, only to ask "whether the sister, important as she was, could be at the center of his nuclear self? When she died, he wept not at her grave but at the poet Lermontov's. Ultimately, did he weep for her, or for himself?" (1984, 38). His doubts suggest that he rejects the use of the crypt as an explanatory device, especially since on the previous page he accurately explained that in the crypt young Sergei had incorporated the sister as "the only way of harmonizing his ego ideal and his love-object; it was Stanko's only way to love his sister so as not to kill her, and to kill her so as not to love her" (37). Accepting this as an accurate description of the Wolf Man's fragile psyche also

as outlined in *The Wolf Man's Magic Word*, we can be more specific. We shall note, to begin with, that the revelation which Mahony finds "startling" is precisely the very first step on the path down which Abraham and Torok tread in interpreting the account of the wolf dream. The first words of the account are "I dreamed." The verb "to dream" is spelled out in Russian as *"vidiet son,"* a phrase which resonates with the noun "witness" (*vidietz*) and the English word "son," indicating that the phrase "I dreamed" might also mean "the witness is the son" in the Wolf Man's polyglottal crypt. (Abraham and Torok [1976] 1986, 34). From this beginning, they are able to deduce that what the content of the account recalls is not simply the wolf dream, but the circumstances to which this dream cryptically refers: an occasion on which the boy was called upon to act as witness to some misdeed. That the "son" is referred to in the third person suggests to them that the words spoken by the Wolf Man are from the mouth of someone other than the young boy: in this case, the words are the mother's and they are being directed at the English governess (35). These revelations become the first index of the crypt, pointing to two of its defining features: the capacity to conceal unspeakable words behind series of cryptonyms, and the capacity to make the Wolf Man speak on behalf of any number of the characters involved in the family drama, centered upon the sister and the seduction.

For Abraham and Torok, the initial question which leads them to the crypt is this: "In whose mouth does this shred of dialogue belong?" (35). For our purposes here, the more immediate question is, why was this shred of dialogue repeated in its cryptic form to Freud? We might assume for one moment that the ambiguous term *"Überzeugung,"* with its German root "witness" and the consequent cryptonymic link to the Russian "to dream," may have been sufficient to prompt the Wolf Man to echo "I dreamed." Yet it is not in the Wolf Man's nature to deliberately hold himself up as a mirror to the other, as the crypt has already closed off the mouth with which he might reach out with words to the other. Instead, his (non-)response is to present himself as a statement from which whatever terms the other presents are excluded, in order to preserve the crypt. The Wolf Man's "I dreamed" excludes Freud's *"Überzeugung"* because the latter's ambiguity arises as a consequence of matching the verb "to witness"

---

means recognizing that Pankeiev could not weep for his dead sister without compromising the crypt's integrity.

with "to father," by placing emphasis upon the masculine role in pro-creation. Yet, as Abraham and Torok suggest, the father is absent from the scenario to which "I dreamed" refers (35, passim). The dream account is thus an attempt to deny, in advance, the father-complex toward which Freud will lean as a consequence of his "conviction."

This initial failure to correspond established the pattern for the remainder of the analysis, and for the various attempts each would make at writing their own lives on the template of their relationship with the other. In Pankeiev, Freud saw a simple, passive reflection of his own troubled past, yet it was the Wolf Man who spoke these words and, in doing so, refused Freud entry into the crypt. To state that the Wolf Man was compliant and obliging is of course correct, for this was how the "sister" locked in the crypt wanted to be perceived, but this does not also mean that he was *responsive*. In Freud, instead, the Wolf Man saw the Jewish swindler that he had described in his early transference description. Accordingly, he resisted his analyst at the level of the crypt, with the result that the Wolf Man's words contradicted Freud's. After analysis, as we have seen, such contradiction often became explicit gainsaying, but the enigma that the Wolf Man presented to analysis, *in analysis*, was a contradiction expressed not in so many words but in so many *allosemes*. "Allosemes" is the term Abraham and Torok used to describe "the lexical contiguity of the various meanings of words . . . as they are catalogued in a dictionary" ([1976] 1986, 19). Instead of constructing a rebus from the constellation of free associations pertaining to representations of an event, cryptonymy buries material at least another level deeper in representation, "replacing a word by the synonym of its alloseme," the result being "not a *metonymy of things* but a *metonymy of words*" (19). Behind such a crypto-metonymic displacement, the Wolf Man's words may easily have seemed internally, to the satisfaction of the crypt and its occupants, to contradict what they externally confirmed: Freud's complex conviction.

In the degree to which I focus more upon the resistant function of the crypt, I have of course diverged from Abraham's and Torok's image of the desperate and enamored patient for whom psychoanalysis represented a final resort: "He placed all his hopes in the Professor. He would tell him everything. Everything, yes, except . . . one thing: the unsayable" (23). What I am attempting to do here is explore the degree and the manner of this exception to the "everything" that the

Wolf Man would tell Freud. The basis for my divergence is Abraham's and Torok's characterization of the Wolf Man as a construct or a conglomeration of incorporated (because unassimilable) substitutes for externalized realities. In this sense, however much Pankeiev—or indeed, perhaps, yes, even the "Wolf Man"—wanted or needed to tell everything, none of the characters occupying the crypt ever really spoke *to* Freud through Pankeiev's mouth. Instead, they spoke to (and on behalf of) "the Professor," the most recent addition to the short list of those with whom the Wolf Man had populated this internal world. The incorporated Professor thus became a device enabling mediation between the unsayable and the will to speak. I suggest that if Pankeiev—or was it little Stanko? or Tierka?—was enamored with Freud and the psychoanalysis that he offered, the occupants of the crypt were still ready at all times to preserve the secrecy of Stanko's incriminating testimony.

(Dear) Anna Left (Herself): The Burden of *Psychanalyse*

Does Freud, in "From the History of an Infantile Neurosis," misinform readers? This is not the same as asking whether his interpretation is accurate, or even whether it is adequate. Rather, it is a question of whether he knowingly embellished the testimony of his only witness or fabricated material from the case history in order to legitimize his interpretation. I do not doubt that the case history was written with the legitimization of a particular set of concepts against potential detractions, characterized within the text as Freud's version of the views held by Adler and Jung, as a key motivation. What I have been arguing here, however, is that such a motivation was not a key to the analysis which the case history describes, nor does it explain why Freud withheld the history for four years. "Withholding" is, of course, the crucial term here. In Stanley Fish's reading of the case history, Freud's many dissimulations are defined as "rhetorical" so as not to exempt them from the charge of tendentiousness (Fish 1987). Freud does not persuade the reader so much as he posits the reader in the role of the resistant patient (along with the dissidents Adler and Jung) "as a proof of the independence of the analysis," to create an illusion of our right to reject interpretations based on "such paltry but unimpeachable facts as these" (in Fish 1987, 169). As Fish notes, these "facts" which sway us toward accepting the interpretation are anchored by "the *assumption* of the primal scene" (169). Freud thus disregards the burden of proof, preferring to withhold this assumption that he later calls upon as evidence against his staged accusers.

Yet Fish equivocates on the matter of whether Freud *knowingly* misinforms us, as the analyst, like the analysand, "can only know what he knows within the rhetoric that possesses him and he cannot be criticized for clinging to that knowledge even when he himself could demonstrate that it is without an extra-discursive formation" (171). Fish concludes, therefore, that Freud's rhetoric is grounded inescapably in the rhetorical tradition dating back to Seneca, just as the arguments he makes with this rhetoric issue from his own personal anxieties: "The thesis of psychoanalysis is that one can not get to the side of the unconscious; the thesis of this essay is that one cannot get to the side of rhetoric. These two theses are one and the same" (171). What Fish is describing, in other words, is what I have been calling life-writing. Yet the description of the case history as life-writing remains incomplete if we assume that the persons "to, for, with, and/or against" whom it was written are none other than those accusers it so elaborately puts forward as its most obvious targets. The delay between the termination of the analysis and the release of the case history is as crucial to understanding the production of this text as is the production itself. Thus, we are more likely to locate the "other" to Freud's life-writing in this text if we search not only for the persons against whom it was written, but for the person *from whom it was being withheld*.

The most direct answer to this question would seem to be the Wolf Man. This leads to another question: why should Freud withhold anything from this one patient to whom he had already given so much and to whom, as Derrida (1986) and Lukacher (1986) have argued in their readings of *The Wolf Man's Magic Word*, he feels deeply indebted? I shall argue here that within the terms of Freud's legacy both "withholding" and "giving" amount to much the same thing, after we consider the consequences for psychoanalysis of the encounter between the Wolf Man (*this* crypt) and Freud (this false crypt). We shall see that the accumulation of debts ultimately represents one function of the burden weighing heavily upon both participants, a burden by the name of Anna (with its myriad associations).

As Abraham and Torok have suggested, the Wolf Man's burden rested in the secretion of the guilty wish for the sister Anna to rub little Stanko's penis. Conversely, we shall see that Freud's guilt is expressed in a phrase that seeks to absolve him of guilt, a phrase that we shall locate in the last place we may expect to have found it (since it is the most visible of all the expressions we encounter in psychoanalysis): the term "psychoanalysis" itself. The cryptic phrases impact so heavily upon the analytic relation because "psychoanalysis" emerges as a key stake in the relationship between our protagonists.

To understand how psychoanalysis itself was to become the specific object with which Freud speculates in his rivalry with the Wolf Man—indeed, to understand how this relationship could be characterized as a rivalry—we need to return to the analytic moment in which the wolf dream *is being* recalled by the patient. We have already seen that with those first words by which the Wolf Man states that he is recalling a dream, he is already delineating a contradiction. "I dreamed" means that the father is absent from the primal scene of bearing witness to the guilty secret, although it is a secret, like the fort/da game, that continually recalls the father by virtue of his absence: sister, rub *my* penis, not daddy's, and cut off (let *us* do the castrating in this place) this threat of being convicted-if-convinced (conviction, *Überzeugung*). By drawing attention to the degree to which the dream account contradicts Freud's conviction, I hope to have filled in a significant gap in Abraham's and Torok's interpretation of the cryptic message concealed behind (and therefore partly revealed by) the dream account. Yet one other obvious gap remains in their attempts to decipher the Wolf Man's cryptic language. Confronted with the claim that there were "six or seven" wolves, Abraham and Torok hear the "sister" (*siestorka*) echoed in the Russian word for a pack of six or "sixter" (*shiestorka*), yet the "or seven" is left unexplained ([1976] 1986, 37). I suspect that they may have decided, as I have, that this extra number is no more than a red herring, thrown up to put the wolf-hound professor off the scent of the wolves (the *"goulfik"* or "open fly" of the guilty wish statement). I contend, however, that the presence of just such a red herring compromises the image of a compliant patient who desired to tell everything to the analyst, who would later betray this trust for the sake of the institution.

It is of course possible that Freud's penchant for details compelled the patient to shift from the assertion of a simple multiplicity—"*some white wolves*"—to a guess at precisely in what number this multiplicity consisted. Confronted, perhaps, by Freud's insistence on knowing how many wolves were in the dream, Pankeiev freely spoke the number which directly hinted at Tierka's presence, only to retract under pressure from the crypt. Alternatively, this "six or seven" might be read as early flirtation by Tierka, of the sort described by Abraham and Torok:

> The man in the chair was now named Father and the man on the couch automatically took on the complementary role, Tierka's role. This was the unexpected but inescapable effect of the analytic situation. His depression vanished, and with his extravagant request began a flirtation between Father and Sister that was to last four and a half years. (23)

"Six" is not only the sister but the German "*sechs*," sounding like the English "sex," a bold flirtation that with a flippant dismissal—"or seven" (*oder sieben*)—is passed over as nothing more. Either way, the Wolf Man learned very quickly how willing Freud was to be diverted away from the *siestorka/shiestorka* (sister/sixter). Freud did not wish to hear the metonymy of words. He wished only to bear witness to the free association which functions, as Gilles Deleuze and Félix Guattari have stated, "at the level of the representation of things" (1977, 138). This "six or seven" had clearly interested his analyst, so the Wolf Man gave him another—the five wolves in the drawing—and then another—the age of four to which the dream can be dated. Seven, six, five, four . . . the analyst had his reduction; he could break the rest down into the Oedipal threesome on his own, with no further help from the Wolf Man.[8]

---

[8] Deleuze and Guattari suggest that in Freud's reductionism we witness "how the wolves will have to be purged of their multiplicity," in order to prove what he had decided from the outset, his conviction (1977, 138). The impression put across in their essay is that the analytic relation consisted of incompatible entities: on the one hand, there was Freud, dominated by Oedipus and the diagnosis of psychotic episodes; on the other, there was the "becoming-wolf" whose schizoid multiplicity manifested itself outside of psychoanalytic discourse. In the following passage, I will argue that what Deleuze and Guattari also tell us about the relation of the Wolf Man to his psychoanalytic proper name suggests the opposite: that the "becoming-wolf" gave itself to Freud as a "not-wolf" (the singularities arising from Freud's reductionism) precisely so that it can be given the proper name which actualizes the wolf presence.

The analytic relation thus presented the Wolf Man with a space into which all of his guilty secrets and all of the occupants of his crypt could project themselves and still not be heard. The desire to tell everything is at least comfortably set against the desire to not be heard—a double role that Freud provided so adequately. Yet one other benefit would accrue from being in psychoanalysis: a proper name. Deleuze and Guattari have argued that the proper name "is the instantaneous apprehension of a multiplicity," from which we begin to glean some understanding of the importance for the Wolf Man of his analytically appointed name, "a real proper name, an intimate first name which refers to becomings, infinitives, and intensities of a depersonalized and multiplied individual" (1977, 146). It is significant that in his later life, long after others had discovered Sergei Pankeiev's name and tracked him down, he continued to sign the name "Wolf Man," even though this pseudonym clearly no longer served as a cover for his identity. Is it possible that he considered his given name insufficient to account for the multiplicity he had become and was continually becoming with further incorporation? With Freud, though, he had an opportunity to be given another name that would be legitimate in the eyes of the world. After all, he knew in advance that Freud was no mere clinician, that analyses with *this analyst* (the "father" of all analyses) had a major tendency to become published case-studies and significant pawns in theoretical debates. He may even have been familiar with one of Freud's most recent acts of nomenclature, the naming of the "Rat Man."[9] If his own case was of sufficient interest to Freud, then perhaps—and this was indeed quite a gamble—he had also given his analyst the animal content from which to derive a new name: the "Wolf Man."

With this name he will have realized several ambitions. The "wolf," as Deleuze and Guattari suggest, names multiplicity. Their patient Franny Schizo states the matter plainly, capturing the importance of the pack or "the mass position": "That's stupid, you can't be a wolf, you're always eight or ten wolves, or six or seven" (1977, 139). In the image of an insatiable gatherer of incorporated roles, we face the internalization of this mass position. Yet the special value of "Wolf" for

[9] Though no other phrase than "the patient" is used to refer to the subject of the case history in "Notes upon a Case of Obsessional Neurosis" (1909), Freud had begun referring to his patient as the "Rat Man" in correspondence with Jung throughout early 1909, before he began to write the case history.

the Wolf Man is that this name for a multiplicity can also function as one of the cryptonyms which conceals (as it also speaks) little Stanko's guilty secret, since the "wolf" is also the *"goulfik"* or wide-open fly which exposes the penis to the sister-Tierka-Anna. How better to shore up the crypt than to become an embodiment of the word which captures this crypt's multiplicity and which performs *the concealment of the act of exposure*? By taking on the proper name of the wolf, Pankeiev may also have been actualizing what he had once been told would be his destiny: to give over his blood ties (abandoning the name given by the father) as he passes into kinship with the wolfen. I have already noted the disagreeement between Carlo Ginzburg and Whitney Davis over the status of the werewolf myth: for Ginzburg, the myth adds a dimension to the interpretation of the childhood dream for which Freud had failed to account; for Davis, the "wolf man" in the story is the adult in analysis who gives to the myth, "now, and in part retrospectively, [a] significance it would never have had" as a result of the psychoanalytic encounter (190). Davis admits that we may only ever guess at the balance of *Vorträglichkeit-Nachträglichkeit* in the Wolf Man's psychic history, yet in arguing for this balance, he places greater emphasis upon the *Nachträglichkeit* than on the *Vorträglichkeit* informing Ginzburg's argument (1995, 191). By characterizing an incorporation as a movement in what Deleuze and Guattari call "becoming," however, I am arguing here for a slight restoration of the balance in our hypothetical description of the Wolf Man's role in the analysis: where the child had once imagined that the dream of the wolves marked his initiation into the becoming-wolf of his lycanthropic vocation, the recollection in analysis restores to the dream some of its initiatory value, as it marks the beginning of the Wolf Man's entry into the constellation of names that are proper to psychoanalysis.

From Freud's introductory remarks to the case history, we gain some insight into the patient's investment in, at the very least, creating an impression that he was telling all. In just the second paragraph of the case history, Freud takes the remarkable step of directly implicating his patient in discussions on what was to be included in writing the material for publication: "In spite of the patient's direct request, I have abstained from writing a complete history of his illness, of his treatment, and of his recovery, because I recognized that such a task was technically impracticable and socially impermissible" (1918, 8). Such a "direct request" for the "complete history" to be made available for general perusal seems an extraordinary measure by an analysand, except if he or she views the analysis as a means to some other end, such as public exposure or social acceptance. The publication of the complete history would legitimate the Wolf Man's analytic name, suggesting that the transference onto Freud was not in itself sufficient as a guarantor of such legitimacy. Yet through the machinations of the psychoanalytic institution he had a path to legitimacy, hence the request: to you, Herr Professor, I have said all that I can; the rest is your responsibility . . . publish it; *institute* it.

It is absurd, however, to imagine that Freud would have related everything to the reader in writing the case history, not simply because such a task was "impracticable" or "impermissible." After all, the full details of his patient's treatment and recovery had to include admissions from the analyst that very special favors had been granted to this patient in order to maintain the analysis, at a time when other patients were being asked to reduce their hours or terminate their analyses. Even if we are to leave to one side the ethical concern that such an admission obviously raises, we cannot ignore the damage that this admission would make to Freud's polemical stance, by bringing into question the *general* validity of observations made about one particular (and clearly very *special*) patient. Yet, almost in spite of himself, Freud indicates the special status of this patient simply by saying anything at all about his request, and by suggesting that this request had entered into his own calculations in selecting or deleting material for publication. The text thus states from the outset the two directions in which it attempts to orient itself: the first footnote (which was added in 1918) states that its polemical orientation supplements "On the History of the Psycho-Analytic Movement" (1914a)—an essay he admits was "of a personal character"—by providing an "objective estimation" (insofar as it draws upon analytic material) of ideas expressed more subjectively in the earlier polemic; and a statement made in the second paragraph, (which we must assume was written in 1914) suggests with the term *trotz* (meaning "in spite of," but with emphasis on defiance) that at the time the text was written its primary motivation, particularly with respect to its "patient" (in spite of whom Freud included or omitted material), was far from objective.

"From the History of an Infantile Neurosis" is "fragmentary," as Freud states the matter, because it is defiant, openly flying in the face of its subject's wishes (1918, 7). Might Freud also have withheld the text from publication for four years for precisely the same reason? If we are to make this assertion, we need to be more certain of the Wolf Man's position as a rival to Freud. We have already determined that when he first came to Freud, Pankeiev was in some respects already a "Wulff-Man," whose arrival coincided with the crucial fifty-second anniversary (the "dog" anniversary) of the death of Julius. Both his initial transference and recollections from childhood, including the wolf dream, will have been catalysts for Freud to form the same identification with this patient that had seen him previously cast others as arch-revenants of Julius. For reasons that Freud himself could not possibly have missed—unless, of course, he had a blind-spot the size of a crypt diverting his conscious perceptual activities—*this* revenant was different from the others. Rather than providing Freud with an image of his younger brother, this revenant seemed more insistently to present him with a mirror reflecting himself in his own past. Specifically, I shall be arguing in the next few pages that although Freud was looking for Julius to be reflected in Pankeiev, he saw instead the Wolf Man, a reflection of himself insofar as this was a reflection of his own (false) crypt and the material it screened. In a bold strategic move, however, Freud addressed this reflection directly in the life-writing of the case history, to produce a text which enabled him to reconcile or synthesize the false crypt with the material that it screened at the same time as it convinced its reader of the primacy of the primal scene (the Wolf Man's and, by association, his own).

I shall begin by arguing that the "dog" anniversary—which has appeared to be so important an association in shaping Freud's Julius identification in 1910, just as images and imagery relating to dogs had shaped the Julius identification with Silberstein in the formation of the "Academia Castellana"—also contains crucial links to the rivalry with the sister Anna and the object-loss which triggered the formation of the false crypt.[10] In some further material added to *The Psychopathology of Everyday Life* (1901), we find evidence that during the

[10] It is possible to assert a clear link between the events of 1910 and the "Academia Castellana": in April 1910, for the first time since abruptly ending his correspondence with Silberstein in 1881, Freud wrote his old friend a letter, in which he laments that "life is running out" for him, but that he is, if not a financial success, the leader of a

first two years of his analysis with the Wolf Man, from 1910 to 1912, Freud continued to work through the complex Anna-Amme material that Julius material had been screening. The eleventh example of the forgetting of sets of words, added in 1912, refers to Freud's visit to Sicily with Sándor Ferenczi in September of 1910. The anecdote describes a debate the two men had concerning the name of a town (Castelvetrano) through which they passed yet whose name neither could recall (30–32). In his account of their debate, Freud claims that he (the "older man" described in the account) had first thought of the name Caltanisetta, which, he confessed, "certainly isn't right," and then tried to find a suitable substitute, based on having forgotten many Sicilan names already: "what was the name of the place on a hill that was called Enna in antiquity? Oh, I know—Castrogiovanni" (30–31). After he had been reminded of the forgotten name Castelvetrano, according to Freud, "it was for him to explain why he had forgotten it," which he does by suggesting that the second part of the name sounds too much like "veteran," a reminder of his own increasing age (31). As a sign that his resistance was directed only against the second half of Castelvetrano, Freud adds that only "the initial sound recurred in the substitute name Caltanisetta."

As Ernest Jones recounts in his biography of Freud, this trip had been an unhappy one, and it was primarily only the result of Freud's "generosity and tactfulness" that he and Ferenczi were to remain friends (1974, 361). According to Jones, Ferenczi had stayed quiet and introspective throughout the journey, a characterization that seems to be confirmed by Freud's recollection of having to make all the running in providing explanations and his claim that no interpretation had been made of "the motive for the similar failure of the younger man's memory" (Freud 1901, 32). Yet we may question Freud's generosity and tact if we consider that Ferenczi's introspection was due to what Jones called an "inordinate and insatiable longing for his father's love," and in Freud's first letter to Ferenczi after the trip he states that he could no more have disciplined his younger companion "than I could have my three sons because I am too fond of them and should feel sorry for them" (in Jones 1974, 360). As in other correspondence, we see here that Freud's "tact" is far more tactical than

---

great movement that has received widespread recognition (in Grosskurth 1991, 29–30).

tactful. Moreover, his tactics in this particular instance give us a clear indication of how this letter and the anecdote added in 1912 to *The Psychopathology of Everyday Life* position their subject as a non-respondent, such that the other against whom they are written is not Ferenczi but the sister Anna. Despite his (and Jones's) characterization of Ferenczi as having been the less revealing of the two during the trip, Freud states in his letter that his companion had noticed, "but also understood, that I *no longer* [that is, since "Fliess's case"] have any need to uncover my personality completely," by which he explains that a "part of homosexual cathexis has been withdrawn and made use of to enlarge my own ego. I have succeeded where the paranoiac fails" (in Jones 1974, 360). The message to Ferenczi is clear: I, the Father Professor, am not a paranoiac. We might also add the following: not like Fliess, not like Adler or Jung, not like my Russian patient, and not like you.

Of course, the account that Freud adds to *The Psychopathology of Everyday Life* is far from revealing, except on the matter of his fear of his own mortality, a theme upon which (as we have seen) he had already expanded at length, dropping hints about Julius and his guilt along the way. In particular, Freud's claim that there is no resistance against the first half of the name Castelvetrano is less than convincing, and he does not explain why "Enna" was thrown forward as a substitute when "Castrogiovanni" offers the most immediate rationalization. In terms of the enlargement of the ego through the withdrawal of a part of homosexual cathexis, however, the *placement* of the anecdote in the body of the text is revealing. To the readers of the fifth and subsequent editions of *The Psychopathology of Everyday Life*, the anecdote seems nestled in the middle of the long third chapter, but in 1912 this example was the last in the chapter, followed only by the brief summary (dating to 1907) explaining that the mechanism of forgetting names consists in interference by a complex associated with an alien train of thought (Freud 1901, 39–40). This summary was followed immediately by the fourth chapter, "Childhood Memories and Screen Memories," which refers at the outset to Freud's "Screen Memories" (1899), an essay that I have already discussed here at some length in connection with a renewal of the drama played out in the false crypt. The example that is used first is of a "man of twenty-four" who recollects that in his fifth year he experienced "difficulties over the difference between *m* and *n*" (1901, 48). This memory apparently "only acquired its meaning at a later date, when it showed itself suited to represent symbolically another of the boy's curiosities," that the major difference between boys and girls is similar to that between the *m* and the *n*: "that a boy, too, has a whole piece more than a girl" (48). This concern with the difference between *m* and *n* also registers the key linguistic precursor for Freud's first traumatic object-loss: the confusion over Anna and Amme. As the Castelvetrano parapraxis is placed soon before this example in the text, the emergence of the name "Enna" as a substitute for Castelvetrano seems to hint at another complex interfering with the recollection of the correct name, a complex represented by the name "Emma" (an inversion of Amme) and its various associations.[11]

Immediately following this anecdote (save for a paragraph which Freud added in 1920), the text provides us with a detailed account of a screen memory that had formed part of the basis for Freud's self-analysis: a memory of having been crying in front of a cupboard, which his half-brother was holding open, and of his mother entering the room looking slim and beautiful, from which Freud reconstructed a link between his nanny's disappearance and the birth of his sister Anna (49–52). A key term in Freud's reconstruction is the pun his half-brother had used to state the nanny's whereabouts: *eingekastelt* ("boxed up"). Here we find evidence that the first half of Castelvetrano points to more than one association for Freud and should therefore be considered as one of those names which, as he explains, "consequently belongs to more than one group of thoughts (complexes) [and which] is frequently interfered with in its connection with one train of thought owing to its participation in another, stronger complex" (40). The first half of "Castel-vetrano" *is* resistant since it echoes the second portion of *einge-kastelt*, thereby throwing up associations of the traumatic loss of the nanny. It might be no coincidence that the

[11] In addition to the Anna-Amme connection I am drawing here, the name Emma will also have been an important and direct reference to females implicated in two of the main rivalries I have discussed: prior to 1911 the name will most likely have been associated with Fliess through the ill-fated Emma Eckstein, but during that year Jung's wife, Emma, will have become more prominent as she tried to intervene through a secret correspondence on her husband's behalf. For a concise discussion of the way in which Freud used the correspondence with Emma Jung in forming a theory of object-choice, see Klaus Theweleit's *Object-Choice (All You Need Is Love . . .)* (1994, 68–81). Indeed, by being cast as the "younger" (*jünger*) man, Ferenczi may have been substituted in this document for Jung, with whom Freud had more recently been having conflict.

Castelvetrano parapraxis is positioned immediately prior to references to the essay "Screen Memories," and to the *m/n* and *eingekastelt* memories, as these latter pieces of text (though written previously) indicate that what Freud had stated in a private letter to Ferenczi—that he conceals a part of his personality in and through his revelations—also applies to what he adds to his published text in 1912.[12] The Father Professor's claim to tell all provides clues to what he is concealing even as he denies that anything at all is being concealed. In his account of the Castelvetrano parapraxis, Freud repeats his confession, though it is performed differently and less explicitly. Here, the form of his confession is the *placement* of a document—which contains a claim that all has been revealed by the older man (if only by implication, since nothing has been revealed on the part of the younger)—alongside some existing documents which cast doubt on the suggestion that the newer document reveals all.

By now it should also be clear that by taking both sets of documents together we gain new insight into the meaning of the name "Castellana" that Freud adopted for his private academy with Eduard Silberstein. As Freud mused over Castelvetrano in 1910 and 1911, prior to inserting the account of this parapraxis into *The Psychopathology of Everyday Life* in 1912, he must have realized that his academy—which had been a very private device for legitimizing the false crypt through a myriad of associations—carried a name comprising two keys (*kastelt*-"Anna") to unlocking the traumatic scene that the false crypt had been erected to screen. What I have shown here, however, is nothing more than that Freud's false crypt was dangerously unraveling around the material that it was designed to screen, at around the same time that he was in analysis with the Wolf Man. The precise relation between this Anna material and the Wolf Man analysis is yet to be established. With *The Psychopathology of Everyday Life*, though, we are given a good starting point for establishing such a relation, given that we know Freud had been grappling with the relevance of fairy tales throughout the first three years of the Wolf Man analysis. In Freud's

[12] The *m/n* memory seems to insist on being read in connection with the Castelvetrano parapraxis, since a similar linguistic confusion is raised in this text: the younger man claims to encounter difficulties between the letters "w" and "v" in shifting from German to Italian, a confusion that represents an inversion of *m/n*. Note also that by drawing our attention to the shift from German to Italian and back again, Freud seems to invite the translation that I suggested in the previous footnote, from *"giovane"* ("young") to *"jung"* (1901, 31).

interleaved copy of the 1904 edition, in which he recorded numerous examples that were to be added in subsequent editions, we find the following observation inserted between the accounts of the *m/n* and *eingekastelt* memories:

> Dr. B—— showed very neatly one Wednesday that fairy tales can be made use of as screen memories in the same kind of way that empty shells are used as a home by the hermit crab. These fairy tales then become favorites without the reason being known. (49n2)

Again, we should not think that the placement of this fragment is incidental, especially when we note that "fairy tales" in German is *"Ammenmärchen."* The importance of the first half of this word should by now be self-evident, but we shall also begin to glimpse the importance of the second half when we note that it was most likely in late February or early March that Freud's sixth child Anna would have been conceived, and that in either possibility he almost certainly will have not learned of her conception until early in March.

The role of Anna in the early development of psychoanalysis has been well documented before now. Even the fact of her unwanted conception has been listed by Anna Freud's biographer, Elisabeth Young-Bruehl, as one of the day residues for the specimen dream of interpretation, that of Irma's injection (1988, 27–28). Martha's new pregnancy was an unwelcome one, as neither parent was in full health at the time, and the practice was barely bringing in enough money to support the already large Freud contingent. This combined with other events—the Emma Eckstein saga and a growing disenchantment with Josef Breuer throughout the writing of *Studies on Hysteria*, among others—to produce a composite figure, Irma, as the target for Freud's ill-wishes. Since Martha's pregnancy was unwanted, it is also an early indication of Freud's developing ambivalence toward Fliess that he had expressed his intent to name the child Wilhelm if it was a boy (26–27). This claim makes sense, so why has the same thing never been suggested (to the best of my knowledge) for Freud's choice of the name Anna?

I do not doubt Freud's claim to have named the child after Anna Hammerschlag is quite legitimate, but I question whether this name is a product *only* of "the domestic side of his temperament and of his preference for social companionship, which was largely Jewish," as

Peter Gay has suggested (1990, 60). Patrick Mahony has suggested that the proliferation of the nasal letters "m" and "n" in Freud's correspondence and writing in 1895 is indicative of a "nasal obsession" that determined his ambivalent identification with Fliess, complicated by both Emma Eckstein's troublesome nose and Freud's own nasal operation (1987, 121). Mahony's catalogue of Freud's use of these letters is worth particular attention:

> The reception in the dream was a birthday celebration for Freud's wife, pregnant with her sixth child, who could be named An*n*a if a girl and Wilhel*m* if a boy. Acting as a symbolic link, the nasal letters also figure in:
> Ir*m*a/E*mm*a/A*nan*as
> Sig*m*u*n*d
> M. (Breuer, "the leading figure in our circle")
> Methyl/a*m*yl,/tri*m*ethyla*m*i*n*/A*m*alie. (122)

Viewed together like this, the uses of the nasal letters may strike us as a rationalization for the Amme-Anna complex that we have been discussing. Significantly, it suggests also that Freud's ambivalent relationship with Fliess—which I have described here as a key formation for Freud in legitimating associations derived from the Julius complex—belongs itself among the constellation of associations deriving from the Amme-Anna complex, of which the choice of the names Wilhelm and Anna for Freud's sixth child is a direct expression.

Given that Freud's disenchantment with Josef Breuer—"M." in the Irma dream—also finds expression in a nasal letter, it seems unusual that the name of the specimen patient of psychoanalysis is not mentioned in the catalogue of nasal words. Anna O, as Freud (or Breuer) had named Bertha Pappenheim, is simply too obvious to omit, and yet Freud himself seemed reluctant to include her name among those he extracted from the Irma dream.[13] By the time Freud completed *Studies in Hysteria* in 1895, of course, Anna O had become a vital pawn in his imaginary battle with Breuer to claim control of the new psy-

[13] My suspicion is that Freud devised the name Anna O, since it was he who had the greatest to gain by doing so (at least symbolically): as Pappenheim's father was named Sigmund and a brother was named Wilhelm, Freud could have used the name in 1895 (the year in which he completed *Studies in Hysteria*) to recast Breuer's patient in a new drama being played out with Fliess in the role of arch-revenant. By casting Pappenheim as Anna, Freud is elevated to the role of the father while Fliess remains the brother.

chology. Rachel Bowlby has demonstrated that in "On the History of the Psycho-Analytic Movement" (1914) and *An Autobiographical Study* (1925) Freud provides an ambiguous account of the "untoward event" which prompted the sudden end to Breuer's treatment of Anna O, with the most direct diagnostic explanation being that a sexualized "transference love" had befallen the treatment and that Breuer shied away from this sexualization of the relationship and from its analytic implications (Bowlby 1991, 11–12). Bowlby's reading of these texts demonstrates, however, that the true character of this "untoward event," a phantom pregnancy carried for the full term (pseudocyesis), is all too casually reflected in the language with which Freud portrays Breuer's "contretemps," countered by his own success in delivering psychoanalysis. For our purposes, the striking feature of Freud's words in 1914 (the year he terminated the Wolf Man analysis), in which he recalls the events leading up to the publication of *Studies in Hysteria* in 1895 (the year of the birth of his sixth child, Anna), is the degree to which they attempt to transform the traumatic phantom pregnancy endured by the suggestible Anna O into a symbolic victory of the father of psychoanalysis over his rival.

This transformation is, I think, quite purposeful and deliberate (at least within the mode of improvisation): I suggest that during 1895 the choice of the name of Anna for his sixth child had allowed Freud to imagine that his wife's pregnancy was merely a phantom, as Anna O's had been. This possibility can be taken further, suggesting that the use of the name Anna in the accounts of two quite unrelated cases of unwanted pregnancy echoed a wish from Freud's own childhood. Yet in 1914, Freud could reflect upon both the victory that Anna O had given him over Breuer and the improvement in his analytic practice that seemed to accompany the birth of his sixth child. Soon after Anna's birth, Freud boasted to Fliess that her arrival seemed to have brought about "an increase of my practice, doubling what it usually is" (1985, 154). Within three weeks, Freud had also completed "Draft K. The Neuroses of Defense," which he mailed to Fliess with a letter marking the beginning of the new year. This document, coming so soon after *Studies in Hysteria*, also marked the start of a new phase in Freud's life, in which his family life and practice became increasingly utilized as the subjects of a glut of theoretical writings, peaking with *The Interpretation of Dreams* (1900) and *The Psychopathology of Everyday Life* (1901). Not long after the beginning of this phase, as we have seen, anniversary reactions tied to the death of Julius had also begun to intensify, most notably in the cardiac episode stemming from an identification with the sculptor Tilgner. The boon accompanying the birth of his daughter also demanded its sacrifice: all that glistened was not gold.

I have also argued that Freud was quite anxiously awaiting the release of "Further Remarks on the Neuro-Psychoses of Defense," in which he claimed property rights over "the laborious but completely reliable method of psycho-analysis used by me in making these investigations" (162). I will speculate further that this anxiety is tied to the presence in this essay, and in "Heredity and the Aetiology of the Neuroses," of a phrase locked within the name Freud gave to his "completely reliable method": with the term *"psychanalyse"* (as it will have first appeared in the French publication), we hear the echo of a child's lament: *"sich Anna ließ"* (Anna left [herself]). I class this as a lament, rather than a wish, because the verb is clearly given in the past tense (in the imperfect indicative) and cannot be mistaken for *"Verlassen"* (leave), and because the verb *"ließ"* has a close visual resemblance to an expression of fondness, *"lieb"* (dear). Rather than a wish for Anna to leave, this phrase is thus rendered as a regret that (dear) Anna has left. I claimed earlier that with the first part of the name that Freud gave to psychoanalysis, he had also given a name to the crucial investment of his therapeutic method in life death. We see now that with the remainder of the name that he gave to this method, he also concealed those words with which he confesses (by virtue of his lamentation) his complicity in the most hurtful object-loss of his early childhood.[14]

Whether or not the reader accepts this speculation, we must not forget that Freud had sent "Draft K," from which he drew material for the essays released in February, to Fliess with the suggestive subtitle "(A Christmas Fairy Tale)." His first concentrated articulation of a general theory of sexuality (including the assumption of infantilism and sexuality) was thus declared a *Weihnachtsmärchen*, another of the

[14] Patrick Mahony suggests that similar processes are at work in Freud's refusal to give to the death drive its appropriate name: "Freud's conscious or unconscious censorship rebelled against having his favorite daughter formally inscribed and contained in Th*a*natos" (1984, 164). We can add here that such an inscription would conflict with the inscription of his daughter (as a function of Amme-Anna, the mother-nanny-sister complex) in the name of psychoanalysis, and insofar as *this* name also articulates a lamentation *against* death wishes.

gifts that had accompanied the arrival of his March-daughter. Confirmation of this association came in a most unsuspecting manner on 21 April 1896, after Freud delivered "The Etiology of Hysteria" to his colleagues, when Richard von Krafft-Ebing dismissed the lecture as a "scientific fairy tale" (*"wissenschaftliches Märchen"*) (Freud 1985, 184). This lecture was the "one prior commitment" to which Freud had referred in his letter of 16 April 1896—the Tilgner letter (181). These associations seemed to gravitate together at an alarming rate after Anna's birth, producing a tight knot that would not begin to unravel until the critical periods between 1907 and 1910. Then, as Freud approached the last *termin* in April 1910, something miraculous presented itself to enable the false crypt to draw the unraveling threads together again. Davis suggests that "the Wolf Man's fairy-tale associations to the Christmas Eve dream could not have failed to remind Freud of his own 'Christmas Fairy Tale' " (1995, 69). The key to unlocking the Wolf Man's secrets would thus provide proof of infantile sexuality—but more importantly, for our purposes, this proof could be situated once again in association with *Ammenmärchen*.

For Freud, though, not just any fairy tale would suffice. Despite the Wolf Man's insistence that his dream had been triggered in part by a picture used to illustrate "Little Red Riding Hood," we have seen that Freud also insisted with some authority that the catalyst must have been "The Wolf and the Seven Little Goats." Freud's particular investment in this tale can be traced to his observations of his daughter's development: in a letter to Fliess of 23 February 1898 he mentions both directly: "Recently Annerl complained that Mathilde had eaten all the apples and demanded that her [Mathilde's] belly be split open (as happened to the wolf in the fairy tale of the little goat)" (1985, 300). It is difficult to tell from this account whether it is the father or the daughter who draws the parallels between the splitting open of a full belly and the fairy tale of the little goat, but we can be certain that the father records the link, thereby inscribing *for himself* the association between this particular tale and his little Annerl. For this reason, I suggest that when he inserted a statement to the effect that fairy tales can be used as screen memories into his interleaved copy of the 1904 edition of *The Psychopathology of Everyday Life*, between accounts of the *m/n* and the *eingekastelt* memories, Freud was himself thinking of "The Wolf and the Seven Little Goats" by way of example.

We find that *this* fairy tale above all others resonates with suggestive material if at least two languages are taken into account. For example, a "mother-goat" or *"Geiß"* is also known as a "nanny-goat," providing an all too obvious reference to his earliest object-loss.[15] More complex associations may be found in the words which describe the type and number of little goats: in *Ziegenbock* or *"billy*-goat," we hear an echo of the name Wilhelm; and, in the number of goats, we find the same number as in the brood of which Freud was himself a member—that is, if we count only *Amalie's* children (as Jakob had two sons from a previous marriage) and, of course, if we discount Julius. Such word play enables the mother of seven (Amalie) and the nanny to merge, in a conflation that mimics the earlier Amme-Anna confusion. The third character in this composite figure (the sister) *and* the ill-wishes that accompanied her arrival are also incorporated into the fairy tale in the form of the "clock-case" in which one of the children hides in order to escape being devoured by the wolf. By having encased (*eingekastelt*) itself, the little goat determines that it shall be returned to the mother-nanny. From Freud's own analysis of the *eingekastelt* memory, references to the birth of his sister are clear.

What he does not tell us in *The Psychopathology of Everyday Life*, yet which he stated plainly in discussing a different problem in *The Interpretation of Dreams*, is that imagining anything "boxed," with a "Schachtel (box), Loge (box at the theatre), Kasten (chest), Ohrfeige (box on the ear)," symbolizes both childbearing *and* the wish "that the child might die before its birth" (Freud 1900, 154–55). Thus, *this* fairy tale can be seen as a device by which Freud might have incorporated his March-child completely into the composite figure Amme-Anna (mother-nanny-sister). To put this another way, the fairy tale enables Freud to project the *whole* of the composite figure torn asunder by his early object-loss onto the figure of his little Annerl. While these associations (this knot) remain tied together, the effects of the object-loss are deferred and the false crypt can continue to direct guilt toward Julius.

As we might expect, then, the account and the drawing of the wolf

---

[15] In the mother-goat or *Geiß*, we hear a sharp echo of Jung's "polter*geist*," although both of these terms may have been triggered as associations by the Wolf Man's claim to have only been able to draw caricatures such as those of a "drunkard" (the literal translation is *Trinker*, although an alcoholic drink is *geistig*) or a "miser" (*geizhals*).

dream present an opportune moment before the critical fifty-second Julius anniversary to reprise these fairy tale associations. Freud's conviction is thus *Überzeugung* because it is directed at that initially unwanted child: Herr Father Professor is *too* potent, too much the begetter of new things, in contrast to his capacity to take life simply by wishing someone away. As life-writing, the case history presented Freud with the further opportunity to absolve himself of his complicity in the loss of the nanny by instituting *this* fairy tale within his own ongoing Christmas fairy tale, psychoanalysis. Yet in order for this absolution to be instituted *absolutely*, Freud will have known that several conditions must be met by the case history, one of which is that it be presented as a polemic against dissensions from Freud's two arch rivals. To meet this condition would of course mean that the material which had initially offered a simple alternative to the rivalries being played out with the Julius revenants Adler and Jung would now be channelled back into these rivalries.

Positing the Rival in "From the History of an Infantile Neurosis" and Beyond

Given the imposition of a false crypt at the core of psychoanalysis, the most important requirement of the case history must be that the contents of the crypt will not be exposed or compromised by what this history reveals. Whether Freud was conscious of this requirement or not, the case history does proceed with extreme caution through material which might point to either the Amme-Anna complex or the supposed infantile scene of rivalry with Julius. What Whitney Davis calls the *Nachträglichkeit* of Freud's writing in the case history is, in this sense, shaped by the tension within the life-writing between two very important imperatives: enough suggestions must be made that this history is *not* about Julius to give the speculators sufficient evidence to suggest that it is all about Julius (the guilt of the survivor manifesting in a denial of repressed material); and, without giving the same speculators any clues that this is about Amme-Anna, as much about the sister must be written as is needed to dismiss any suggestions that she is the key to the crypt—therefore, confess everything but say nothing. Amme-Anna functions in Freud's life-writing in the case history as a very *deliberate* crypt screen, by which I mean that it is not a crypt screen proper but does draw attention to itself as if it were a crypt screen, in order to throw the analyst off its scent (to use the language of the wolves, to which it had become accustomed).

We can expect, then, that wherever clues to Amme-Anna are left in the case history, there shall also be a negation of Julius, simply because such a negation will inevitably be read as an affirmation. Accordingly, when we identify the wolf dream symbolically as a Christmas fairy tale, we find the denial of Julius even here in the symbolic heartland of the sister-mother-nanny-daughter composite: the date of the Wolf Man's birthday and of the wolf dream are given here as Christmas eve, but this is only according to the Gregorian (*not the Julian*) calendar. The relation between these Christmas dates and the reconstructed primal scene also becomes significant, as the Wolf Man's condition—"He was suffering at the time from malaria" (Freud 1918, 36–37)—refers the event to the summer, an observation enabling Freud to "assume that his age was $n + 1\frac{1}{2}$ years" (37). A footnote is added at this point by the editor to qualify this equation:

It might perhaps be clearer to say "$n + \frac{1}{2}$". The point is that owing to the interval of 6 months between the patient's birthday and the summer, his age at the time of the trauma must have been 0 years + 6 months, or 1 year + 6 months, or 2 years + 6 months etc. The $0 + \frac{1}{2}$ is, however, already excluded in the footnote on p. 36." (37n3)

It *might* be clearer to say "$n + \frac{1}{2}$," but clarity seems at this point to be what is at issue in Freud's argument. Here, we find an example of life-writing performing for the reader the processes described in "The Psycho-Analytic View of Psychogenic Disturbance of Vision," since the equation (by virtue of being the product of mathematical calculation) seems to provide clarity on the matter, but obscures a crucial problematic. As Strachey suggests, Freud had on the previous page dismissed the possibility that his patient had been only six months of age at the time of the primal scene. Instead, he "established" the relevant age at "about one and a half years" (36). If the age has been established at one and a half years it seems redundant to provide a variable "n" to state that the age can be calculated as "$n + 1\frac{1}{2}$ years," as the equation could only hold true if this variable is taken as a constant equal to zero. The equation does now speak the language of the Amme-Anna complex, however, since it holds true only where *an n =* *a o* (Anna O, the death wish against the unborn child). Yet the false crypt intercedes, since the equation also only holds true where this nasalized death wish against the unborn is appended to the age of one and a half years, a figure linked to estimates of little Sigismund's own age at the time of Julius's death.

Were it not for Strachey's editorial clarification, which transcribes Freud's "$1/2$" as the interval measured by a factor of "6 months," we might also overlook precisely what Freud's equation seems designed to avoid: the number six. Indeed, of the few numbers given by the Wolf Man for the various estimates of the number of wolves in his dream, the number six is given the most cursory treatment in the case history. With reference to his subject's age at the time of the primal scene, we have seen that Freud dismisses the number six from his equation. Elsewhere, he does little more than use the number six as justification for pursuing "The Wolf and the Seven Little Goats" in the dream interpretation: "Here, the number seven occurs, and also the number six, for the wolf only ate up six of the little goats" (31). The number six—now the number of *Schuld* and of Freud's March-daughter—seems more important here for its capacity to be deducted from the number seven to produce a singularity on which to focus; or, more accurately, to reduce the ten major characters in the fairy tale (the seven goats, their mother, the wolf and the cutter) to the four Oedipal figures compressed into the triangulation of the nucleus of a single family unit (the child, the mother, and two fathers—a castrating and a castrated father).[16] The most important thing for Freud here is that

[16] These two fathers upon which I only touch briefly here may be derived from the difference between the castrating father (which Freud knows must be at the top of the Oedipal triangle and at the core of the superego) and the castrated father (Jakob) that he remembers from his own experience. For further explanation of this interpretation, see Leonard Shengold's *"The Boy Will Come to Nothing!" Freud's Ego Ideal and Freud as Ego Ideal* (1993). Alternatively, the two fathers may be derived from Jakob and the more vigorous Philipp who, according to some commentators, may have had an affair with Amalie which Freud and/or the nanny may have suspected and/or witnessed. See Paul Vitz's *Sigmund Freud's Christian Unconscious* (1988). On the other matter of the relation of the number seven to the number six, the reader may also be interested by an exchange between Karl Abraham and Freud, in letters and essays, in which the prime numbers and common superstitions pertaining to the number seven are traced

any clues linking the fairy tale or the dream interpretation (the reconstructed primal scene) to events in his own life are carefully inserted only as a negative. Even the fairy tale is eventually forced to the background by Freud's decision to focus in greater detail upon visual associations with the number five (or the "V" of the butterfly's wings and nanya's legs) in the latter half of the case study, during which all material that might have pointed us toward the Wolf Man's own sister Anna is directed instead toward the parents. That this Roman V is a castrated "VI" or "W" is overlooked throughout the text. The only occasion on which the "W" is discussed in relation to castration is in the mutilation of *"Wespe"* to form *"Espe,"* indicative of "S.P.," and in this the letter is subtracted from the entire word (94). This allows Freud to *not* allude to *The Psychopathology of Everyday Life*, in which Castelvetrano (including the slippage between the Germanic "w" and "v"), *m/n, Ammenmärchen,* and *eingekastelt* had been raised in close proximity to each other.[17]

In the case history, then, Freud provides enough clues to suggest that this text is a device enabling him to work through several sets of associations pertaining to material from his own life, yet this life-writing is everywhere answerable to the false crypt and the secrets that it protects. As a result, much of the material that later points Abraham and Torok in the direction of the Wolf Man's crypt is also left lying in the background of Freud's text. Using Fish's reading of the case history as a guide here, we might state that Freud convinces us to accept the primal scene of parental coitus *a tergo*, rather than the seduction by the sister, by overwhelming the reader with the reconstructed "fact" of the primal scene. Yet even here, in the language with which Freud lays out such a fact before us, we find that the Wolf Man's crypt (and, consequently, the sister Anna) states its case as clearly as possible: in the *siesta* to which the parents are supposed to have retired for their afternoon lovemaking, we cannot help but hear the resonances of the *siestorka/siestra* (sister) and, therefore, the *shiestorka/shiestiero* (six) which represent the two keys to unlocking the secrets of the crypt (Abraham and Torok [1976] 1986, 17). The *Nachträglichkeit* of

---

to an earlier system of counting to base six—see Max Schur's *Freud: Living and Dying* (1972).

[17] Recall that the difficulty associated with the letters *m* and *n* is attributed in *The Psychopathology of Everyday Life* to a boy in his *fifth* ("v," the castrated "vi") year.

Freud's writing is thus intimately linked to his attempt to integrate the language of the false crypt screen with that of the absolution he seeks for the more primary (though far less "primal") scene of rivalry and guilt.

Indeed, even where Freud runs up hard against the Wolf Man's crypt, he restores material from his own crypt at the core of his interpretations. In what had originally (in 1914) been the final block of material in chapter five—"A Few Discussions" (1918, 48–57)—Freud argues that the Wolf Man's sister may have also witnessed a scene similar to that witnessed by her brother, a claim based on her "remarkable calumny against his good old nurse, to the effect that she stood all kinds of people on their heads and then took hold of them by their genitals" (56). He concludes that the possibility of the sister's having also witnessed a primal scene of sexual intercourse "would also give us a hint of the reason for her own sexual precocity" (57). As a claim with which to conclude one whole chapter of his work, this is a quite remarkable one from Freud, since it gives rise to a very precise connection between the Wolf Man's primal scene and the sexuality of the sister. Yet we have already noted that one of the functions of the primal scene is to allow Freud (or at least the language of the false crypt) to divert the reader's attention away from the relation with the sister as a factor in the wolf dream. Accordingly, then, he adds a new block of material prior to publication, in which he argues that the primal scene of parental coitus *a tergo* may not by necessity have been an actual scene, and he suggests instead that the "scene" in question may have been based on the patient's having observed sheep dogs copulating (57–60). In support of this, he adds that "the wolves in the dream were actually sheep dogs and, moreover, appear as such in the drawing" (57–58). For Allen Esterson, as we have seen, such wavering over the type of animal in the dream—in contrast to the Wolf Man's insistence in 1957 that what he had drawn were "not wolves at all but white Spitz dogs with pointed ears and bushy tails"—is proof of either contradiction or even intentional misrepresentation of the truth by Freud. Yet Esterson fails to point out that Freud's alternative interpretation is put forward so as to prompt further investigation of the "analytic findings" (Freud 1918, 59). Where Freud had hinted at the possibility that it was the sister's primal scene experience that had been relayed to the Wolf Man through her sexual behavior, all this talk of sheep dogs allows Freud to reassert the "correctness" of the primal scene hypothesis, in such a way that attention has been shifted away from any consideration of the sister yet again.

It may be that in the Wolf Man's statement we find the source of Freud's "sheep dogs." I have already stated, in agreement with Whitney Davis, that the dogs sketched by the Wolf Man in the drawing of the dream of the wolves gave Freud reason to recall both the wolf and the hounds depicted by Friedrich von Tschudi in *Animal Life in the Alpine World*. The Wolf Man's open fly (the *goulfik* or wolves) is transformed on the analyst's side into the ambivalent wolfhound as the symbol of analysis. Yet I want to speculate even further here, by suggesting that the Wolf Man's "Spitz dogs" may have been a reconstruction from a somewhat ambiguous phrase entailing a homonymic, bilingual confusion encountered somewhere in the analysis. Freud's sheep-dogs are of course *Schäferhunden*, while the Wolf Man's Spitz dogs are *Spitz hunden*, either (or both) of which may have emerged by name from the observation of the "pointed ears" of the dogs in the drawing, as "pointed" translates literally as *"spitz"* and figuratively (as in a "pointed" remark) as *"spitz"* or as *"scharf"*—the similarity of *"Schärfe"* (sharpness) to *"Schäfer"* (shepherd) could easily have led to some degree of confusion between the patient (for whom German was a third or even a fourth language) and the analyst (for whom dogs carried particular symbolic value in 1910).

The point is of course that where potential cryptonymic confusion arises, we can only speculate on the matter of where the source of the confusion lies. What we can do with a greater degree of certainty is trace the effects of this confusion within the writing whose apparent contradictions draw our attention to the possibility of such confusion in the first instance. In "From the History of an Infantile Neurosis," Freud clearly refers to sheep dogs in order to situate the witnessing of the coital scene within the landscape of the Wolf Man's domestic environment. Whereas the term "sheep dogs" may serve as a generic marker for any breed used in protecting a flock, the German *"Schäferhunde,"* however, does refer to a particular breed of dog (Alsatian, or German shepherd), which localizes the scene of witnessing more directly within Freud's cultural experience, from which his own false crypt has drawn its associations. In the section of the case history with which we are dealing here, there is a movement from the meanings of the wolf dream and the Wolf Man's drawing for the analysand to their meanings for the Father Professor (*this* analyst). The case history inscribes this tension between one particular subject of psychoanalysis (the "Wolf Man") and the Father Professor. Even as Freud asserts the interpretative adequacy of the primal scene hypothesis, he shifts focus from the specifics of the Wolf Man's case to that which is generally "the same in every case" (59). We can see now that in the word used to designate this generalization, the Wolf Man's magic word and Freud's Anne-Amme material are presented in synthesis: while sheep dogs had been specified as a target of the infantile gaze in the Wolf Man's case, Freud suggests more generally that the intercourse imagined by the child in most cases is invariably aroused "by an observation of the sexual intercourse of animals" (59). In the use of this term "animals" ("*Tiere*"), Freud may seem to be echoing the Wolf Man's magic "*tieret*" words (chief among which is of course the sister Tierka), yet he does so with a word that translates into English with a nasalized Anna-Amme word: "animal."

In this way, "From the History of an Infantile Neurosis" synthesizes material that would otherwise be incompatible: the case history allows the false crypt to continue to throw up Julius material as a screen for the Anne-Amme material in the form of words in which *both* sets of words are concealed-so-as-to-be-revealed. Furthermore, the text inscribes the Wolf Man's cryptonyms within the contours of its own false cryptonymy, producing a fold within these contours: the text performs the blockage of metaphorics, but only inasmuch as it blocks the Wolf Man's crypt from concealing-revealing itself in or through analysis.

So why would Freud withhold this text which achieves so much toward resolving his own dilemma? We now have the clues from which to construct an answer to this pressing question. In order for the case history to block the Wolf Man's crypt even as it synthesizes Freud's, it must give the "life" of Freud's own life-writing over to the insatiable Wolf Man. It does not matter that Freud is the consummate non-respondent, never giving his life-writing over to another except to serve his own ends, since he knows that his own capacity to write irresponsibly to, for, with, and/or against others is reflected in the Wolf Man's incorporating crypt. Clearly, if what Freud says about the Wolf Man's request is accurate, the pair had obviously discussed publishing the details of the case history, and Freud may have guessed from this request that his own wish to tell nothing by telling everything was mirrored in the patient's wishes. In spite of his attempts to address himself (insofar as he addressed Julius and Amme-Anna at once) in the case history, Freud may have suspected that this example of life-writing directly addressed the Wolf Man. In this respect, withholding the case history would be keeping everything for himself, maintaining the assumption (*Annahmen*) of the burden, an *assumption* that would remain an entirely appropriate mode of operation for the false crypt since it also *names* Anna-Amme.

The question of the accumulation of debts between analyst and analysand is thus refigured here as a question of the degree to which, in the analysis (and, indeed, in the transference-countertransference) and in a manner appropriate to analysis—say nothing or say everything, either way, talk to me—the two incorporating rivals compete for the right, assuming everything, to accept the burden unto himself. Another way of saying this is to state that what was at stake in their rivalry was nothing more or less than the institution of psychoanalysis itself. Expressed as a function of this rivalry, then, "From the History of an Infantile Neurosis" is not a gift given to Freud by the Wolf Man as an attempt to erase the debt, it is Freud's legacy, his attempt to unburden himself. This would be reason enough to withhold the text while it was possible for the Wolf Man to accept the legacy and, therefore, to assume the whole of the burden of psychoanalysis.

Indeed, I suggest that the case history might never have been published, were it not for one crucial turn of events in 1918. While it is of course true that the delay between termination of the analysis and publication of the case history coincides almost exactly with the duration of the war, I suggest that this relation is secondary rather than direct, since the war stood in the way of the one condition that Freud required before he could unburden himself. After the inconveniences placed on the Freud family by the war had eased, Anna asked her father if she could undergo what has since become known as the training analysis, and Freud agreed to analyze her himself. In 1914, in "On Narcissism: An Introduction," Freud had included among the types of obvious female object-choice those women who do not have to wait for a child in order to progress from secondary narcissism to object-love: these are women who, as Klaus Theweleit adduces, "do not marry and remain childless, who have identified with a superior father in a masculine way and who (in the most fortunate cases) become the father's successors; just right for the type of daughter which Anna Freud actually became" (1994, 89). In 1914, it seems, Freud had no intention of unleashing his Wolf Man in the war against Adler and Jung. In "On Narcissism," which directly attacks his rivals, Freud had outlined a different weapon, which Theweleit summarizes as a "sort of secretary/aide/successor daughter" (89).

Yet the war years were clearly a cause of anxiety for Freud, if for no other reason than that the war posed a direct threat to members of his immediate family. In the case of his fairy-tale daughter, however, Freud's anxiety seems to have stemmed from fears that had more to do with the domestic politics of psychoanalysis than with any physical threat. Elisabeth Young-Bruehl suggests that Freud shared his daughter's concern with being left in charge of the household at the tender age of eighteen (1988, 63–64). Yet Freud's own anxieties, as he expressed them differently in letters to Lou Andreas-Salomé and Ernest Jones, suggest somewhat more egoistic motives behind the ways in which he addressed his daughter's concerns. Jones had, of course, attempted to court Anna during the first months after the outbreak of war, although Freud had warned him directly of the futility of such an attempt as soon as he learned of Jones's first meeting with Anna: "There is an outspoken understanding between me and her that she should not consider marriage or the preliminaries before she gets 2 or 3 years older. I don't think she will break the treaty" (Freud and Jones 1995, 294). This "outspoken understanding" seems to have endured well beyond the next two or three years, since Jones's fate also fell to Hans Lampl after 1920 (Young-Bruehl 1988, 95–97). Though both father and daughter were very fond of the potential suitor in each of these cases, the father's disapproval of any marital vows was echoed by the daughter in word and in deed, despite the possibility that in each case marriage might have eased the growing burden that the young Anna faced in the Freud household.

To Salomé, Freud proposed an alternative solution, which more neatly fits within the guidelines laid down for the secretary/aide/successor daughter in "On Narcissism." In April 1915, Anna's name begins to appear with some degree of frequency in Freud's letters to Salomé, and by 1917 he starts hinting at his wishes that his correspondent may become closer with his daughter. François Sirois notes that Freud is ambiguous in these letters, and that it is not altogether certain whether he was "seeking a mentor, a protector, or a woman friend for her" (1998, 282). It is possible that Freud had hoped Salomé might become for the younger Anna what Dorothy Burlingham later became: while Anna and Dorothy were not a lesbian couple, according to Young-Bruehl, the American did provide Anna with the chance to take on the "paternal role" in a close relationship "with a suitable daughter from an American family" (Theweleit 1994, 93). What Freud wanted for his daughter was no more or less than what he himself wanted from his relationship with Martha, and it may be no coincidence that at different times he compared both his wife and Anna with King Lear's Cordelia (Young-Bruehl 1988, 62–63). The Cordelia-like love displayed by Martha Bernays (together with Bernays family connections) had made her into an ideal object-choice for the man who would be the begetter of an institution, and the same approach to love now made Anna the ideal successor.

When Freud wrote "The Theme of the Three Caskets" between 1912 and 1913, as Young-Bruehl suggests, he was visibly depressed, and must have considered himself to be a Lear (63). We have seen here that this was also the time at which he was working through the fairy tale material that paved the way for the synthesis of his Amme-Anna material with the Julius screen. This was also the time at which the situation with Jung had come to a head, and Freud's thoughts were clearly on the problem of succession in the face of being caught up in a "tragedy of ingratitude" of his own (in Young-Bruehl 1988, 63). With the departure of the older daughters into marriages, then, Freud faced Christmas 1913 with only the one daughter left, yet the "Three Caskets" essay had been in part an injunction to keep himself from "asking too much of his youngest daughter—who loved her father as deeply and exclusively as any Cordelia" (63). When Freud wrote "From the History of an Infantile Neurosis" in 1914, he was still guarding against forcing too much of his legacy too soon onto his daughter. In the years that followed, he grew more anxious of the possibility that this daughter might also be lost, until she declared that she was ready to accept the father's legacy—a legacy that had already inscribed the daughter's name within its own name. After this, Freud published the Wolf Man's history, thereby instituting the life-writing in which he had synthesized the false crypt and the material it screened.

We should also note that it was on 27 May 1918 that Freud received the message from Pankeiev in which he requested Freud's authorization for foreign travel for reasons of health (Mahony 1984, 10). This message is the first occasion on which Freud would have learned that his not-yet-famous patient had *not* been cured when the treatment had been arbitrarily terminated four years earlier. Within a year of receiving this message, Freud was to take the Russian back into analysis, a situation which may prompt us to wonder whether the return of the Wolf Man in 1918 was also a primary catalyst for publication of the case history in the fourth volume of his *Sammlung kleiner Schriften*. Yet I have been arguing here that the more important factor was Freud's growing anxiety over his daughter Anna's future role in (and for) psychoanalysis. Her request to her father meant that Freud's little *Ammenmärchen* (this composite fairy tale figure) had announced that she was ready to assume (*annehmen*) the burden of psychoanalysis. By the same token, or another way of saying the same thing, the *sixth* child was ready to inherit the legacy of *Schuld* (the burden of "guilt") associated with this number. Within this constellation of associations, the Wolf Man is significant only insofar as *this* crypt functions as a foil to Freud's false crypt, and Pankeiev (the patient himself) is really not very significant at all. Indeed, Pankeiev's letter signals more of a complication than a catalyst, by marking the return not of the Wolf Man but of the individual from whom this subject of the case history was to be withheld.

As life-writing, "From the History of an Infantile Neurosis" enshrines the Wolf Man at the core of psychoanalysis only by withholding this "Wolf Man," the subject of the case history (Freud's legacy), from the Wolf Man Sergei Pankeiev. Here then is the paradox of the Wolf Man's burden: when we read the case history as life-writing, we find that the Wolf Man is central to psychoanalysis only when he is posited as the other or limit from which psychoanalysis withdraws in order to institute itself. What I call the Wolf Man's burden is this necessary (inasmuch as it is functional) symmetry between an unburdening of oneself and the vouchsafing of one's legacy, inscribed in the text of the case history, and yet guaranteed by the (non-)movement in which the text has been withheld. The burden is that aspect of the Freudian legacy, conceived and transmitted through the course of a life-writing, which marks this legacy as *having been withheld* in advance of having been passed on. To inherit the legacy is to assume the burden, which means that one marks oneself as the rightful heir, set apart from this other from whom the legacy is to be withheld in perpetuity.

That the other from which the legacy is withheld is necessarily different from the other for whom it is designated clearly institutes a triangulation within the analytic or intersubjective relation. To assume the burden is also, therefore, to necessarily assume a relation to a third, whose rivalry with the Father Professor is a condition upon which the institution of psychoanalysis, including the legacy itself, remains consequent. As we have seen, in the degree to which the case history of the Wolf Man is an example of Freud's improvisational life-writing, this text not only institutes rivalry at the heart of psychoanalysis—we have seen that texts with which "From the History of an Infantile Neurosis" engages provided necessary precursors to the rivalry in which it implicates itself—since this text gives rivalry as the *modus operandi* and rationale for the Father Professor's legacy. My point here is that in the case history of the Wolf Man, more so perhaps than in any other, we witness the transition *from* a life-writing in which rivalry is given as the ground upon which to authorize psychoanalysis—that is, to legitimize psychoanalysis and to endow it with a proper name, the name of the Father Professor—*to* a form of life-writing in which the rival is posited as one whose rivalry prompts the need for legacy *and* as one from whom this legacy must be saved if it is to be inherited by the next generation of analysts.

We can see how successfully Freud assimilated the syntheses of the Wolf Man case history by looking at the way in which he passed the burden of analysis onto the next generation of analysts. We observe, for example, that dogs became an important part of Freud's life and his analytic practice. His favorite breed was the chow, and his favorite among these was one named Jofi.[18] Martin Freud recalls that his father always kept Jofi by his side, even during analytic sessions, which is significant given the symbolic role that dogs played in the manifestations of the Julius screen and in the synthesis of this screen material with the Amme-Anna material in the Wolf Man case history (1973, 379). It is also significant that in 1926 Freud passed his famous Wolf

[18] The nanny who was primarily responsible for Anna during her infancy was named Josefine Cilharz, in which we see the name of one of the most recurrent of Freud's Julius revenants (Josef) repeated yet again. According to Elisabeth Young-Bruehl, Freud apparently paid for the hospitalization his daughter's former nursemaid received during her later life and prior to her death in 1925 (1988, 465n24). The name Jofi may have recalled for Freud the diminutive form of this particular Josef-figure, the one who had on more than one occasion been what Young-Bruehl calls the "dearly beloved rescuer" of Freud's fairy-tale daughter (33).

Man to Ruth Mack Brunswick for further analysis, and not to Anna. To his daughter, instead, he had already given the gift of an Alsatian named Wolf, which became this analyst-daughter's constant companion.[19]

These two "gifts" may be read in terms of the legacy understood as a function of rivalry, as it had been inscribed in "From the History of an Infantile Neurosis" and then realized in the withholding of the text. Paul Roazen claims that the referral of the Wolf Man to Brunswick represented Freud's "one great personal gift to her," with which he "paid her the highest compliment" (1984, 426). Yet we may wonder if this compliment is not also a somewhat ambiguous one. The Wolf Man had been referred to Brunswick because he needed treatment for an acute paranoia which (as the patient himself later recalled in a letter to Muriel Gardiner) may have been connected to Freud's remarkable request for verification of the dates and details concerning the recollection of the wolf dream (in Abraham and Torok [1976] 1986, 53). What Freud had requested was for his former patient to verify the claims that were made in "From the History of an Infantile Neurosis," in response to the attacks by Otto Rank that I discussed earlier. As Abraham and Torok point out, however, Freud's request struck the Wolf Man as a request for "nothing less than a truthful testimony," thereby implicating the patient once again—as he had been implicated during the formation of the crypt—in a scene of witnessing, the truth of which held the castration-conviction together (53). Father Professor, to whose ear the Wolf Man had purported to tell everything in order to protect the crypt, was thus transformed into the father accuser-castrator, and it is no surprise that the Wolf Man's reply to Freud, while furnishing him compliantly with the testimony that he required, also contained two recollections in which castration is configured directly: "One was a conversation with the coachman about the operation that is performed on stallions, and the second was my mother's story about a kinsman born with six toes, one of which was cut off immediately after birth" (52).

It is also no surprise that castration is figured through the number

---

[19] Young-Bruehl notes that a Viennese newspaper gossip columnist commented with delight on the irony of the situation in which this gift arrived soon after Anna's former suitor Hans Lampl had announced his engagement to Jeanne de Groot, a trainee of Freud's: "Lampl got his Jeanne and Anna got her Wolf" (in Young-Bruehl 1988, 99). By 1925, it seems, Anna was well aware that her role in psychoanalysis would prevent her from ever finding companionship of a more conventional kind.

six, the number repeatedly overlooked by Freud in the case history: the *shiestorka-siestorka*. The Wolf Man's reply to Freud foreshadows his memoirs in that it attempts to restore to Tierka a central role in the cryptic narrative of his life. It was not long after he was reminded of this letter, more than thirty years later, that the Wolf Man began writing these memoirs which consign psychoanalysis to a secondary role in comparison with the sister. In this sense in which the Wolf Man Sergei Pankeiev (alias Stanko, alias Tierka) resisted the case history as anything like his (or their) life-writing, we close upon a reciprocation of the rivalry that had been cultivated previously in the preparation of the case history for publication and in the delays which protracted its release. Patrick Mahony records the reaction of Brunswick upon first meeting her newly referred patient: "She reacted with dismay and disbelief, and at first she found it difficult to think the patient was the same one described by Freud" (1984, 140). As her expectations had been shaped by the text of the case history, Brunswick was initially disappointed by the patient. Only later, in her analysis of the Wolf Man's dreams and of the transference, did Brunswick begin to consider that this discrepancy between patient and case history was in part due to the active resistance by the patient to *this particular representation*.[20] By instituting rivalry, Freud had placed the insatiably incorporating Pankeiev in an impossible situation: to be passive and compliant would be to accept the role of the rival; active resistance to this role would mean opposing the Father Professor, thus confirming his characterization of the patient as an enemy of truth. The clever, incorporating Wolf Man had been "taken in" by psychoanalysis, in the sense both of being incorporated and of being duped. With the referral of his patient, Freud utilized an internal mechanism to keep the Wolf Man within psychoanalysis without undoing the rivalry he had inscribed within the life-writing that shaped the most famous of his case histories. Brunswick seems therefore to have been more of a patsy than a patrimonial beneficiary, since her "gift" was this Wolf Man who is internal to the symbolism of the legacy only to the extent that he is marked internally as its external point of reference. Brunswick received the remainder that was left over by the calculation of the legacy, measured against a point of rivalry. Alternatively,

[20] Abraham and Torok detail the effect of Brunswick's changing views on the analysis and, therefore, on the Wolf Man's cryptonymy, in particular, in chapters six and seven of *The Wolf Man's Magic Word: A Cryptonymy* ([1976] 1986, 55–76).

Anna's gift of an Alsatian named Wolf can be situated at the symbolic heart of this legacy, as it manifests some of the terms that Freud had managed to synthesize in "From the History of an Infantile Neurosis." To his fairy-tale daughter he gave the gift of a "sheep dog," the "animal" central to psychoanalysis (as is Anna's name), and which had been crucial in enabling Freud to contain the Wolf Man and his sister Tierka in the case history. To Anna, then, Freud passed the symbols marking the link from his past to the future of psychoanalysis, this legacy. Befitting its role, this Wolf-dog gift arrived in the Freud household within a day or two after 15 April, this most fated of anniversaries (Young-Bruehl 1988, 469n66).

Conclusion: *Last* Words

I have maintained that this book is not an attempt at a cryptonymy of Freud, and that such a procedure would indeed be impossible. Nevertheless, these speculations do hinge upon considering some further implications for psychoanalysis of Abraham's and Torok's revised psychoanalytic topography. It is for this reason that I am obliged to discuss the work of Nicholas Rand and Maria Torok whose extraordinary *Questions for Freud: The Secret History of Psychoanalysis* represents a culmination of more than twenty years of theoretical investigations, begun soon after Abraham's death in 1975 and based in part on his suggestion that Freud's theories might have been formulated under the sway of a "family secret (perhaps similar to the Wolf Man's)" (1997, 164). Rand and Torok suggest that psychoanalysis is rife with internal contradiction because Freud was himself unprepared to come to terms with his own family secrets, which they trace ultimately to the criminal history of Freud's Uncle Josef. To be sure, they contend that these contradictions are methodological first and foremost:

> The contradictions we see arise from the methodological crux of
> Freudian theory. Many practitioners are still wondering today how im-
> portant a role the psychoanalysis of real traumas as opposed to fantasies
> should play in therapy. Freud's vacillation on this fundamental question
> has affected every aspect of his theory; unknowingly, we still labor
> under its influence. (2–3)

Their investigations proceed fluently from some of the implications of *The Wolf Man's Magic Word*, though this prior text is (perhaps appropriately) hardly mentioned after twenty years of subsequent inquiry. The "break" explored by Abraham and Torok is echoed in the "methodological rifts" upon which Rand and Torok focus, and in both of these texts the methodology of psychoanalysis is never separable from the unconscious processes it takes as its object. Where the more recent investigations go beyond the earlier ones is in their aim, "to halt the nearly unconscious transmission of Freudian methodological rifts" (3). *Questions for Freud* is thus no "sequel" to Abraham's final work with Torok, since its stated aim is clearly interventionist in a way that *The Wolf Man's Magic Word* had avoided.

That Rand and Torok clearly direct their comments *toward* psychoanalysis, with a view to effecting a change within that institution, allows us to identify the main point at which the present speculations diverge from this recent work with which it might seem otherwise to have so much in common. An obvious consequence of the reading of the Wolf Man's crypt was always going to be the observation that *this* crypt was central to the development of the second topography and, therefore, to psychoanalysis, at the time that it began to develop as a worldwide institution. Rand and Torok explore the general methodological principles and uncertainties of psychoanalysis, from which we might go so far as to say that their later work is an exploration into the condition of instability that made the engagement with the Wolf Man possible: in this sense, the later work of Rand and Torok is more like a "prequel" to *The Wolf Man's Magic Word*.

Accordingly, they recognize that their investigations into the sources of Freud's methodological principles have profound implications for Freud biography, but also for the way in which we look at the history of psychoanalysis as a body of transmissible practices and theories. Where Abraham and Torok hoped to "cure" psychoanalysis by bringing to the surface that cryptic topography which marked *the* break in the history of the institution, Rand and Torok now identify the more general structure of contradiction underlining all of psychoanalysis, leading them to question "whether a clean theoretical break ever occurred, either in 1897 or at any time afterward" (157).[1]

---

[1] Rand and Torok reject the popular notion that the self-analysis from 1896 to 1897

My own project is admittedly far more myopic. Its focus returns inevitably to the text which Abraham and Torok had identified as the very moment of the break. Where they had identified the Wolf Man's crypt as the source of this break, and suggested that this crypt could be read (by the cryptonymic method) as that which the text of the case history inscribes, in spite of itself, as its own "unreadable" parameter, I have attempted to explain this condition of unreadability in Freud's writing as the condition of the false crypt shaping his life-writing. I have demonstrated here that if we are to understand the reasons for Freud's failure to come to terms with the Wolf Man, we must recognize the importance of the figures represented by the name "Anna" in the development of both Pankeiev and Freud. Given that this figure was a key to unlocking the crypt in Torok's work with Abraham, it seems all the more unusual that the name of Anna is kept almost completely suppressed in her work with Rand on the secret history of psychoanalysis—or, perhaps, it is not so unusual, as it may be an index of the desire of the more recent project to avoid all comparison with the earlier one. In fact, the only time that Anna is mentioned by Rand and Torok is in reference to the role played by Freud's *daughter* in censoring the publication of letters pertaining to the Emma Eckstein affair in the Fliess correspondence (101).

As I suggest, however, the role played by the figure of "Anna," within the Anna-Amme complex, is distilled through the false crypt screen which posits Julius's death as a primary trauma. While they neglect the figure of Anna in Freud's personal (or his family) history, Rand and Torok recognize the need to take Julius's death into account, albeit only briefly. They contend quite rightly, I believe, that gaps in Freud's writing and, therefore, in the theory of psychoanalysis reflect the gaps in the stories that his family were willing to tell about itself. This leads them to make the following claim, based on speculations about family silences, to lend support to their decision to assign primacy to the crime of Uncle Josef in Freud's traumatic past:

---

was the key moment in the development of psychoanalysis, since this analysis "coincided with a period of intense theoretical vacillation" (1997, 157). For them, everything that came after 1865 (the year of the "trauma" of Uncle Josef's criminal charges) will have been characterized by ongoing internal contradiction and blindness: the self-analysis was no more likely to get to the root cause of Freud's problems than the "theoretical fluctuations" of all the later work, with which it shared a common point of origin.

There are, of course, types of traumas or misfortunes about which one can talk freely, for example the death of a sibling or a grandmother, a car accident, an illness, the loss of livelihood, destitution. These misfortunes can be more or less easily absorbed into a family's topography because talking about them is not forbidden. However, a dishonor, a stain on the family's reputation, leaves behind a permanent silence and malaise. (170)

In an endnote appended to this statement, they note that several scholars, "among them Alexander Grinstein in *On Sigmund Freud's Dreams* and Didier Dumas in *L'Ange et le fantôme*, isolate the death of Julius, a baby brother of Freud's, as the principal trauma of his life" (233n7). Rand and Torok thus dismiss any thought that Julius's death could be seen as the "principal" trauma of Freud's life because it will have been remembered explicitly within the family's discourse about itself. Like them, I have suggested here that his brother's death will have continued to be remembered throughout the first few years of Freud's life, but this visibility represents, for me, the very reason why Freud is likely to have used this event as a convenient screen to cover over the gaps produced by a later trauma.

I also agree that a stain upon the family's reputation will leave a silence, and it is for this reason that I believe that the disappearance of the nanny is so significant. There can be no doubt that her disappearance was censored within family discourse, since it is only through reconstructions during his self-analysis and a confrontation with his aging mother over the matter that Freud later confirmed the traumatic circumstances in which the nanny was dismissed—and even then, we now believe, his mother invented a lie to conceal the truth of these circumstances from the mature Freud. The lie she used to conceal the truth in this matter was to claim that the nanny had been guilty of using the young Freud to steal from the family. The crime of which Amalie accused the nanny is a domestic equivalent of the crime for which Josef Freud was convicted. The lie becomes even more intriguing when we recall that the year in which Josef was charged with counter-feiting (1865) is also the one that I have listed as the first in which the anniversary of Julius's death will have fallen close enough to Easter to prompt a potential association between the two in the Freud family remembrances. If this was the year in which what Paul Vitz calls Freud's Easter-Pentecost complex first became attached in his mind to the death of his brother, then it is likely that the incrimination of Josef (which happened two months *after* Easter) was quickly absorbed into the same set of associations.

Amalie's choice of lie lends weight to Rand and Torok's claims about the lasting impact of Josef Freud's crime on the other members of his family, though it is also a sign that at the very least Sigmund's mother hoped to continue to keep something from him about the dismissal of the beloved nanny of his first few years of childhood. My belief is that the family's silence about Josef is something in which Sigmund would have also been complicit, since he was already an articulate young man by 1865—his father later recalled to Freud that it was "in the seventh year of your age that the spirit of God began to move you to learning" (in Jones 1974, 47). By his ninth and tenth years, during which time the scandal surrounding Josef erupted, Freud was no longer going to be the simple pawn capable of only mutely internalizing his family's silence. By 1865, he was an active participant in the creation of the stories that the Freud family chose to tell itself, and indeed it was Sigmund who is supposed to have given the name Alexander to the youngest of his siblings, at the age of ten. If Freud was himself silent about Josef's misfortune, then it was either by choice or, perhaps, because he simply integrated Josef into the false crypt, as yet another way that he could avoid talking about the deeper past.

Indeed, Rand and Torok describe Freud's analysis of the *non vixit* dream as a key to understanding the importance of Josef, since it is here that he attributes the nephew-uncle relation (between John and Sigmund) as the source of the intensity of all his later relationships, though he does this in the dream through various repetitions of the name Josef (190–91, 233n9). Yet we have seen that Freud's published interpretation of the *non vixit* dream echoes the prior claim he had made privately to Fliess, that it was in his relationships with John and Julius that subsequent relationships had their blueprints. My intention here is not to argue the point, however, by insisting on the primacy of one or another of the manifold traumatic events in Freud's life. Rather, my concern is with the degree to which all such events are reconstructed *a posteriori*, and in such a way as to seem as if the event in question has priority status in the associative chain into which it has been integrated. In this sense, my concern is with demonstrating that the primacy of traumatic events is itself an illusion brought on to sustain a fantasy, as indeed may be their status *as events*.

Already I imagine that with this last claim I am inviting criticism for disregarding the reality of traumatic events, from those who, for example, attack psychoanalysis for turning a blind eye to the crippling reality of the abuses or seductions it finds lodged in the fantasy lives of its patients. Yet it should be apparent here that my claims do not emerge directly from psychoanalytic speculations. Unlike Rand and Torok, for whom "Freud" is posited as a psychoanalytic subject, I have been *reading* "Freud" after the manner of Derrida or Abraham and Torok. While the reading of "life-writing" purports to read the "life" in writing, as if to revive the dead, there can be no doubt that the focus upon reading and writing here designates a textualized subject of analysis, fashioned in the course of improvising self-representations, and the life that we find is understood to be an effect of this reading. Yet this book uses a methodology based on a reading of life-writing precisely so that it might demonstrate the degree to which unconscious or ego processes—as they are read in the associations within and between texts—produce real effects at the levels of both the individual and the institution. It is to this end that I have used the notion of a false crypt to describe the sort of psychic structure which may be capable of producing the broad-reaching institutional effects psychoanalysis presents to us.

The notion of the false crypt emerges directly as a result of trying to explain the discrepancy between the discovery of the crypt in the ego, *using Freud's words* as a key to unlocking this crypt, *and* Freud's failure to discover the crypt himself. The false crypt thus enters into discussion as an explanatory tool, enabling us to describe Freud's blind spot as the cultivation of a deeply mythologized sense of self constructed in *and for* psychoanalysis. Yet for all this myopic attention to the writing of Freud's life, in his rivalries and analyses, I shall not attempt to shield myself from some of the effects of this mode of reading—at least not from those that I can anticipate here. Readers might have observed, for example, that on several occasions in this book I have cited any one of numerous sources in attributing facts, interpretations, or quotations—the choices sometimes being manifold, as so many books and articles have been written about the life and works of Freud. While the choices I make in this respect are often incidental, based on whichever book I happen to have with me at the moment that I am writing about a particular fact or supposition, for instance, I nevertheless admit that there are times when the selection of information is calculated and strategic.

The rationale behind such calculations is not simply a matter of the constraints of having to write to certain academic or scholarly protocols. Indeed, the terrain on which this book has maneouvred was outlined from the beginning, and I have at times clearly selected this or that source for a particular item both for the relevance of the item *and* because an engagement with this source presented an opportunity to position myself in particular ways, in relation to (or within) the field of Freud biography. There is in an admission of this sort a further suggestion of the despair hinted at in the introduction—the despair, that is, associated with after-the-fact reconstructions as an unwanted staple of the biographical enterprise. No matter how much we might wish, like William Beatty Warner, to be able to read the life in life-writing, if we are to maintain the historicity of a text as a marker of value (as a way of gaining legitimacy for our biographical text), then we must recognize that the *reading* of life-writing designates that it comes after the life. It is, in this sense, the inscription of death.

The notion of the false crypt has been a device for this inscription here, enabling us to think in terms of erasures and deferrals at the same time as we posit a biographical subject capable of being submitted to sustained scrutiny. The result is of course that the biographical subject merges imperceptibly in this mode of reading with the texts that we read, leaving our subject never more devoid of "life" than in the very place we had sought to find it. If this effectively sets the present text apart from those biographies on which I rely so heavily for the "facts" of Freud's and Pankeiev's "lives," then we might instead cling to the thought that the mode of reading which produces these effects also complements a psychoanalytic reading, at least insofar as it distances itself from a mode of reading that Freud himself claims to have never tolerated. With this thought, we introduce yet another major reading effect that it will be necessary to take into consideration before I close here: we must wonder how much the present text is the product of my own intractable transference onto Freud.

There are of course several ways in which I might attempt here to avoid facing up to this issue directly, or even to refute the "charge" of failing to account for my relation to the master in defining my position from the outset. In some sense, the reader might suspect that by setting my own project apart from that of Rand and Torok, I have been building throughout this conclusion toward the claim that I have no wish to engage with the institution of psychoanalysis in any direct way. Perhaps the same could be said of my use of François Roustang's characterization of psychoanalytic discipleship as dire mastery in the opening section to the first chapter. Yet if I am to stand by what I have written, then I cannot deny that in many ways this text also writes "me," after the manner of life-writing, and it is in this respect that the present text addresses "Freud" throughout the course of its speculations.

It may be more appropriate, then, to discuss the question of my own transference onto Freud by considering the implications of what has been written here for a general understanding of the transference relation. In a footnote to the third chapter of this book, I noted that on at least one occasion Freud used the term *Übertragung* to refer to "conviction," whereas the term is more commonly given as "transference," the state in which the patient forms an attachment to the analyst, as to an ego-ideal. Based on this observation, I claimed that Freud's use of the term indicates the degree to which the description of a psychoanalytic modality (the transference) also describes what this modality produces in analysis (conviction). I also noted that this term for transference and conviction extends the notion of the burden through the root *tragen* (to bear). We see how this burden is calculated in the transference in the Wolf Man analysis, wherein the principal components of the ego-ideal attachment represent the very "word-things" (as Abraham and Torok call these products of incorporations) which neither Freud nor his patient could afford to give over to the other.

The notion of the Wolf Man's burden enabled us to picture a transference relation with dire consequences for the survival of psychoanalysis at a broad institutional level, such as the establishment of this rivalry as a necessary condition for Freud's legacy. It may also enable us to imagine the transference relation in general as an intersubjective one, where subjectivity is constituted in the performance of this relation. In the light of what has been said about the relation between Freud and Pankeiev here, constitutive of the "Wolf Man," this performance may be understood as something that is more deeply textualized than, for example, simply the playing of roles. Here, analyst and analysand represent positions within the analytic situation, which reduces intersubjectivity to an intensely concentrated site of negotiation. Yet for all this concentration, we might note that the negotiation in question does not occur in a vacuum: as we have seen in the case of both "Freud" and the Wolf Man, the construction of the self within analysis involves the revision and reworking of substantial amounts of baggage. We would of course be mistaken to presume that every analysis involved the encounter between a crypt and a "false" crypt, but in the degree to which *this* analysis produced the Wolf Man's burden (the more general structure of rivalry and legacy shaping the birth of psychoanalysis) I suggest that all subsequent analyses do address this encounter in some way. For this reason, I should perhaps defer at the very last here to Rand and Torok's more pragmatic concerns. If the particular transference I have described is so encrypted as to have enabled both a cryptonymy of the Wolf Man and a reading of Freud's life-writing in terms of the supposition of a false crypt, then we must wonder how either an analyst or an analysand could ever occupy a sufficiently stable point of reference, from which anything like a psychoanalysis of a human subject might hope to proceed. In my own reading of this relation, I have been more concerned with psychoanalytic theory and less with its clinical application, because it seemed to me that concentration upon the classical analytic situation ignored the potential for the unstable and performative subject negotiated within the analysis to have entered into this contract with an ulterior motive. Rand and Torok suggest, however, that the more psychoanalysts learn of these motives which underline and undermine their institution, the greater will be their need to sever their ties with the origins of psychoanalysis. As for those of us who may wish to remain aloof from this challenge, there can be no doubt as to the widespread role of psychoanalytic theory in our own critical practices. Now, perhaps as much as ever, we must all assume the challenge of the Wolf Man's burden.

Works Consulted

Abraham, Nicolas, and Maria Torok. [1976] 1986. *The Wolf Man's Magic Word: A Cryptonymy*. Translated by Nicholas T. Rand. Minneapolis: University of Minnesota Press.

———. [1987] 1994. *The Shell and the Kernel: Renewals of Psychoanalysis*. Translated by Nicholas T. Rand. Chicago: University of Chicago Press.

Balmary, Marie. [1979] 1982. *Psychoanalysis Psychoanalysed: Freud and the Hidden Fault of the Father*. Translated by Ned Lukacher. Baltimore: Johns Hopkins University Press.

Bernardi, Ricardo E. 1989. "The Role of Paradigmatic Determinants in Psychoanalytic Understanding." *International Journal of Psycho-Analysis* 70:341–57.

Blum, Harold P. 1980. "The Borderline Childhood of the Wolf Man." Pp. 341–65 in *Freud and His Patients*, edited by Mark Kanzer and Jules Glenn. New York: Jason Aronson.

Borch-Jacobsen, Mikkel. 2000. "How a Fabrication Differs from a Lie." Review of *Der Fall Freud: Die Geburt der Psychoanalyse aus der Lüge*, by Hans Israëls. *London Review of Books* 22 (8):3–7.

Bowlby, Rachel. 1991. "A Happy Event." *Paragraph* 14 (1):10–19.

Bronfen, Elisabeth. 1989. "The Lady Vanishes: Sophie Freud and *Beyond the Pleasure Principle*." *South Atlantic Quarterly* 88 (4):961–91.

Brooks, Peter. 1979. "Fictions of the Wolf Man: Freud and Narrative Understanding." *Diacritics* 9 (1):73–81.

Carotenuto, Aldo. 1984. *A Secret Symmetry: Sabina Spielrein between Jung and Freud*. London: Routledge and Kegan Paul.

Clark, Ronald. 1982. *Freud: The Man and the Cause*. London: Granada.

Davis, Whitney. 1995. *Drawing the Dream of the Wolves: Homosexuality, Interpretation and Freud's "Wolf Man."* Bloomington: Indiana University Press.

Deleuze, Gilles, and Félix Guattari. 1977. "May 14, 1914. One or Several Wolves?" Translated by Mark Seem. *Semiotexte* 2 (3):137–47.

———. 1983. *Anti-Oedipus: Capitalism and Schizophrenia*. Translated by Robert Hurley, Mark Seem, and Helen R. Lane. Minneapolis: University of Minnesota Press.

De Beer, Sir Gavin. 1969. *Hannibal: The Struggle for Power in the Mediterranean*. London: Thames and Hudson.

de Man, Paul. 1979. "Autobiography as De-facement." *MLN* 94:919–30.

Derrida, Jacques. 1978. "Freud and the Scene of Writing." In *Writing and Difference*. Translated by Alan Bass, 196–231. London: Routledge.

———. 1980. *La Carte Postale: de Socrate à Freud et au-delà*. Paris: Flammarion.

———. 1984. "My Chances/*Mes Chances*: A Rendezvous with Some Epicurean Stereophonies." Translated by Irene Harvey and Avital Ronell. In *Taking Chances: Derrida, Psychoanalysis, and Literature*, edited by Joseph H. Smith and William Kerrigan, 1–32. Baltimore: Johns Hopkins University Press.

———. 1985. *The Ear of the Other: Otobiography, Transference, Translation*. Edited by Christie McDonald, translated by Peggy Kamuf. Lincoln and London: University of Nebraska Press.

———. 1986. "Foreword: *Fors*: The Anglish Words of Nicolas Abraham and Maria Torok." Translated by Barbara Johnson. Pp. xi–xlviii in *The Wolf Man's Magic Word: A Cryptonymy*, by Nicolas Abraham and Marie Torok, translated by Nicolas Rand. Minneapolis: University of Minnesota Press.

———. [1980] 1987. *The Post Card: From Socrates to Freud and Beyond*. Translated by Alan Bass. Chicago: University of Chicago Press.

———. 1989. "Psyche: Invention of the Other." Translated by Catherine Porter and Philip Lewis. Pp. 26–59 in *Reading de Man Reading*, edited by Wlad Godzich and Lindsay Waters. Minneapolis: University of Minnesota Press.

———. 1990. "Let Us Not Forget—Psychoanalysis." *Oxford Literary Review* 12 (1–2):3–7.

Dimock, George. 1995. "Anna and the Wolf-Man: Rewriting Freud's Case History." *Representations* 50:53–75.

El Saffar, Ruth. 1984. *Beyond Fiction: The Recovery of the Feminine in the Novels of Cervantes*. Berkeley: University of California Press.

Esterson, Allen. 1993. *Seductive Mirage: An Exploration of the Work of Sigmund Freud*. Chicago and La Salle: Open Court.

Fiebert, Martin S. 1997. "In and Out of Freud's Shadow: A Chronology of Adler's Relationship with Freud." *Individual Psychology* 53 (3):241–69.

Fish, Stanley. 1987. "Withholding the Missing Portion: Power, Meaning and Persuasion in Freud's *The Wolf-Man*." Pp. 155–72 in *The Linguistics of Writing: Arguments Between Language and Literature*, edited by Nigel Fabb, Derek Attridge, Alan Durant, and Colin McCabe. New York: Methuen.

Forrester, John. 1990. *The Seductions of Psychoanalysis: Freud, Lacan, and Derrida*. Cambridge: Cambridge University Press.

Freud, Harry. 1973. "My Uncle Sigmund." Pp. 312–13 in *Freud: As We Knew Him*, edited by Hendrik M. Ruitenbeek. Detroit: Wayne State University Press.

Freud, Martin. 1973. "Freud: My Father." Pp. 378–84 in *Freud: As We Knew Him*, edited by Hendrik M. Ruitenbeek. Detroit: Wayne State University Press.

Freud, Sigmund. 1895a. *Studies on Hysteria*. In *The Standard Edition of the Complete Psychological Works of Sigmund Freud*. Edited by James Strachey, translated by James Strachey, Anna Freud, Alix Strachey, and Alan Tyson. London: Hogarth Press and the Institute of Psycho-Analysis, 1953–74 [hereafter given as *Standard Edition* only].

——. 1895b. "Project for a Scientific Psychology." *Standard Edition* 1: 283–398.

——. 1896a. "Heredity and the Aetiology of the Neuroses." *Standard Edition* 3:142–56.

——. 1896b. "Further Remarks on the Neuro-Psychoses of Defense." *Standard Edition* 3:159–85.

——. 1896c. "The Aetiology of Hysteria." *Standard Edition* 3:189–221.

——. 1899. "Screen Memories." *Standard Edition* 3:299–322.

——. 1900. *The Interpretation of Dreams. Standard Edition* 4–5.

——. 1901. *The Psychopathology of Everyday Life. Standard Edition* 6.

——. 1909. "Notes upon a Case of Obsessional Neurosis." *Standard Edition*. 10:153–320.

——. 1910a. *Five Lectures on Psycho-Analysis. Standard Edition* 11:3–56.

——. 1910b. *Leonardo da Vinci and a Memory of His Childhood. Standard Edition* 11:59–137.

——. 1910c. "The Psycho-Analytic View of Psychogenic Disturbance of Vision." *Standard Edition* 11:209–18.

——. 1913a. "The Occurrence in Dreams of Material from Fairy Tales." *Standard Edition* 12:281–90.

——. 1913b. "The Theme of the Three Caskets." *Standard Edition* 12:291–301.

——. 1914a. "On the History of the Psycho-Analytic Movement." *Standard Edition* 14:3–66.

——. 1914b. "On Narcissism: An Introduction." *Standard Edition* 14:69–102.

——. 1915. "Papers on Metapsychology." *Standard Edition* 14: 105–258.

——. 1917. "Mourning and Melancholia." *Standard Edition* 14:239–60.

——. 1918a. "From the History of an Infantile Neurosis." *Standard Edition* 17:3–123.

——. 1918b. *Sammlung kleiner Schriften zur Neurosenlehre, Vierte Folge*, Leipzig-Wien.

——. 1920. *Beyond the Pleasure Principle. Standard Edition* 18:3–64.

——. 1921. *Group Psychology and the Analysis of the Ego. Standard Edition* 18:67–143.

——. 1923. *The Ego and the Id. Standard Edition* 19:3–66.

——. 1924. "The Economic Problem of Masochism." *Standard Edition* 19:159–70.

——. 1925a. "A Note upon the 'Mystic Writing-Pad.'" *Standard Edition* 19:225–32.

——. 1925b. *An Autobiographical Study. Standard Edition* 20:3–70.

——. 1954. *The Origins of Psycho-Analysis: Letters to Wilhelm Fliess, Drafts and Notes 1887–1902*. Translated by Eric Mosbacher and James Strachey, edited by Marie Bonaparte, Anna Freud, and Ernst Kris. London: Imago.

——. 1985. *The Complete Letters of Sigmund Freud to Wilhelm Fliess: 1887–1904*. Translated and edited by Jeffrey Moussaieff Masson. Cambridge, Mass.: The Belknap Press of Harvard University Press.

Freud, Sigmund, and Karl Abraham. 1965. *A Psycho-Analytic Dialogue: The Letters of Sigmund Freud and Karl Abraham 1907–1926*. Translated by Bernard Marsh and Hilda C. Abraham, edited by Hilda C. Abraham and Ernst L. Freud. New York: Basic Books.

Freud, Sigmund, and Ernest Jones. 1995. *The Complete Correspondence of Sigmund Freud and Ernest Jones 1908–39*. Edited by R. Andrew Paskauskas. London and Cambridge, Mass.: Harvard University Press.

Freud, Sigmund, and Carl Jung. 1974. *The Freud/Jung Letters: The Correspondence between Sigmund Freud and C. G. Jung*. Translated by Ralph Manheim and R. F. C. Hull, Edited by William McGuire. London: Hogarth and Routledge and Kegan Paul.

Freud, Sigmund, and Oskar Pfister. 1963. *Psycho-Analysis and Faith: The Letters of Sigmund Freud and Oskar Pfister*. Translated by Eric Mosbacher, edited by Heinrich Meng and Ernst L. Freud. London: Hogarth Press and the Institute of Psycho-Analysis.

Freud Bernays, Anna. 1973. "My Brother, Sigmund Freud." Pp. 140–47 in *Freud: As We Knew Him*, edited by Hendrik M. Ruitenbeek. Detroit: Wayne State University Press.

Gardiner, Muriel, ed. [1971] 1973. *The Wolf-Man and Sigmund Freud*. Harmondsworth: Penguin Books.

——. 1983. "The Wolf Man's Last Years." *Journal of the American Psychoanalytic Association* 31:867–97.

Gasché, Rodolphe. 1994. *Inventions of Difference: On Jacques Derrida*. Cambridge, Mass. and London: Harvard University Press.

Gay, Peter. 1990. *Reading Freud: Explorations and Entertainments*. New Haven: Yale University Press.

Gedo, John E., and Ernest S. Wolf. 1976a. "The 'Ich.' Letters." Pp. 71–86 in *Freud: The Fusion of Science and Humanism: The Intellectual History of Psychoanalysis*, edited by John E. Gedo and George H. Pollock. New York: International Universities Press.

——. 1976b. "Freud's *Novelas Ejemplares*." Pp. 87–111 in *Freud: The Fusion of Science and Humanism: The Intellectual History of Psychoanalysis*, edited by

John E. Gedo and George H. Pollock. New York: International Universities Press.

Geertz, Clifford. 1975. *The Interpretation of Cultures: Selected Essays*. London: Hutchinson.

Ginsburg, Lawrence M., and Sybil A. Ginsburg. 1987. "A Menagerie of Illustrations from Sigmund Freud's Boyhood." *The Psychoanalytic Study of the Child* 42:469–86.

Ginzburg, Carlo. 1986. "Freud, the Wolf-Man, and the Werewolves." Pp. 146–55 in *Clues, Myths, and the Historical Method*, translated by John and Anne C. Tedeschi. Baltimore: Johns Hopkins University Press.

Greenblatt, Stephen. 1980. *Renaissance Self-Fashioning: From More to Shakespeare*. Chicago: University of Chicago Press.

———. 1992. *Learning to Curse: Essays in Early Modern Culture*. New York: Routledge.

———. 1997. "The Touch of the Real," *Representations* 59:14–29.

Grinker, Roy R. 1973. "Reminiscences of a Personal Contact with Freud." Pp. 180–85 in *Freud: As We Knew Him*, edited by Hendrik M. Ruitenbeek. Detroit: Wayne State University Press.

Grinstein, Alexander. 1968. *On Sigmund Freud's Dreams*. Detroit: Wayne State University Press.

Grosskurth, Phyllis. 1991. *The Secret Ring: Freud's Inner Circle and the Politics of Psychoanalysis*. Reading, Mass.: Addison-Wesley.

Haynal, André. 1988. *Psychoanalysis and the Sciences: Epistemology-History*. Translated by Elizabeth Holder. Berkeley: University of California Press.

Jones, Ernest. 1974. *The Life and Work of Sigmund Freud*. Edited by Lionel Trilling and Steven Marcus. Harmondsworth: Penguin Books.

Jung, Carl Gustav. 1963. *Memories, Dreams, Reflections*. Edited by Aniela Jaffe, translated by Clara and Richard Winston. London: Collins and Routledge and Kegan Paul.

Kanzer, Mark, and Jules Glenn, eds. 1980. *Freud and His Patients*. New York: Jason Aronson.

Kerr, John. 1994. *A Most Dangerous Method: The Story of Jung, Freud, and Sabina Spielrein*. Edited by Peter Dimock. New York: Vintage Books.

Klein, Melanie. [1932] 1975. *The Psychoanalysis of Children*. London: Hogarth Press.

Lacan, Jacques. 1955. "Function and Field of Speech and Language in Psychoanalysis." Translated by Alan Sheridan. London: Tavistock Publications. *Écrits* 30–113.

———. [1973] 1994. *The Four Fundamental Concepts of Psycho-Analysis*. Translated by Alan Sheridan. Harmondsworth: Penguin Books.

Lacoue-Labarthe, Philippe. [1979] 1993. "The Scene is Primal." Translated by Karen McPherson. Pp. 99–115 in *The Subject of Philosophy*, edited by Thomas Trezise. Minneapolis: University of Minnesota Press.

Laplanche, Jean. 1976. *Life and Death in Psychoanalysis*. Baltimore: Johns Hopkins University Press.

Laplanche, Jean, and Jean-Bertrand Pontalis. 1988. *The Language of Psychoanalysis*. Translated by Donald Nicholson-Smith. London: Karnac Books and the Institute of Psycho-Analysis.

Lauzun, Gérard. 1965. *Sigmund Freud: The Man and His Theories*. Translated by Patrick Evans. Greenwich, Conn.: Fawcett Publications.

Lukacher, Ned. 1986. *Primal Scenes: Literature, Philosophy, Psychoanalysis*. Ithaca: Cornell University Press.

Mahony, Patrick J. 1984. *Cries of the Wolf Man*. New York: International University Press.

———. 1987. *Psychoanalysis and Discourse*. London: Tavistock Publications.

Marcus, Steven. 1984. *Freud and the Culture of Psychoanalysis: Studies in the Transition from Victorian Humanism to Modernity*. Boston: George Allen & Unwin.

Marini, Marcelle. 1992. *Jacques Lacan: The French Context*. Translated by Anne Tomiche. New Brunswick: Rutgers University Press.

Masson, Jeffrey Moussaieff. 1984. *The Assault on Truth: Freud's Suppression of Seduction Theory*. New York: Farrar, Straus and Giroux.

McGrath, William J. 1987. *Freud's Discovery of Psychoanalysis: The Politics of Hysteria*. Ithaca: Cornell University Press.

Nägele, Rainer. 1987. *Reading after Freud: Essays on Goethe, Hölderlin, Habermas, Nietzsche, Brecht, Celan, and Freud*. New York: Columbia University Press.

Obholtzer, Karin. 1982. *The Wolf Man Sixty Years Later*. Translated by Michael Shaw. London: Routledge.

Offenkrantz, William, and Arnold Tobin. 1973. "Problems of the Therapeutic Alliance: Freud and the Wolf Man." *The International Journal of Psychoanalysis* 54:75–78.

Pontalis, Jean-Bertrand. 1981. *Frontiers in Psychoanalysis: Between the Dream and Psychic Pain*. Translated by Catherine Cullen and Philip Cullen. London: Hogarth Press.

Rand, Nicholas. 1994. "Introduction: Renewals of Psychoanalysis." Pp. 1–22 in *The Shell and the Kernel: Renewals of Psychoanalysis*, by Nicolas Abraham and Maria Torok. Chicago: University of Chicago Press.

Rand, Nicholas, and Maria Torok. 1997. *Questions for Freud: The Secret History of Psychoanalysis*. London and Cambridge, Mass.: Harvard University Press.

Riviere, Joan. 1973. "A Character Trait of Freud's." Pp. 353–56 in *Freud: As We Knew Him*, edited by Hendrik M. Ruitenbeek. Detroit: Wayne State University Press.

Roazen, Paul. 1984. *Freud and His Followers*. New York: New York University Press.

Rosenberg, Samuel. 1978. *Why Freud Fainted*. Indianapolis and New York: Bobbs-Merrill.

Rosenzweig, Saul. 1994. *The Historic Expedition to America (1909): Freud, Jung, and Hall the King-maker*. St. Louis: Rana House.

Roudinesco, Elisabeth. 1990. *Jacques Lacan & Co.: A History of Psychoanalysis in France, 1925–1985*. Translated by Jeffrey Mehlman. Chicago: University of Chicago Press.

Roustang, François. [1976] 1982. *Dire Mastery: Discipleship from Freud to Lacan*. Translated by Ned Lukacher. Baltimore: Johns Hopkins University Press.

Schur, Max. 1972. *Freud: Living and Dying*. New York: International University Press.

Shengold, Leonard. 1993. *"The Boy Will Come to Nothing!" Freud's Ego Ideal and Freud as Ego Ideal*. New Haven: Yale University Press.

Sirois, François. 1998. "A Look at the Freud-Salomé Correspondence." *International Journal of Psycho-Analysis* 79 2): 269–86.

Smith, Robert. 1995. *Derrida and Autobiography*. Cambridge: Cambridge University Press.

Sprengnether, Madelon. 1990. *The Spectral Mother: Freud, Feminism, and Psychoanalysis*. Ithaca: Cornell University Press.

——. 1998. "Reading Freud's Life." Pp. 139–68 in *Freud 2000*, edited by Anthony Elliott. Melbourne: Melbourne University Press.

Theweleit, Klaus. 1994. *Object-Choice (All You Need Is Love): On Mating Strategies and A Fragment of a Freud Biography*. Translated by Malcolm Green. London and New York: Verso.

Vitz, Paul C. 1988. *Sigmund Freud's Christian Unconscious*. New York: Guilford.

von Tschudi, Friedrich. 1865. *Das Thierleben der Alpenwelt*.

von Tschudi, Johann Jacob. 1845. *Untersuchungen uber die Fauna Peruana*. St. Gallen: Scheitlin and Zollikofer.

Warner, William Beatty. 1986. *Chance and the Text of Experience: Freud, Nietzsche, and Shakespeare's Hamlet*. Ithaca: Cornell University Press.

Weber, Samuel. 1982. *The Legend of Freud*. Minneapolis: University of Minnesota Press.

——. 1984. "The Debts of Deconstruction and Other, Related Assumptions." Pp. 33–65 in *Taking Chances: Derrida, Psychoanalysis and Literature*, edited by Joseph H. Smith and William Kerrigan. Baltimore: Johns Hopkins University Press.

Wolf Man. 1957. "Letters Pertaining to Freud's History of an Infantile Neurosis." *Psychoanalytic Quarterly* 26:449–60.

Young-Bruehl, Elisabeth. 1988. *Anna Freud*. London: Macmillan.

Index

185